Praise for *Hunting LeRoux*

"An investigative masterpiece. . . . A fascinating look. . . . LeRoux is . . . one of the most intriguing and frightening criminals I've ever read about. . . . A stunning work by a master investigative journalist."
—Don Winslow, *New York Times* bestselling author of *The Border* and *The Force*

"The New Now of transnational crime. Elaine Shannon's incisive, you-are-there account of cyber-crime syndicate godfather Paul Calder LeRoux is a scorching, hair-raising glimpse into a new kind of criminal who's altogether terrifying because he's altogether real."
—Dennis Lehane, *New York Times* bestselling author of *Mystic River* and *Gone, Baby, Gone*

"An amazing story, inhabiting a global world of crime."
—Mark Bowden, author of *Black Hawk Down*

Hunting LeRoux

ALSO BY ELAINE SHANNON

THE SPY NEXT DOOR

NO HEROES

DESPERADOS

Hunting LeRoux

The Inside Story of the DEA Takedown
of a Criminal Genius and His Empire

ELAINE SHANNON

MICHAEL
MANN
BOOKS

WILLIAM MORROW
An Imprint of HarperCollins*Publishers*

For my husband, Dan Morgan, and our son,
Andrew Shannon Morgan, my earth and my sky;
For my brother Edward Hogan Shannon, force of nature;
For my brother Michael Willard Shannon
and my nephew Michael Willard Shannon II,
who are in the stars.

A hardcover edition of this book was published 2019 by William Morrow, an imprint of HarperCollins Publishers.

FIRST WILLIAM MORROW PAPERBACK EDITION PUBLISHED 2020.

Library of Congress Cataloging-in-Publication Data has been applied for.

ISBN 978-0-06-285914-3

20 21 22 23 24   LSC   10 9 8 7 6 5 4 3 2 1

CONTENTS

I saw the inconceivable mystery of a soul that knew no restraint, no faith, and no fear, yet struggling blindly with itself.

—Joseph Conrad, *Heart of Darkness*

You must make a friend of horror. Horror and moral terror are your friends. If they are not, then they are enemies to be feared. . . . You have to kill without feeling . . . without passion . . . without judgment . . . without judgment! Because it's judgment that defeats us.

—John Milius and Francis Ford Coppola, *Apocalypse Now*

All non-state actors, whether malign or benevolent, are both finding enormous profit in two related phenomena. The first has been the amazing global growth of the free flow of information, goods, services, and people. The fact that you can be anywhere in the world, buy something, and have it delivered to you within three days is simply amazing, but increasingly commonplace. The second has been the arrival of the so-called "Digital Age," where it is now possible to have a supercomputer and high-speed access to information about virtually anything wherever one happens to be around the world at one's fingertips. The power and advantage this is generating has been enormously beneficial for most of mankind, but malign actors can profit just as much.

One of the results we're now seeing unfold before us is that non-state actors, whether malign or benevolent, can accrue power, influence, capability, and reach that were once exclusively available only to nation-states.

—*Lieutenant General Michael K. Nagata, director, Directorate of Strategic Operational Planning at the National Counterterrorism Center and veteran of the U.S. Army Special Forces*

FOREWORD
BY MICHAEL MANN

WE'RE SITTING IN A GULFSTREAM II, STARING AT A STEROID-POPPED, MUSCLE-bound ex–NATO sniper in handcuffs. He looks out the window. We lift off from Monrovia, Liberia. That look of ennui on his face decays into self-pity, because he knows he's bound for long-term incarceration in the United States. He hasn't uttered a word about the irony. He and his part-ner, Tim Vamvakias, a former U.S. Army military policeman, flew from Phuket, Thailand, to murder a Libyan sea captain and drug transporter turned informant and the DEA agent for whom he worked. The "Libyan informant" has just arrested him. The targets were a setup. So were the coordinators who supplied staged surveillance photos of the targets, a daily log of their movements, the opportune kill spot, and the French mercenary in charge of their West African transportation and the sup-plier of silenced .22 caliber pistols and Heckler & Koch MP7s.

On that Gulfstream, the man opposite Dennis Gögel, the hired killer, is "Taj." Taj is a superstar undercover DEA agent, working with the agency's elite and secretive 960 Group. Taj and the group's boss, Lou Milione, staged themselves as targets. Another pair of mercenaries just as dangerous as Gögel and Vamvakias have been arrested simulta-neously in Tallinn, Estonia. Yet another team of killers, including their leader, Joseph "Rambo" Hunter—a retired US Army sniper trainer—is being apprehended at this very moment in Phuket. We have been dropped inside a complex operation in which five separate undercover stings, involving three different nations' police forces in different parts of the world, all needed to be synchronized to conclude with arrests—

simultaneously. That was so that none of LeRoux's teams could alert any of the others.

Elaine Shannon's *Hunting LeRoux* delivers us into close proximity to dangerous people in the most ungoverned places on the planet. The moment-to-moment, heartbeat-to-heartbeat suspense of the five take-downs pervades many sections of Shannon's book. Fiction would be hard pressed to match the tension and color and the new dimensions of crim-inality revealed here. There is nothing else quite like it. Its authenticity is based on her knowledge of federal and transnational law enforcement, criminal enterprises, and the trust of her sources, who are exclusive to her.

It, simply, is better than most crime stories people can make up. Shannon has the magical ability to write from inside the flow of actual events, making them come alive. You know it's real, and you are there.

Reading Shannon's partial manuscript almost two years ago, I felt I had never been taken inside an organized criminal empire within day-to-day proximity of its lethal and brilliant entrepreneur with such spec-ificity. The atmosphere of danger and continual scrutiny is tangible. It's as if we're captive in a series called *Lifestyles of the Rich and Malevolent.*

Equally, the manuscript parachutes us into the lives of Tom Cindric and Eric Stouch, the two agents in the DEA's secretive 960 Group, who initiated and are the protagonists driving the mainstream investigation into LeRoux. Across continents and time zones, in dark motel rooms and in dangerous countries, we are with law enforcement's most major-league big-game hunters.

The revelation at the center of this true-crime saga is Paul Calder Le-Roux and the transformation he innovated. LeRoux is a cybertech genius turned crime lord—committing cold-blooded murders along the way. He created a revolution in how transnational organized crime organized itself. LeRoux deconstructed the conventional ways even sophisticated drug cartels or arms merchants operated. They still had "farm-to-the-arm," vertically integrated business models often locking them to physical locales. Infrastructure and personnel hierarchies made them vulnerable, visible, and out-of-date to LeRoux. He deconstructed that model and created something completely different. His criminal enterprises—linked by a dark web of his own invention—were like a cutting-edge Silicon Valley start-up, using the gig economy, pivoting quickly off failed ideas, capable of rapid scalability, and climbing a hockey-stick curve of success.

He—and those who have followed—traffic in advanced weapons systems, tonnages of drugs, and exotic fissile materials, and engage in money laundering. They corrupt struggling small countries into failed nation-states to provide transport hubs and service regional conflicts. This new world's innovator and its architect is Paul Calder LeRoux.

Early on, the 960 Group came to the realization that LeRoux was the Elon Musk, the Jeff Bezos of transnational organized crime. They believe LeRoux is the "new now" as well as the near future.

Many in LeRoux's presence describe his lethal aura of brilliance, deviance, and sociopathy.

As a dramatist, it is this additional quality of *Hunting LeRoux* that appeals to me, perhaps even more compellingly than its revelations. That is, our proximity. *We are there.* We are brought there because people trust Elaine Shannon. She has a reputation among intelligence agencies and top-echelon law enforcement as a highly respected journalist who courageously goes where the story is, never betrays confidences, and gets it right. Their confidence in her, their openness, and the acuity of her insight—plus her irony and charm—is why the book has its unique ambiance and close-up engagement.

The agents driving the investigation—Cindric and Stouch; their bosses, Lou Milione and Derek Maltz; the undercover DEA agent Taj—share their first-person perspectives, diaries, memos, documents, personal feelings, intuitions, suspicions, fears, and, sometimes, triumphs with Shannon. Their perspectives are woven into the compelling fabric of this narrative.

So, too, is the perspective of "Jack," the man LeRoux calls his "golden boy." Through the eyes of Jack, we are taken into LeRoux's strangely empty, twin luxury Manila penthouses and read his body language and experience the brainstorm-a-minute outbursts of this blond three-hundred-fifty-pounder. We're flattered by his seductive speech and feel the danger of his MRI-like stare. Threat is redolent in the heat and humidity.

Jack built the compound and the militia for LeRoux in Somalia, helped him move money, and buy sumptuous safe houses. Jack flipped to Agents Cindric and Stouch and became their undercover source, reporting on and surreptitiously recording LeRoux at enormous personal risk. Not only had LeRoux created squads of killers, he'd begun pulling the trigger himself.

The image of LeRoux on this book's cover is one frame from a surveillance video Jack recorded through a lens in a small device hidden in his clothing.

Overseeing Agents Cindric and Stouch is ASAC Lou Milione, one of the founders of the 960 Group under Special Operations Division chief Derek Maltz. Milione and his right-hand man, Wim Brown, have taken down some of the world's most insulated and sophisticated criminal figures, including the arms merchant Viktor "Merchant of Death" Bout, Monzer al-Kassar, and Haji Juma Khan, an Afghani heroin kingpin. The 960 Group, quietly, is law enforcement's heavy-hitter.

In *Hunting LeRoux,* Shannon creates a work in which we walk in the shoes, live in the skins, and see through the eyes of these people. It is a revelatory true-crime saga.

Michael Mann is an acclaimed four-time Oscar-nominated director, writer, and producer. His credits include *Thief, Manhunter, The Last of the Mohicans, Heat, The Insider, Ali, Collateral, Miami Vice, Public Enemies,* and *Blackhat.* He produced Martin Scorsese's *The Aviator* and *Hancock,* and the television series *Miami Vice, Crime Story, Luck,* and *Witness*—as well as the Emmy-winning miniseries *Drug Wars: the Camarena Story,* based on Elaine Shannon's bestselling 1988 book, *Desperados,* about the murder of DEA agent Enrique Camarena in Mexico.

INTRODUCTION: MALIGN ACTOR

TO UNDERSTAND THE SIGNIFICANCE OF PAUL CALDER LEROUX, THE CRE-
ator of the Innovation Age's first transnational criminal empire, start at
the other end of the evolutionary scale.

When the last cocaine cowboy went down, it wasn't classy.

On the run from the Mexican marines, Joaquin "El Chapo" Guz-
mán emerged stinking from a sewer pipe. His idea of keeping a low
profile was to steal a fire-engine-red Ford Focus from a grandmother.
Black-clad Mexican federal police intercepted him in a matter of
minutes and locked him in a fetid rent-by-the-hour sex motel until a
government helicopter took him back to the prison he had tunneled
out of six months earlier.

El Chapo, taken into custody on January 8, 2016, was one of the last
relics of the first phase of the cocaine invasion—call it the *Miami Vice*
era—when cocaine cowboys built their brands by festooning themselves in diamond-encrusted guns and belt buckles and by surround-
ing themselves with cars, corpses, trucks, SUVs, dealerships, whores,
horses, hotels, nightclubs, soccer teams, TV stations, zoos, boats, and
more corpses. The most famous and fabulous shot and betrayed one
another until nearly all of them were dead or in prison.

Phase Two began in the first years of the twenty-first century. The
global black market in illegal drugs had become a vast, mature industry estimated to generate $400 billion a year (and probably much
more), exceeding the combined profits of the underground trade in
arms, humans, and blood diamonds. Responding to attractive profit

opportunities on the dark side as well as in the visible economy, the underworld globalized. As traffickers militarized, militants criminalized, and they met in a borderless swamp. Colombian cartels joined forces with Lebanese syndicates and Hezbollah operatives in South America, Africa, and Europe. Colombia's Marxist guerrillas, the FARC (Fuerzas Armadas Revolucionarias de Colombia, or Revolutionary Armed Forces of Colombia), went into cocaine production on an industrial scale; by the early 2000s, DEA officials estimated that the FARC supplied more than half the world's cocaine. Mexican organizations turned up in Nigeria and China. The Serb mafia posted gun runners on every continent. The Russian mafia laundered money, smuggled, bribed, intimidated, and launched cyberattacks for profit. Afghanistan's Taliban insurgency was founded with money from Afghan heroin kingpins.

The men and women at the top of transnational organized crime had evolved for the era of globalization. They were discreet and smart enough not to go to war with one another. They were in the game to make money, not news. They embraced the tools of the Digital Age—encrypted mobile devices, satellite phones, cloud storage, the dark web. They were ardent capitalists who worshipped no god but money. They drank alcohol, gambled, whored, raped, and blasphemed. Radical ideology left them cold, except as a means of destabilizing governments that threatened their impunity. They invested strategically, in chaos, because the threat to their existence was not rivals or soldiers or cops but peace. They paid off armed bands who held territory, who controlled roads, ports, rivers, border crossings, and air strips. They were never the face of conflict. But they were the money in the back room, and it was the money that kept things boiling.

However sophisticated the infrastructure, during Phase Two, most criminal organizations were still working within an industrial model of organized crime. They had to control the supply directly and supervise the steps of production, from farm to arm. That meant lots of people and facilities to grow, harvest, refine, transport, reprocess, produce, guard, smuggle, protect with internal security and counterintelligence, distribute, collect money, and launder money. Lots of people. Lots of organization. Lots of aboveground and belowground infrastructure, all of which was vulnerable to discovery and attack by adversaries and law enforcement.

Now Phase Three—the model for transnational organized crime of tomorrow—has emerged, and it is changing everything. It is the innovation of Paul Calder LeRoux, who has introduced the principles of twenty-first-century entrepreneurship to the dark side of the global economy.

Born in the outlaw colony of Rhodesia, LeRoux has a complicated psyche and near-genius intelligence. With his imposing 350-pound physique, anvil-shaped forehead, and blue-black eyes that gleam like lit cigarettes, he strides into a room and takes command, projecting the menacing gravitas of an absolutely powerful medieval monarch, a Gilded Age robber baron, or a Wagnerian antihero. His mannerisms evoke Marlon Brando's Colonel Kurtz, the renegade Green Beret turned warlord in Francis Ford Coppola's Vietnam War epic, *Apocalypse Now*. LeRoux conveys the tension roiling his soul just as Brando/Kurtz did, by rubbing his pale shaved head, twisting his neck, and smiling when there is nothing to smile about. These are gifted, seductive souls who have weighed good and evil and chosen evil, justifying it as more honorable than hypocrisy. "There's nothing that I detest more than the stench of lies," Brando/Kurtz told his interlocutor, boasting that he had surrounded himself with warriors "who are moral . . . and at the same time who are able to utilize their primordial instinct to kill without feeling . . . without passion . . . without judgment! Because it's judgment that defeats us." Of course, for Kurtz, it was really about power. No judgment meant no reason and no remorse. That was madness, but who has more power than a madman?

LeRoux understood the usefulness of fear very well. In a similar vein, he bragged of buying an island off the Philippines coast because "every villain needs his own island." The password that unlocked his laptop was "Hitler." He sought alliances with malefactors he admired—Colombian cartels, Russian oligarchs, Somali pirates, the Serb mafia, and Chinese Triads. He surrounded himself with enforcers as pitiless as Kurtz's headhunters.

For years, the chief operating officer of LeRoux's empire was a hard-drinking, meth-smoking English sadist named Dave Smith, who, LeRoux said, "got great pleasure in torturing animals and killing people and torturing people. Obviously, he is very violent, and he is the type of person I needed." LeRoux instructed Smith to hire more men like himself—men who "enjoyed killing and torturing and beating."

Brando's Kurtz adorned his jungle dwelling with human skulls. LeRoux updated the concept, loading his laptop with digital snapshots of the bloodied corpses of people he ordered killed. Inside his sparsely furnished penthouse, he toiled in lonely splendor, obsessed with accumulating dollars, euros, rands, rubles, dirhams, and rupees by dealing in chemicals, drugs, gold, timber, and arms. His customers, he said proudly, were "warlords, criminals, essentially anyone who had money."

Greed and cruelty are as old as humankind. What is groundbreaking about LeRoux is his unique combination of dazzling intellect and absence of conscience. These qualities have allowed him to develop a formidable business style. He is transnational organized crime's supreme innovator. He is Netflix to Blockbuster, Spotify to Tower Records.

For LeRoux, money is just a way of keeping score. He dresses with the ironic downscale look known as Silicon Valley billionaire—battered khakis and primary-colored polo shirts that can be seen from space. He stuffs himself with Domino's pizza and Big Macs. His women are expendable and interchangeable. For LeRoux, sex is a snack, like an energy bar or a stress reliever.

When doing business, he is crisp and focused. He has racked up numbers that Silicon Valley's forward leaners would envy. Starting in 2004, when he emerged in East Asia as the brash young founder of a new kind of e-commerce business, he built a criminal empire stretching from Manila and Hong Kong, across Jerusalem and Dubai, to Texas to Rio. By 2012, he employed close to two thousand people. His first venture generated at least 3 million orders valued at close to $300 million total. More recently, he has developed numerous unquantified cash streams for various criminal enterprises and legitimate fronts.

Yet, typical of Silicon Valley style, in his operations there is little or no infrastructure. He wants no permanent administration, locale, or means of production; no retinue, no partying, no posse. He uses the gig economy to procure contract mercenaries and temp workers. He issues orders to them by email or text in his own unbreakable encryption, sending them to distant corners of the earth to sequester assets, bribe officials, and negotiate business agreements. At any given moment, his hired hands never know where he is or even what he looks like. Loyalty, the adhesive of mafias, Chinese Triads, and cartels, isn't in his playbook. Once he is done with people, he abandons them or, if they annoy him, has them executed. He calls his Filipino, African, and Israeli subordinates "marginals," meaning less than human and expendable.

Phase One and Phase Two criminal organizations tended to be linear, logical, and tied to physical geography. LeRoux is the first crime lord to operate in the realm of pure cyberspace. He browses among clients, suppliers, fixers, and networkers, meeting them wherever fiber optic cables and satellite links take him. His strange big brain empowers him to juggle multiple projects at once and remember everything. His ambitions are unrestrained by conscience and second thoughts.

His entrepreneurial style might be compared to his fellow South African Elon Musk and to Jeff Bezos, founder of Amazon, ranked among the world's richest men. Like Musk, who zigzagged wildly from business directories to PayPal to outer space to electric cars to self-driving cars to tunnels, LeRoux's brain vaults effortlessly from online casinos to e-commerce in pharmaceuticals to small arms to missile technology to North Korean crystal meth.

And like Bezos, who created the Everything Store, the online superstore that aspired to sell anything anybody might want, LeRoux set out to build the Amazon for arms, with an ultraefficient fulfillment and transshipping facility in a sparkling new, entirely self-sufficient, heavily armed planned community in the Somali badlands.

Most of the buzzwords of twenty-first-century entrepreneurship apply to LeRoux—contempt for tradition, disruption, lean management, global reach, and rapid scalability. He knows how to find and exploit unfilled niches, upend markets, travel light, move fast, and stay nimble.

He has kept his dealings clandestine by creating his own, virtually uncrackable dark web. He is not a hacker. He never bothered to break into government or business systems, though he could have easily learned the knack. To him, computers are tools, like ballpoint pens and can openers. He used an old Dell that he configured himself. He was confident it couldn't be breached, and he wasn't so sure about newer models. Hackers as a rule don't kill people. LeRoux did, personally and by proxy.

For years, LeRoux was a ghost, flickering on and off the screens of the Drug Enforcement Administration, the CIA, and United Nations, yet evading becoming a target of counterterrorism and global crimefighting units. He went almost unnoticed even when he started dealing with Iran and North Korea. The monitoring systems of the U.S. government and its allies were alert to signs of conventional criminal groups, with their predictable, visible hierarchies. The DEA agents who started hunting LeRoux in early 2012 saw only a spectral outline, far more mysterious and challenging than any crime lord they had faced before. "He was creating a whole new industry that transcended the concept of drug trafficker and gun runner and was becoming something original," said Lou Milione, head of the unit that tracked him. "With the economies of scale of which he was capable, he was going to reach a point where, if nobody took him out, he would have continued to get stronger and more powerful, and God knows what he would have been involved in. And He. Would. Not. Have. Cared."

The hunt began with a tip to two of Milione's best agents, Tom Cindric and Eric Stouch, who had been partners for years and at that point were assigned to track international drug trafficking across Africa.

Cindric, Stouch, and their fellow agents in the 960 Group, a secretive element inside the agency's Special Operations Division, are some of the boldest and most creative criminal investigators in the U.S. government. Milione was, in his youth, an actor with serious off-Broadway and film credits. Within the DEA, he was famed for taking down Monzer al-Kassar, the so-called Prince of Marbella, his story splashed across the pages of *The New Yorker*. The ultimate arms merchant, Kassar, a Syrian, supplied every generation of terrorists and rogue leaders, from Abu Abbas, leader of the Palestinian Liberation Front and leader of the 1985 *Achille Lauro* Mediterranean cruise ship hijacking, to Iraqi dictator Saddam Hussein. Milione and his agents also arrested Haji Juma Khan, a kingpin of the Afghan heroin cartel. Most spectacularly, in 2008 Milione and his agents staged a sting that captured the Russian arms merchant Viktor Bout, the vaunted "Merchant of Death" who inspired the film *The Lord of War*.

Milione handpicked agents who were smart, curious, capable of deception, in constant motion, enterprising, irreverent, and not what they seemed. They revered the law but didn't mind breaking rules. These qualities were personified by Cindric and Stouch. Their hunt for LeRoux, detailed for the first time in this book, is revealing and unsettling. With bold imagination, highly specialized partners, some luck, and faith in their own gut instincts—qualities that can't be learned and can't be taught—they recruited one of LeRoux's confidants and penetrated his hidden world.

The ability to sense what's over the horizon is not necessarily a blessing. The deeper they went down the rabbit hole, the more ominous their discoveries, the more acute their foreboding.

"Paul is who's coming," Cindric said. "He is steps ahead of everyone. And we are not ready for that."

CHAPTER ONE

SEPTEMBER 25, 2013

THE BLOND GIANT WEPT RACKING SOBS, FAT TEARS SOAKING THE FLOW-ered turquoise board shorts and flip-flops that were his idea of keeping a low profile.

Dennis Gögel, a former German army sniper and crack shot, had just arrived in Monrovia, capital of Liberia, on an errand for his employer, Paul Calder LeRoux, an eccentric entrepreneur who had made his first fortune with a scheme to sell pharmaceuticals on the Internet.

LeRoux was branching out into ventures of geopolitical significance—Colombian cocaine, North Korean meth, advanced weapons systems, war profiteering, and Iran sanctions busting. For settling scores, he recruited a team of mercenaries from the swelling ranks of American and European military warfighters who had seen combat in Afghanistan, Iraq, and NATO peacekeeping missions. Most vets settled into civilian life without incident, but a few, like Gögel, remained adventure-addicted Lost Boys in search of Neverland. LeRoux, happy to play Captain Hook, put them up in a safe house in the rowdy Thai beach resort of Phuket and financed their adrenaline-charged revels. All they had to do in exchange was occasionally get rid of people who threatened him or impeded him.

As the best shot on the team, Gögel was to be assigned the trickier contract hits, called "bonus jobs" because they paid extra. The job in Monrovia, his first for LeRoux, was to kill a DEA agent named Joey Casich, who was posted to the U.S. embassy there, and his informant, a Libyan ship captain and professional smuggler named Zaman—Sammy to his pals in Colombia. LeRoux complained that Casich and Sammy were interfering with him and his new business partners, a Colombian organization that was setting up a cocaine route from South America to West Africa and then to Europe.

LeRoux's head enforcer, Joseph Hunter, a retired U.S. Army sniper trainer and drill sergeant, had received covert photos of Casich and Sammy and a detailed surveillance report of their routine movements. The photos showed Casich and Sammy meeting in various places in Monrovia. Hunter, who took pride in his cold-blooded efficiency as LeRoux's head hit man, posted the photos on a wall in the mercenaries' safe house and told Gögel and his wingman, Tim Vamvakias, a former U.S. Army military policeman, to memorize the faces and come up with an attack plan.

The mercenaries figured that Sammy wouldn't be hard to spot. He was a cocky young dude with walnut skin, black eyes, and a devilish grin. He dressed flashy, West Coast gangster style, in a black T-shirt, black cargo pants, and Oakley shades.

Recognizing the American agent would be tougher. Pale and middle-aged, average height, average weight, dressed in a zippered windbreaker, polo shirt, and khakis, he looked like every traveling business pro striding through any airport concourse and hotel lobby anywhere in the world. His colorless appearance was not an accident. As players on both sides knew, the first rule of traveling anonymously was to blend in. For a DEA agent, that meant dull tan slacks or utilities, cut loose for striding purposefully, kicking doors, climbing walls, and jumping out of windows; shoes for sprinting, plain, not neon; tan shirts and jackets with pockets for a sidearm, badge, cuffs, and two or three mobile phones. An agent had to have at least one phone per identity. No shorts—they were for the weight room. Suits were for kids' graduations, weddings, divorce court, and funerals.

During the four flights from Phuket to Monrovia, Gögel ignored

Hunter's blend-in rule and also his grandmother's folk saying—"*Man soll das Fell des Bären nicht verteilen, bevor er erlegt ist.*" *Don't sell the bear's fur before you've killed him.* His festive beachwear getup was his way of celebrating the $80,000 he and Vamvakias were about to make for the bonus job—the first of many, he expected. LeRoux and the Colombians had plenty of enemies. Knocking off a few of them was going to make him rich.

"Actually, for me, that's fun," Gögel told Hunter as they were planning the hits. "I love this work. . . . I am very happy with my job right now."

Only, things hadn't gone the way the young German planned. Now his steroid-swollen forearms torqued uselessly inside handcuffs that tethered him to the seat in an executive jet, idling on the tarmac while the pilot and copilot set a course for a small private airfield in White Plains, New York. From there he would be taken to federal court in lower Manhattan.

The shackles gave him just enough slack to move his hand to his lips. Every so often he kissed a scrap of paper that bore the scrawled cell phone number of the Russian girl he had met in Phuket. She must have been something, because that high-pitched wail didn't sound like a noise that would come out of such a big guy. You'd think that years of looking at the human race through crosshairs would crush all romantic impulses. Love is strange.

Vamvakias was tied down in the rear of the jet, sagging and close to inert. A skinny forty-one-year-old from San Bernardino, California, he'd been around the track longer than Gögel. As he would eventually tell the court, he had spent thirteen years in the service, eight of them on active duty as an explosives-detection dog handler and on a military police SWAT team. He had never deployed to a war zone as a soldier, but after his retirement from the U.S. army in 2004, he had worked as a contractor, running bomb dog operations in Doha, Qatar, and Kandahar, Afghanistan. He was fired from the last job for lying about his diabetes. His health was failing, and he sensed that this time, he wasn't going to catch a break.

The younger man couldn't sit still. He fidgeted and grimaced. It didn't help that Taj, an intense thirty-four-year-old DEA agent, had settled into the seat directly across from him and explained, not unkindly, that he would take care of all Gögel's needs during the trip. Buckling himself in across from Gögel, Taj smiled at the flight attendant and told her to give Surfer Dude another Pepsi, and no, she couldn't comfort the guy, pitiful as he looked. The good-looking German was just twenty-seven, and life as he knew it was over. He was looking at maybe twenty years in an eight-by-ten cell. He'd be a pasty, flaccid fifty-something by the time he got out. (In fact, both Gögel and Vamakias would plead guilty to conspiracy to murder a law enforcement agent and a person assisting him and other serious crimes. Each would be sentenced to 240 months in prison.)

Taj didn't feel sorry for Gögel. He thought that a couple of decades in the slammer was better than the macho piece of shit deserved. Taj had recently returned from Afghanistan, where he had spent four years in disguise, recruiting a network of informants inside the Taliban and the Afghan heroin cartel that supported it. He had often deployed to the front lines with American and allied special operations troops. He had seen good men die, men younger than Gögel or himself, bleeding out from the kinds of bombs Gögel's boss, LeRoux, sold to Iran for terrorists. The agent looked at the prisoner with a mix of cold fury and detached irony. They had been in Afghanistan at the same time, supposedly on the same side. Taj wondered how many civilians the German had shot just to see if his gun worked.

Shortly before takeoff, Taj, wearing a navy raid jacket with huge yellow letters that shouted DEA, leaned into Gögel, glared at him with eyes that burned like hot needles, and snapped, "You recognize me?"

Gögel stared and shook his head.

Then, Gögel's eyes widened. *WTF? Sammy the Libyan? He's got a badge?* That's when the German started sobbing. He realized that this was a sting, street theater, a snare, and he had taken the bait. Taj was the man Gögel had come to Monrovia to kill. They stared at each other across an unbridgeable gulf.

Taj had enjoyed certain advantages that had eluded his target. Gögel's youth had been sad but conventional. Taj's was extreme, inside, warmed by the unconditional love of family but, beyond the walls, besieged by a society going up in flames. He was born in Kabul in 1979, a few months before Soviet tanks rolled in. He spent the first ten years of his life in the crossfire between mujahideen fighters and Soviet troops occupying Kabul. Many evenings, he huddled with his family in a dank subterranean bomb shelter they had dug underneath their dining room table. Bombs went off daily outside the house and his elementary school. His uncle, a doctor, was killed by a rocket attack on the hospital where he was treating the injured. His grandparents and another uncle were bayoneted and shot by Soviet soldiers rampaging through their farm.

In February 1989, during the last days of the Soviet occupation, the communist regime's secret police set out to kill his father, an engineer who worked in the political section of the U.S. embassy. The father had already been accused of spying and had been tortured. He and his wife got a warning from a friend in intelligence—get out of the country *now!* They were forced to make a terrible choice. They sent Taj, who was ten at that point, and his two teenage sisters with a smuggler who promised to take them across the Khyber Pass to Pakistan. The parents bundled up the baby and climbed into a truck driven by a second smuggler. They split up the family, hoping that if they were intercepted and shot, their older children would survive.

Taj left his childhood on the frozen slopes of the Hindu Kush mountains above Tora Bora. His father had lectured him that he was the man of the family now and had to get his older sisters through the treacherous mountain passes to safety. Taj knew that virgins brought a high price in the bazaars. He knew what he had to do—watch, hide, never sleep, and keep the three of them moving. Miraculously, the family reunited in Peshawar. A couple of years of wandering led them to a melting-pot California town of *taquerias*, *pho* shops, and tattoo parlors. His father found work as an engineer for an American oil company, but money was tight. Taj worked two and three jobs to pay for books, shoes, tuition, and anything else he wanted. He grew to adulthood revering the God of Muhammad, Abraham, and Jesus, the U.S. Constitution, the American educational system, the American work ethic, Willie Nelson, and Harley-Davidson, not necessarily in that order.

After the attacks of September 11, 2001, he set out to join the U.S. Marines but acceded to his mother's tearful pleas—"No more war!" He earned a master's degree in criminal justice and signed on with the DEA because the agency promised to put him on the street instead of sticking him at a desk and making him translate and write reports. He was allergic to desks. He went undercover the first week on the job, playing meth and heroin dealers of vaguely Mediterranean ethnicity. He became adept as passing as a Mexican cartel operative, though he didn't speak a word of Spanish, only the Spanglish he picked up from high school friends.

To play Sammy the Libyan, he didn't even have to fake an Arabic accent, just pose for a few photos, looking flush and seedy. What mattered, he discovered, was not facility with language but the way he carried himself. As long as he swaggered, coldly menaced, and bragged about the money he and his targets were about to make, nobody dared question him about his family background.

In 2009, he returned to the land of his birth with a mission to infiltrate the Taliban and the heroin cartel that supported it. The countryside's flourishing poppy fields had transformed what should have been a limited conflict into a permanent, self-funding quagmire. He could recruit informants in Farsi, Dari, and Pashto, so he decided to use his languages and street smarts to do something about the pain of ordinary Afghans—those kids flung out into bitter cold, begging for food and coins amid minefields, graveyards, and open sewers. Call it altruism or survivor's guilt, he knew that but for an incredible string of good fortune, he would have been out there with them.

Like all plans in all wars, the DEA strategy to break up the cartel, shorten the conflict, and clear the way for stability and reconstruction didn't survive the first skirmish. Few in the U.S. government but DEA agents gave priority to stopping the heroin trade. Heroin supported both sides of the war. Prominent figures in Afghanistan's nominally pro-Western power elite were getting a fat slice of the heroin action. American and NATO military commanders feared that attacking the drug trade would cost hearts and minds. Taliban insurgents relied on drug profits as their main source of financing for weapons and logistical support. Osama bin Laden and his followers weren't directly selling heroin, as far as the DEA agents knew, but Bin Laden was protected by the Taliban and Pakistan's leadership, both of which benefited from the burgeoning South Asian heroin trade. In addition to figuring out how the drug trade worked, Taj and his partners focused their informants and wiretaps on helping American and NATO forces locate IEDs and arms caches, on heading off ambushes and bombings, and on pinpointing locations of high-value targets. At the request of U.S. special operations commanders, Taj sent informants across the border into Pakistan's North Waziristan to locate several hostages, including U.S. army private Bowe Bergdahl and American tourist Caitlan Coleman, her Canadian husband, and their children, born in captivity. The Afghan sources returned with GPS coordinates of the compounds where the hostages were being guarded by Afghan insurgents affiliated with the Taliban.

In 2012, after four years in the war zone, Taj transferred to the DEA's Special Operations Division. Milione tapped him for his 960 Group. That was the best job in the agency, if you didn't mind living out of your suitcase. Milione's team had a license to go anywhere in the world to find and stop transnational drugs, arms, and money-laundering networks that played critical roles in the operations of terrorist groups and rogue regimes.

The agents sometimes found themselves in direct conflict with the CIA. DEA agents wanted to arrest smugglers of drugs and arms, but sometimes the CIA wanted to hire the same people and keep them in play as sources. The CIA could do that because its missions were overseas, covert, and outside the legal system. DEA agents played by American laws, rules, and procedures John Adams and Wyatt Earp would recognize. Everybody got his day in court. No drones, no renditions, no secret prisons, no torture, no illegal intercepts, no clandestine judgments, no summary justice, and no targeted killings.

Wim Brown, Milione's alter ego, led the 960 Group's Africa team when it started looking into the LeRoux organization. Midway through the investigation, he transferred to Nairobi. He was gray-haired, engaging, quick-witted, and unfazed by just about everything except Washington, which he despised. Under Milione and Brown were the two case agents for LeRoux—Cindric, energetic, garrulous, charming, and hot-tempered; Stouch, thoughtful, meticulous, coolheaded, and utterly reliable. Cindric went wide-angle. Stouch zoomed in.

Taj played utility. For the Gögel-Vamvakias takedown, he pulled double duty, first, as Sammy the Libyan, and later, as Gögel's escort and guard. Taj wasn't as big as Gögel—nobody in the DEA contingent was—but he had been under fire, in places most soldiers never got to see, and he wasn't about to let this blond slacker ruin his day by trying to escape.

Gögel came from the sleepy German town of Stadthagen, an hour's drive from Hanover. His mother died of asthma when he was three and his father left him to the care of his grandparents. In 2007, at the age of eighteen, after graduating from trade school, he enlisted in the German army, where he discovered that he had talent as marksman. He became a sniper in the Panzergrenadier division, the equivalent of the U.S. Army Rangers, with two deployments to Kosovo and an honorable discharge in 2010.

Ex-soldiers trained in communications and electronics could find work in corporations, information technology, or civilian law enforcement. Airmen became civilian pilots and flight engineers. In Western Europe, there wasn't much call for sharpshooters. Gögel drifted into what ex-commandos called "the mercenary Facebook" of footloose American and European vets. It wasn't literally a Facebook page, but it served the same function for restless, underemployed, hard-core warfighters, whose numbers had swelled during U.S. and NATO engagements in Kosovo, Bosnia and Herzegovina, Iraq, and Afghanistan. Action-loving men of many nations met and mingled while working in combat or intelligence-gathering units and in command-and-control centers. After they left active duty, many of those who craved more high-risk assignments took jobs in security companies that protected diplomats, UN employees, foreign officials, businesspeople, and aid workers in war zones. Smartphones and encrypted messaging apps like WhatsApp, Wickr, ProtonMail, and Signal made it easy for old army buddies to find one another and exchange job tips.

After a short gig as security for a television station in Kabul, Gögel moved on to the Persian Gulf and Indian Ocean, guarding merchant vessels in pirate-infested waters off Somalia. Those long days and nights on cargo ships gave him a lot of time for his favorite activity, body-building. He used ship lines as training ropes, balanced his toes on buckets to perform dozens of knuckle push-ups, and popped steroids.

In early 2013, he connected with Hunter, a brusque Kentuckian who called himself Rambo. With his gleaming bald head, chiseled cheekbones, and ballooned biceps, Hunter looked the part. As he would eventually write the court in New York in a bid for mercy, Gögel was awed by Hunter's tough-guy boasts and claims, mostly false, that he had been in special operations, that he lived an ascetic lifestyle devoted to perfecting his body and mind and that he was now leading what Gögel described as a "highly specialized security group to protect and secure high profile clients." Gögel latched on to Hunter, he later confessed, "not only as mentor but as a father figure, something I never had before. He seemed to offer everything I dreamed of, career development and family. It seemed my life was finally on track."

Gögel misread Hunter. The sour American didn't want to be anybody's daddy. He hired mercenaries to please LeRoux, who had instructed him to find "capable guys who are willing to do black ops jobs." Black ops meant murder-for-hire. What "capable" meant to LeRoux depended on the task. Filipinos and Israelis who worked in his pharmaceutical e-commerce call centers had to be neat, polite, discreet, and adept at taking credit card authorizations.

For his security team, LeRoux wanted U.S. and NATO-trained veterans in superb physical shape, disciplined and willing to take orders unquestioningly. He was not happy with two of Hunter's hires as contract killers, Adam Samia and Carl David Stillwell, out-of-shape civilians who lived in Roxboro, North Carolina, collected guns and fantasized about becoming soldiers of fortune. In early 2012, the pair had carried out a hit demanded by LeRoux, the murder of a young woman named Catherine Lee, who had worked as a real estate broker for LeRoux, finding expensive properties for him to buy through straw purchasers. LeRoux suspected her of skimming and ordered her killed. The North Carolinians bungled the job and left a trail of evidence wide and bright as the Vegas strip at midnight. By the time Gögel set out for Monrovia, the only reason nobody had traced the Catherine Lee murder back to LeRoux was that he had paid massive amounts of protection money to a long list of Philippines cops and other officials.

LeRoux made it clear to Hunter that the next bunch of mercenaries had to be truly battle-hardened sharpshooters willing to kill people they didn't know for $25,000 a head. The list of people he wanted knocked off was growing. He didn't want any more mistakes that would enable corrupt Asian and African police officials to shake him down for even more cash. On the other hand, he didn't want gunmen who were too bright. They might talk back or even refuse hit jobs. LeRoux wouldn't put up with being second-guessed. He didn't want anybody around who could think for himself. He did the thinking for everyone.

Gögel checked all the boxes. He was a bronze god, beautiful, obedient, fun-loving, not too clever and, so it seemed, thoroughly amoral. He was eager for the perks that came with the job—a condo on Phuket Island, sugar-crystal sand, a pocketful of euros, all the ecstasy he wanted, a gym where he could build abs like knuckles, and a welcome at go-go clubs where the bar girls and ladyboys climbed his body like a pole. LeRoux and Hunter had thoughtfully based the mercenary team near Phuket's Patong Beach scene, the sex tourism capital of the world, where every day was Mardi Gras on Whore Island—horns, stench, glare, blinking neon lights, boom boxes, tequila shooters, Suzy Wong's Rock Hard's Crazy Girls A Go Go, Club XTC, and so much more.

Aside from plenty of recreation to distract the sort of young unattached men LeRoux was after, Phuket was an easy place for LeRoux's team to come and go unnoticed. It wasn't a traditional organized-crime hangout. People everywhere, cars all over the place, noisy revelers banging around the streets at all hours. By night, the beach roads were thick with college guys, soldiers and sailors on leave, young professionals escaping from cubicles and mingling with hookers, drag queens, deejays, bar girls, bartenders, women who performed in sex shows with other women, women who performed in sex shows with snakes, masseuses, waitresses, more hookers, women who shot Ping-Pong balls and darts with their vaginas.

On this particular day, though—September 25, 2013—Phuket had extra visitors who weren't getting their freak on in the clubs.

Cindric, Stouch, and Milione were in Phuket, using the resort as a base to run arrests. They had been tracking Paul LeRoux and his henchmen since December 2011 and had designated September 25 as

Takedown Day, when they intended to dismantle the most danger-ous components of LeRoux's operation—his mercenary team and his drugs-and-arms-trafficking team.

The degree of difficulty of their op plan was extreme. Normal law enforcement and military agencies would have called it insane. One problem was that LeRoux's five-man security team operated globally. Its member were practiced at detecting and evading surveillance.

To incriminate two of the five, Gögel and Vamvakias, and make arrests, Cindric and Stouch created the elaborate Liberian undercover sting.

To build the theatrical scenario, Milione, undercover as DEA agent "Casich" and Taj as "Sammy the Libyan," infiltrated into Monrovia. Credible-seeming emails and an hour-by-hour surveillance report had to be crafted to simulate how a Colombian cartel would spy on Casich and Sammy, the "targets" of the assassination plan. The undercover agents playacted surreptitious meetings for low-res iPhone photos in popular Monrovia nightspots. Costumes and disguises were acquired. Evidence of flights, hotel rooms, car rentals, and other logistics had to be generated. Liberian authorities had to be briefed to make the arrests and expel the hit men into DEA custody. It all had to happen amid the anxious awareness that one mistake or leak from anyone would blow the entire operation.

The op plan, difficult enough to pull off on its own, was multiplied by five. A second multilayered sting had to be set up and run in Tal-linn, Estonia, to arrest two more of LeRoux's men, Soborski and Filter, lured there on what they were told was a different mission. And, at three separate locations in Phuket, Thailand, six more LeRoux hench-men had to be taken down.

To further increase the difficulty, each of the targets had to be sur-prised and overpowered and all the arrests had to occur virtually simul-taneously so that no one could alarm the others by texting an *ABORT* signal. Or, if the mercenaries were clever, by not calling or texting at a designated "check-in" time. The cue to vanish might be silence. Each set of arrests had to be prepared and advance like clockwork to Take-down Day. Nothing—from complications with local authorities to the weather, nothing—could cause any of the five operations to delay.

The Estonian operation required theater and logistics similar to Monrovia. The three ops in Phuket—taken down in coordination with a Thai police SWAT team and an elite plainclothes unit—involved intercepting Hunter, as well as rolling up five men identified through messages and undercover meetings as leaders of a branch of LeRoux's empire that smuggled North Korean meth, South American cocaine and small arms from many countries.

In the larger context, Takedown Day was as ambitious and dar-ing as any ever attempted by American law enforcement. For Cindric, Stouch, and Milione, it was another routine, anxiety-ridden 960 Group operation. They lived with the knowledge that if anyone in any of the three theaters of operation put a foot wrong, or if secrecy was blown by an incompetent or corrupt local government official, a jealous CIA officer or a nervous diplomat, the whole scheme would fall apart and shatter like a disco ball. Such disasters had happened before. Who was to say they would not happen again?

Milione, Cindric, and Stouch didn't see any other way to proceed. Milione told the two agents to "plan for as many curveballs as possible" as they were setting up the arrests. "Like a dance—every piece has to be choreographed." Once they gave the "go" signal, there was no turning back.

There was no exaggerating the danger of the arrests, not only to the DEA agents but to their local police partners and innocent bystand-ers. LeRoux's five hit men were battle-hardened military snipers. The five other suspects—LeRoux's smugglers—were professional criminals who had survived for decades on the streets, and they were targets of geostrategic importance, having established a connection to purchase tons of nearly pure meth, industrially produced by a North Korean supplier that appeared to be protected by the regime of dictator Kim Jong Un. The arrangement was worth millions of dollars to a heavily sanctioned, cash-starved rogue nation that was racing to develop nuclear weapons and ballistic missiles that could reach the American homeland. Depriving North Korea of hard currency was the immediate goal. Beyond it, the DEA agents had a longer-term plan. They thought that if they could get inside the North Korean meth/money pipeline, they could gather valuable intelligence about the rat lines that enabled North Korea to evade International controls and raise money to finance its weapons programs.

LeRoux's smugglers had other intrigues in the works. Investigations of these schemes could spin off valuable leads into the small arms underground in unstable countries and regions. They were making deals with Chinese military officers who offered to sell them SAMs, antiaircraft missiles coveted by terrorists everywhere; with white South African arms dealers and mercenaries; and with a gang of Serbian gun runners LeRoux's men nicknamed "the war criminals."

Early on in the setup, working with three accomplished DEA undercover sources, Cindric and Stouch maneuvered Hunter into believing that LeRoux wanted "Casich" and "Sammy" assassinated in Monrovia. The undercover sources—about whom we'll learn more later—were "Colombian cartel representatives" who used the cover names Diego and Geraldo, and Georges, a French bush pilot, who was introduced to the mercenaries as LeRoux's liaison to their unit, their fixer, weapons supplier and transportation. Hunter assigned the Monrovia hit job to Gögel and Vamvakias. He told them to map out exactly how they intended to do the hit, with maximum stealth and no clues to connect the murders back to LeRoux. He gave them a "Colombian surveillance report" that he thought had come from LeRoux and his cartel partners. In fact, the DEA agents had written it and illustrated it with snapshots of Milione and Taj.

Gögel and Vamvakias responded with an assassination plot that was as callous and blood-drenched as the video games the mercenaries liked to play. They discussed it in conversations captured on DEA's hidden bugs and video.

Through Jonathan Wall, LeRoux's U.S.-based purchasing agent, they acquired Hollywood-grade latex masks that would transform their faces into those of black Africans. They intended to pull on the masks and prowl the nightspots until they located their quarries. The fake surveillance report said that Casich and Sammy might be found at a bar and restaurant called the Blue House in Congo Town, half an hour from the city center. Hipster tourists favored the place for its Mexican-African fusion food. The DEA agent and his snitch had been spotted stumbling drunk out of the place, according to the surveillance report. It added that they had also been spotted at the Level 1 Steak House, an upscale place patronized by the political elite, and Bishoftu, an Ethiopian joint that attracted adventurous diners.

Gögel and Vamvakias intended to execute the DEA agent and the informant with shots to the heads from .22-caliber pistols with silencers. Or, if they couldn't get close, they would use Heckler & Koch MP7 "personal defense weapons," which were shrunken submachine pistols designed for special operations forces and security details. Just seventeen inches long and weighing four pounds, the MP7 fired up to forty high-velocity rounds that could pierce NATO-standard titanium body armor. YouTube videos of the H&K MP7 were gun porn that racked up millions of eyeballs. Gögel and Vamvakias lusted after those MP7s the way drunken college guys drooled over the bargirls at the Rock Hard Club on Patong Beach.

"Whatever gets in that kill zone is going down," Vamvakias boasted.

"Even if they wear a Second Chance vest," Gögel said laughing. He referred to a brand of body armor popular with security contractors.

If innocent people who stumbled into the "kill zone" died—tough luck.

The slight hitch was that the MP7 packed so much firepower into a concealable automatic weapon that it was banned for civilian sales. During planning meetings in Phuket, Georges had assured them, no problem, he'd pick up a couple of MP7s on the black market and smuggle them into Monrovia, along with the handguns, masks, and other gear. He'd have everything they wanted waiting in their hotel. They would be back in the Patong bars in a day or two.

After they killed their two victims, the two shooters expected to step out of the blood-drenched bar and into a car waiting to whisk them to the Monrovia airport, where Georges would be warming up a private getaway plane.

They would carry nothing with them that hinted at a murder plot, except for two hollowed-out euro coins, one per shooter. Each coin contained an encrypted microchip. Even if the local cops found the coin and pried it open, they wouldn't be able to read the chip. Hunter had encrypted the data on them because he was afraid that his emails were being intercepted by the DEA or other law enforcement or intelligence agencies. The data was "target package" with photographs of the intended victims, names, descriptions, cell phone numbers, and locations of apartments and hangouts.

The plan got rolling at 9 p.m. on September 24. At that hour, Gögel and Vamvakias took a puddle jumper for the flight from Phuket to Bangkok International and then boarded Kenya Airways 887 for Nairobi. Their flight took off shortly after midnight and landed in Nairobi just past dawn. Gögel and Vamvakias had some breakfast and changed to Kenya Airways flight 508. The plane stopped for an hour in Accra and arrived at their destination, Monrovia, at 3:10 p.m. local time.

They unkinked their knees, grabbed their daypacks, and descended into the blazing sunlight. At the bottom of the steps was Georges, their lifeline. Vamvakias lunged clumsily toward him, as if to embrace him.

"Don't fucking touch me!" Georges snarled. "Just follow me!" He was scowling. As a onetime commander in the French navy, he had professional standards. He thought Vamvakias had been drinking. He whirled on Gögel, who was grinning like an overgrown kid on a visit to Toyland. The German's beach-rat attire offended Georges, whose khaki civvies were trim and just so, as usual.

"Hey, man, you're not supposed to look like that," Georges snapped.

As they crossed the tarmac, Georges explained to Gögel and Vamvakias that he had spread around plenty of LeRoux's money so they didn't have to present themselves to Liberian border control or have their passports stamped. They nodded and grinned, looking forward, after a cramped, swamp-crotch-inducing twenty-five-hour sky-slog, to a decent meal, VIP treatment, a shower, and pressed hotel sheets. They had been around the Frenchman long enough to know that he was sharp-tongued and judgmental, but he was good at what he did, and they needed him. They tagged behind him through the terminal, a dilapidated cargo building that had been pressed into service as Monrovia's airport after the original terminal burned in 1990 during the Liberian civil war.

Georges handed the men's passports to a kindly-looking middle-aged Liberian with dark skin, short salt-and-pepper hair, and a sweet smile. Georges introduced him as Sam, a Liberian immigration officer paid to usher them past border control. Sam beckoned the three men out of the terminal and along a narrow walkway that led to a squat two-room cinder-block hut behind the terminal.

At the door, Georges gestured toward Sam. "He's my buddy. He'll take care of you. I have to talk to immigration for a few minutes. I'll be back, and we'll go into town."

Gögel and Vamvakias stepped inside and found themselves in a dingy room, empty but for a wooden desk and hard, straight-backed chair on one side and a second hard chair on the other. Just as they settled in, the interior door burst open and four figures exploded into the room.

"Police, police, get on the ground, GET ON THE GROUND!" shouted an angular white American man in a T-shirt and jeans. The three Liberians alongside him took up the clamor.

"Police!"

"Get down! Now!"

The startled mercenaries threw up their hands and started to crouch. The cops shoved them the rest of the way until they were prone and face down on the concrete floor.

The American yanked Gögel's arms backward and cuffed them, while one of the Liberians cuffed Vamvakias.

"I'm Special Agent Jim Scott of the U.S. Drug Enforcement Administration," the American said, bending over the pair to show them his credentials. "You guys are under arrest."

Scott stood up, enormously relieved that the mantra he had learned in basic agent training—*surprise, speed, and violence of action*—had worked. He had dreaded wrestling the mercenaries to the floor, especially that blond beast. He asked the Liberian cops to make a ferocious racket, hoping like hell the mercenaries obeyed before they noticed a key detail, that Scott and the three Liberian airport cops weren't armed. American lawmen couldn't carry firearms in most foreign nations. The Liberian airport cops routinely went unarmed.

Scott pulled out a card and read Gögel and Vamvakias their Miranda rights. They had been indicted in the Southern District of New York for conspiring to murder an American official and an American informant, which were federal felonies. The DEA had already presented the Liberian government with a warrant for their arrest. Liberian president Ellen Johnson Sirleaf had declared them "undesirable aliens" and ordered them expelled to the custody of the DEA.

Scott could see that Gögel didn't get it yet. He looked nonchalant, as if this were just another third-world airport hassle. Scott peered into his bag. It was full of anabolic steroids. Gögel said it was time for his dose. Would Scott give him a shot?

"I've got to stay on my regime or I'll get manboobies," he whined.

"You're not going to get any more steroids," the agent said.

With Scott and the cops watching them, the prisoners spent the night on the floor of the airport's presidential lounge, which had been commandeered as a holding cell. The next morning, more DEA agents showed up to escort Gögel and Vamvakias to lower Manhattan for their day in court. Wim Brown pulled off Gögel's T-shirt to photograph his body, to prove he hadn't been tortured. Taj helped him. The German's entire back, shoulder to shoulder, neck to waist, was one big tattoo with splotches of black and enormous Gothic letters that spelled *INFIDEL*.

"What's that?" Taj asked, though he knew. Gögel looked down at his bare tanned toes and shrugged. Did he think *INFIDEL* was a defiant message for Al-Qaeda and the Taliban? If so, the tattoo was just dumb. If an Islamist militant ever got close enough to see the German's naked back, it would be to saw off his head.

Or maybe that enormous *INFIDEL* was meant to impress other soldiers in the showers and hooches. If so, he had insulted the people he was sent to Kosovo and Afghanistan to protect. Good Muslims, and Taj considered himself one, knew that *INFIDEL* didn't mean Christian or Jew. It meant atheist, somebody who believed in nothing.

During these procedures, it started to hit home for Gögel that since he embarked on this job, practically nobody he met was who he said he was.

Brown, the senior DEA agent on the ground in Monrovia, had been sitting knee to knee with Gögel and Vamvakias on the airport tram in Nairobi, then a few rows behind them on the Kenya Airways flight from Nairobi to Accra. Gögel hadn't really noticed him. Brown had looked like any other globetrotting businessman absorbed in his smartphone. Actually, he was DEA's man in East Africa. He had been tailing the mercenaries since they changed planes in Nairobi and texting their movements to Scott and the DEA crew on the ground in Monrovia.

Georges was a bona fide bush pilot and mercenary, but he was also Brown's friend and was working with the DEA, not against it. After his service as a French navy pilot, flying a Crusader interceptor-reconnaissance aircraft, he became a private pilot in Africa, flying for a number of African leaders and strongmen. On the side, he worked gigs for various Western intelligence and law enforcement agencies. In his fifties, he was tanned, fit, and impeccable, even in Monrovia's soggy heat.

Sam, the "corrupt Liberian immigration officer," was Sam Gaye, a retired DEA agent turned security consultant who had been the agency's man in West Africa for many years. Like Georges, he was a pair of eyes and ears for Cindric and Stouch. Born in Monrovia, he moved with his family to the United States when he was fifteen, joined the DEA after college, and volunteered to return to the war-torn region of his birth. Gaye knew just about every West African who mattered, most importantly, his childhood friend Fombah Sirleaf, the stepson of Liberian President Johnson Sirleaf. She had appointed Fombah to the helm of the Liberian National Security Agency. The president and Fombah Sirleaf were in on the sting from the beginning. Sirleaf had posted his own armed, plainclothes agents throughout the airport to make sure the unarmed airport cops managed the arrests of Gögel and Vamvakias without a hitch.

On the DEA-chartered Gulfstream II executive jet that would take the prisoners to New York to face the charges, Taj sat across from Gögel, close enough to hear him breathe. Whenever Gögel needed to go to the head, Taj took him there and stood by. Not the most pleasant part of the job, but the agents couldn't have a prisoner try to rip out wiring that would affect the plane's instruments. Whenever Gögel wanted a drink or food, Taj fetched it. No cutlery, metal, or plastic. Any implement could gouge out an eye in a split second.

Federal agents were required to treat every prisoner with respect, and Taj did. He kept it professional and civil. He served his would-be killer Pepsis and banana pudding and answered his questions patiently. *Yes, he could write the Russian girl. No, American prisons didn't allow conjugal visits. Steroids again? No, he couldn't get steroids in lockup. Yes, he'd probably get manboobs. No, the warden wouldn't help him out on the steroid front.*

But Taj was entitled to his own thoughts, and what he was thinking was, *Fuck you, Gögel. You are the trash of humanity. You want to kill an American citizen for money? Why should you hang out on the beaches of Phuket, enjoying life on my blood, or Lou's blood, or another human being's?*

Taj had seen this show before. He expected that Gögel would throw himself on the mercy of the court and plead that he was practically an orphan. He didn't know any better. He was poor, lost, and confused. Taj had been there—a refugee, penniless, cold, hungry, and hunted, with nothing but what he could carry. But he never felt alone, was never confused and never lost.

Knee to knee with Gögel, he leaned in and asked again, "You recognize me now?"

The German looked down at the floor.

"You have my picture on your wall. You and your pal wrote an op plan about how you were going to kill me."

The German refused to meet Taj's gaze.

"I actually feel sorry for what you're going to go through, as a human being; I really do," Taj said softly, "because you have a long road ahead. It's going to be bad. But imagine if you actually did kill me. I don't think you would've had second thoughts. Where would you be right now? Probably in Phuket, getting drunk and celebrating your actions. Crazy how the world works?"

Gögel still didn't say anything. He put his face up to the window, mashed his cheek against the cold glass, and sobbed.

CHAPTER TWO

MURPHY'S LAW

TEN ARRESTS, THREE CONTINENTS, NINE HOURS. THAT WAS THE PLAN.

What could possibly go wrong? Anything. Everything.

On the morning of September 25, 2013, when Cindric and Stouch gave the signal to start rolling up the LeRoux criminal network, Murphy's law was starting to kick in.

Early in the day, Milione joined the pair of agents in the Phuket Marriott's "honeymoon villa," a secluded cottage on the beach inside the walled hotel complex. It was secure and set apart, with gauzy white draperies that disguised the inhabitants' activities. The agents had rigged up a makeshift command center cluttered with computer cables, socks, and empty water bottles. The love nest had become a man cave, smelling like stress sweat, not runner sweat or sex sweat.

The wall was covered with a map of the world on which the agents had plotted out the locations of their ten targets and a whiteboard with a detailed timeline showing who was supposed to be arrested where and when. The logistics were like a Rubik's Cube with the possibility of live fire.

What Milione was hearing for most of the morning was one of the English language's most versatile words.

"Fuck."

"Fuck fuck."

"What the fuck!"

Cindric and Stouch communicated by expletive and grunt. They'd been together for so long, they didn't need much of a vocabulary.

The agents had arranged for Hunter, the mercenary team leader, to be alone in Phuket. He was first on the list to be arrested, because if the rest of the mercenaries were captured, he would simply replace them and reconstitute the team. He had done it before.

But Hunter solo was not to be underestimated. He was accustomed to killing, was good at it and justified it to himself in a variety of ways. Through his long career in the U.S. Army, he had served as a sniper, sniper instructor, marksmanship and tactics trainer, drill sergeant, leader of air-assault and airborne-infantry squads, and first sergeant. After he retired from active duty, he tried civilian life in Owensboro, Kentucky, the Ohio River town where he grew up, but he couldn't tolerate the peace and quiet. As he told Diego and Geraldo, the Colombian American undercover informants deployed by Cindric and Stouch, "I had twenty-one years of doing the action stuff at high levels. And then I am from a small town in the States. I go back home. I love where I live but once you're there for a while you're like, I got to get back into the [action]."

Hoping to feel young and vigorous again, he took a job with Triple Canopy, an American security contractor (now called Constellis) that placed military veterans in security jobs at American government installations and private companies in locations where robbery, kidnapping, and murder were common. It was a good gig but it was over in early 2008.

Desperate to avoid going home to Kentucky, Hunter canvassed his contacts. The mercenary Facebook came through. Tim Vamvakias, who had served under Hunter, wrote to say that he had recently gone to work as a mercenary for a Manila security company called Echelon Associates. Echelon was a front set up in 2008 by Dave Smith, LeRoux's chief of security. To launder the money he was making in his illegal e-commerce pharmaceutical business, LeRoux hired experts to buy and sell gold, diamonds, timber, and real estate for him. LeRoux moved these valuable assets around, churning the ownership records until his money trail was thoroughly obscured.

LeRoux didn't trust his own experts not to cheat him. To keep them honest, he hired mercenaries to mind them. "The Echelon mercenaries were there principally to ensure that if any of [the experts] stepped out of line, there would be beatings, shootings, intimidation, and, if necessary, killing," LeRoux later explained.

Vamvakias told Hunter that Echelon was assembling a detail of mercenaries and gold experts in Kinshasa in the Democratic Republic of the Congo and the neighboring Republic of the Congo. This team would be buying gold in central Africa and moving it to LeRoux in the Philippines or Hong Kong. Vamvakias said the pay was good—$7,000 to $7,500 a month. He said he was already living the dream, the dream being a teenage boy's fantasy of a treasure hunt, complete with pirates, jungle hunts, and girls in sarongs.

Their adventures could have used the kind of military professionalism Hunter would be expected to bring to the table. For instance, as Vamvakias later recounted at Hunter's trial, while in Papua New Guinea, Smith and Vamvakias screwed up what looked like a simple mission, to set fire to some trucks at a timber mill whose owner, a Chinese businessman, owed LeRoux several million dollars. Their plan looked as if it had been put together by middle schoolers. They went to sporting goods stores and bought a big pile of gear, including hydration packs and machetes, so they could whack through the deep jungle to the mill. It didn't occur to them that they could simply walk down the road to the mill. No, they had to do things the hard way. They made themselves ghillie suits, weaving greenery onto their fatigues to camouflage themselves as foliage, and slithered through the bush for several days, checking out the mill, spotting back doors, and figuring out where they could hide a getaway car. The big night came. They slipped into the mill, but as they were about to torch it, the alarm went off. Security guards rushed in. Smith and Vamvakias dived back into the bush and made their way back to their guest house, bug-bitten, mission not accomplished.

Hunter applied for a job with Echelon and was hired in June 2008. His qualifications as an army sniper and drill sergeant were just what LeRoux and Dave Smith were after. They might have sensed Hunter wasn't terribly creative, but he was capable, a virtue that would delight LeRoux. Hunter liked following orders, he liked giving orders and he loved adventure.

Hunter took to the job of enforcer enthusiastically. "It's just like a military mission," he boasted to his men in a conversation bugged by the DEA agents. "Right? This is real shit. You know, you see everything. You see James Bond in the movie, and you say, 'Oh, I can do that.'"

He had no qualms about murdering people for LeRoux. "I don't kill anyone unless I get paid," Hunter said in a bugged conversation. ". . . It's easy to kill because they can't talk. But when they can talk, you worry."

If that remark sounded strangely specific, it was. One of Hunter's first chores for LeRoux was to kidnap and shoot to wound a LeRoux business associate. He was Steve Hahn, a South African gold expert who, LeRoux thought, had stolen at least $800,000 from him, and maybe more, by faking some losses in a convoluted gold deal. Hunter shot Hahn in the hand, to punish him, and now regretted it because Hahn could testify against him or come after him. Hunter probably wished he had finished Hahn off. Worrying meant anticipating and gaming out a target's next moves. It was exhausting.

After that, Hunter stuck to simple hits. He took part in at least five murders for LeRoux, by the agents' count. They were convinced that he would shed much more blood if he weren't stopped. LeRoux had given him several more "target packages," military jargon for contract hits. He might still try to carry them out. Or he might take another job as a hit man for some other criminal organization. If he were inclined, he could break out into on a one-man killing spree. The nickname Rambo suggested that he nurtured a darkly romantic fantasy of channeling Sylvester Stallone's fictional Vietnam vet who became a patriotic action hero and icon. By *Rambo IV,* released in 2008, his body count topped five hundred people. Could Hunter match that? Would he try?

For all these reasons, the agents wanted to lock Hunter down early in the day. They had made sure he was alone and isolated. Gögel and Vamvakias were in the air on their way to Monrovia, lured by the agents' fake murder-for-hire gambit. Two other LeRoux mercenaries— Michael Filter, an ex-army sniper from Germany, and Slawomir Soborski, a former Polish special operations operator—were in Tallinn, Estonia, dispatched there to stand guard over a weapons deal between LeRoux's Colombian associates and a Serbian mafia boss. This mission was actually a second undercover theater piece dreamed up by Cindric and Stouch.

The problem was, the agents didn't know exactly where Hunter would be at any moment. The satellite cell phone tracker on Cindric's laptop was supposed to tell them. The agents set it to locate Hunter's two mobile phones—a basic Nokia flip phone that Hunter liked because the battery lasted for weeks, and a tricked-out smartphone that Georges had given Hunter and the other mercenaries, for getting in touch with LeRoux and himself. Cindric and Stouch acquired the smartphones through a shady South African company known as a go-to supplier for organized crime. They made the devices look like bona fide bad-guy phones by adding double coding and encryption, just the way LeRoux liked to communicate. Since the DEA agents had the key to the codes, they could read all the mercenaries' texts and emails.

The tracker system turned out to be inconsistent because of poor signal strength or atmospheric conditions or a satellite's position, or because the God of Cops was in a lousy mood. Sometimes the system could establish the GPS coordinates of a phone to within 10 meters, but other times, the radius was 200 or 500 meters.

Takedown Day was shaping up to be a 200-meter day. Murphy's law—if anything can go wrong, it will—was taking hold. Early in the morning, Cindric started pinging Hunter's smartphone with the tracker system. The phone didn't ping back. Was it dead? The flip phone seemed to be emitting faint intermittent signals, but they emanated from the Loch Palm golf course in the middle of the island.

"What the fuck is he doing on a golf course?" Stouch said.

Cindric shrugged. They were pretty sure Hunter didn't like to chase a little white ball. He spent all his spare time in the weight room, jacking up his pecs and lats. Those signals had to be gremlins—electronic malfunctions. Cindric kept pinging.

Nothing.

"Fuck," he said.

"Fuck fuck," Stouch replied.

Cindric kept pinging. Still nothing. The tracker was giving him 200-meter hits on the Nokia, but Cindric wanted a 10-meter hit, or, at worst, a 50-meter hit.

Meanwhile, Colonel Chokchai Varasard, the Royal Thai Police force's best on-scene commander, and one hundred Thai cops—forty men from his own elite unit, who called themselves the Black Monkeys, plus fifty more cops from other units, plus a SWAT team—were waiting in cars and vans in the parking lot of a Buddhist temple at the bottom of the hill below Hunter's safe house. Once they headed up the hill, secrecy would be lost. The safe house, which Hunter had bought with $450,000 of LeRoux's money, was a comfortable two-story family vacation house and a hard target. Situated in the hills in the middle of the island, it was secluded in vegetation and located on high ground, with a long gravel and dirt road leading up to the gate. An approaching car, motorbike, or person on foot would crunch gravel and stir up dust. The house's concrete block walls made it into a fortress.

Chokchai wanted to hit the safe house, now. The SWAT cops were sweating in full body armor. The rest of the cops were in plain clothes, to blend in with the people on the street, but sooner or later, somebody would notice them, and their cover would be blown. With Chokchai were Jimmy Grace, the 960 Group's supervisor for Africa, and Carol

Dillon, 960's intelligence analyst. The parking lot was so thick with adrenaline, the Americans could almost smell it.

Just past 1 p.m., Pat Picciano, an agent who worked in the DEA Bangkok office, called Cindric from his Toyota 4Runner in the middle of the cop cars.

"They want to hit it," Picciano said.

"Hold them off," Cindric said. The satellite still wasn't giving him a solid hit on either of Hunter's phones.

"I don't know if I can."

In a few minutes, Grace, who was riding shotgun with Picciano, called Cindric and Stouch.

"They want to go in. They're getting a hundred-meter hit."

Chokchai had his own cell phone tracking system, which worked by triangulating off cellphone towers. It was usually less accurate than the DEA satellite-based system, but at that moment, it was picking up a signal from near the safe house.

"Stall him," Cindric pleaded.

In a few moments, Grace called back. "We're going in."

"Fuck," Cindric said.

At 2:15 p.m. local time, the convoy sped up the hill and pulled up near the safe house. The SWAT team pulled up to the gate, dashed into the house's walled courtyard, smashed the sliding doors that led from the blue-tiled pool and Jacuzzi into the interior, pounded across the white living room-dining-room-kitchen, raced up the stairs, and slammed into each of the three bedrooms and two baths.

In a couple of minutes, Chokchai radioed Picciano.

"He's not here," he said in Thai. Picciano translated for Grace, who hit speed dial to Cindric in the love nest/command center.

"He's not here."

"What?"

"He's not here!"

Cindric doubled over as if somebody had slammed him in the belly.

His hands gripped his knees. The element of surprise was totally lost. On an island, gossip goes viral without electronics.

"Ohhhh fuuucccckkk!!!" Cindric moaned. "Fuck fuck fuck."

Stouch stiffened in his chair. "What the fuck," he said.

"No! Fuck!" Cindric groaned. "I told them to wait."

Milione, who had been sitting quietly in a corner, saw despair and wildness in their eyes.

"Look, we'll figure this thing out," he said calmly.

Cindric and Stouch stopped cursing and settled down. They weren't sure they'd pull this op out of its tailspin, but it helped to remember that Milione had been here before, hurtling downward, looking out into nothing, fighting gravity and groping around for a big bag of magic.

In fact, Milione harbored more than a casual interest in magicians. As performance artists they created utterly believable, brilliantly fake illusions. Milione was fond of quoting a line from a 2005 film, *The Prestige*, about two ferociously competitive master magicians. The point, said one magician, played by Christian Bale, was, "Simple maybe, but not easy."

That was exactly what Milione and his agents needed to do. After all, what was a sting but an illusion, a bit of theater in the round? Milione knew more than any other person in the DEA about theater. His first career, before he became a lawyer and an agent, was as an actor with bright prospects.

During his college days, electrified by Marlon Brando's Terry Malloy and Stanley Kowalski and James Dean's Cal Trask, and determined to find a place in gritty American realism plays and films, Milione dropped out of college, took off for Manhattan, and enrolled in the Circle in the Square Theater School on Broadway. He got some choice parts— Tennessee Williams, Eugene O'Neill, a little Shakespeare, a bit part as a cadet in Tom Cruise's 1981 film *Taps*, and a washed-up boxer in a summer stock production of Clifford Odets's *Golden Boy*, directed by Joanne Woodward, who sponsored him for membership in the prestigious Actor's Studio. Most uproariously, as his buddies never let him forget, he did a full-Monty nude scene as a gay hustler hooking up with Will Smith in the 1993 film *Six Degrees of Separation*.

All for art, he laughed, but he was serious. He grew up in a house full of books and art. His grandfather, Louis Milione, was a noted sculptor of monuments that adorned public buildings and fountains around Philadelphia. His father, Victor Milione, was the director of the Intercollegiate Studies Institute, originally the Intercollegiate Society of Individualists, a small but influential scholarly institution founded in 1953 by William F. Buckley and Frank Chodorov, the editor of Buckley's groundbreaking polemic, *God and Man at Yale*. They and other conservatives and libertarians created the institute as a counterweight to the societal and academic upheavals of the 1960s. The ISI, now located near Wilmington, Delaware, rejected collectivism, revisionist thinking, and what is now known as political correctness. It championed classical education, traditional values, and personal responsibility. "By the time the Reagan Revolution marched into Washington, I had the troops I needed—thanks in no small measure to the work with American youth ISI had been doing since 1953," President Reagan said.

Milione listened politely to his father's dinner-table discourses on his favorite philosophers, José Ortega y Gasset and John Henry Cardinal Newman, but what really inspired him were the older man's hands, calloused by repairing furniture and restoring the woodwork in the old family house. The message was, there was honor in the blue-collar life. In Manhattan, between acting jobs, instead of waiting on tables or teaching, Milione supported himself, his wife, and child as a meatpacker and club bouncer. One day, a fellow aspiring actor and former bouncer returned to say that he'd found a dream job as a DEA agent— regular paychecks, stories you couldn't make up, cooler guys and better health insurance than the theater and you could serve your country.

Acting! For real! At the time, Milione was appearing at the Joseph Papp Public Theater in Greenwich Village, in an experimental production of *Woyzeck*, an obscure nineteenth-century German pre-Expressionist drama about a military barber driven to madness, mayhem, and murder by cruel superiors. It was a dreary work that appealed to an artsy crowd, not Milione. He was done with angst and yearned to extricate himself. The DEA sounded like just the ticket.

DEA recruiters liked to see advanced academic credentials and law enforcement or military experience. Milione went back to school, earning his bachelor's degree and then a law degree from Rutgers. He paid his way through school by playing in soaps and in 1996 was finally accepted at the DEA.

Once he was on the inside, Milione discovered that the agency culture was not at all the scholarly redoubt envisioned by the recruiters. It was full of ex-marines, ex-soldiers, and ex–street cops, combative, rough-edged, and sometimes dysfunctional as a fractious family. Inside the walls, agents bitched and moaned. "If they're not bitching, they're not breathing," DEA supervisors liked to say. And, "If they're complaining, they're not conspiring." On the outside, they circled around their own like a wolf pack. They revered their alpha wolves.

Milione was pegged as an up-and-coming alpha. He first gained notice in the Manhattan office by starting with a single phone number and connecting dot to dot to dot until he penetrated a major, previously unknown upstate New York drug trafficking network. In 2002, his intellect and tenacity snagged him a promotion to the DEA Special Operations Division outside Washington, D.C.

For ambitious DEA agents, a tour at SOD was an essential credential, just as the best and brightest military officers sought a master's degree at a military war college.

Created in 1992, SOD occupied an unmarked building in a neatly landscaped, generic cubicle farm in the far Northern Virginia suburbs, on the back side of Dulles International Airport. It was about thirty miles due west of the White House, but very few people who worked at SOD would ever see the inside of the president's office.

In the vestibule, seals about the size of buffet plates were mounted on the wall, representing the alphabet soup of law enforcement and intelligence agencies that made up permanent Washington's national security establishment. These agencies posted liaison officers to SOD's Counter-Narcoterrorism Operations Center to study information coming in from around the world about transnational organized crime as it intersected with terrorism.

Another part of SOD consisted of DEA agents called staff coordinators. As the title implied, they coordinated complex cases that involve several domestic and overseas DEA offices. Staff coordinators networked with law enforcement, military, and intelligence officers from all over the world.

Milione was assigned to a small, secretive investigative unit created by Joe Keefe, the chief of SOD at the time. Officially it was called the Bilateral Case Group, but the few at SOD who knew about it called it the untouchables group, DEA jargon for notorious international kingpins who couldn't be arrested by ordinary means because of their wealth, stealth, and power.

The untouchables group started out chasing the usual Latin drug kingpins, but its mission was transformed to national security on April 14, 2003, when U.S. Special Forces troops searching compounds near Baghdad captured Abu Abbas, leader of the Palestinian Liberation Front, an infamous 1980s terror group. Abbas and his followers had been granted safe haven by Iraqi leader Saddam Hussein after they hijacked the Italian cruise ship *Achille Lauro* in 1985 and committed an atrocity that became a cause célèbre in the United States and Israel. Abbas and his fighters shot Leon Klinghoffer, an elderly wheelchair-bound American Jewish passenger, and tossed his body over the side.

After Abbas was incarcerated at Camp Cropper, a U.S. Army–run detention facility outside Baghdad, FBI agents began to build a murder case against him. They realized they needed an eyewitness, so they asked DEA officials to locate and flip an Abbas friend and financial backer—Monzer al-Kassar, a Syrian heroin and arms trafficker known as the "Prince of Marbella" because he lived in the glitzy Spanish resort favored by Arab millionaires. He held forth in a gaudy white marble mansion, called the Palacio de Mifadil, the Palace of My Virtue, with broad lawns, fountains, and a garage for a dozen cars.

Milione was made case agent for Kassar. In other words, he owned the investigation. He dug into the files and saw that Kassar had been on the radar of DEA, Western intelligence, and law enforcement services for decades but never arrested on account of his money and influential friends—a textbook untouchable. Milione found hits on the Syrian's name in no fewer than seventy-five DEA investigative files. After two years, Milione was promoted out of the untouchables unit, to a post higher in the SOD, but he was now officially obsessed with Kassar. He kept his hand in through his best friend, Wim Brown, who had moved to the untouchables team in 2005 and who had taken over from Milione as Kassar case agent.

Though Milione and Brown talked themselves hoarse, Justice Department prosecutors refused to seek an indictment of Kassar, dismissing the evidence against him as thin and legally problematic. Retrying him for the Klinghoffer murder might be construed as double jeopardy.

But, Milione said, what if they got fresh, damning evidence? What if the DEA caught Kassar in *another* conspiracy to kill *more* Americans? That kind of case was usually a slam dunk in American courts, provided the evidence was solid.

With Brown and a third agent, John Archer, Milione began designing a circuitous sting to draw Kassar into their web. To penetrate his inner circle, they deployed an informant named Samir Houchaimi, who had been a member of the Palestinian terror group Black September in the 1970s. Houchaimi had gotten busted for heroin trafficking in Queens in 1984 and had wormed his way out of prison by going to work for the DEA. Recognizing that Kassar was too wily to fall for a direct approach, the agents sent Houchaimi into Hezbollah-controlled southern Lebanon in early 2006, with orders to win the trust of Kassar's business partner, a Syrian named Tareq Mousa Al Ghazi. Milione told Houchaimi to proceed carefully, so as not to arouse Al Ghazi's suspicions. "No problem," Houchaimi said, "I will have him drink the poison slowly, from a spoon."

Houchaimi took months to put Al Ghazi at ease, but finally, in December 2006, the Syrian invited him to a hotel in Beirut, ushered him through a phalanx of guards, and introduced him to Kassar. Kassar was swanning around the city with his claque of thugs as if he owned the place, and he was probably right.

The second act was set in Marbella. There Houchaimi introduced Kassar to two more informants—Carlos, a Guatemalan, and Luis, a Colombian, both posing as arms buyers for the FARC—Fuerzas Armadas Revolucionarias de Colombia—originally the military arm of the Colombian Communist Party, now a jungle insurgency supported by coca refining operations that produced roughly half the world's cocaine supply, according to U.S. government estimates.

Milione, Brown, and Archer agonized over whether to send Carlos and Luis into the Palacio de Mifadil wearing audio cables coiled around their bodies and carrying a bag concealing a video camera. If the electronics were discovered, Kassar would have them shot dead and tossed into the sea before the Spanish police could get there. But Kassar wouldn't come out for the meeting, so Carlos and Luis insisted on taking the risk in order to get credible, incontrovertible evidence.

On March 27, 2007, Kassar welcomed them warmly, whispering to Houchaimi, "These guys are rubes. They're good guys but they don't know how to do business."

As Milione hoped and expected, Kassar's arrogance and avarice clouded his judgment. Kassar didn't need the money, but he was like a gambling addict. He just couldn't leave a $10 million deal on the table.

He draped his arm around Carlos and boasted that he would produce "a thousand men to help fight against the United States." He offered to train FARC fighters to use C-4 military-grade high explosives to make superstrong IEDs. He made a deal to sell Carlos and Luis more than 12,000 weapons, including fifteen surface-to-air missiles—SAMs for short—to shoot down American troops and American helicopters in Colombia helping search for jungle cocaine labs. These were compact, concealable, shoulder-fired rockets that locked in on targets via a heat-seeking guidance system.

By agreeing to sell SAMs to the FARC, which was officially categorized as a terrorist group, Kassar sealed his fate. In 2004, the U.S. Congress had jacked up the penalty for selling SAMs to a mandatory minimum of twenty-five years in federal prison and a maximum of life behind bars. The reason was that these light, portable antiaircraft missiles were the most fearsome weapons desired by terrorists and militants around the world. As a defensive measure, a SAM was unrivaled. An armed group with one or two SAMs could prevent helicopters carrying special operations troops from landing and mounting an attack on the group's stronghold. As an offensive weapon of terror, SAMs were uniquely effective. A ragtag band of extremists could down a single passenger airliner, inflicting mass casualties, then claim that more SAMs were hidden near major international airports. Even if this were a lie, how would anyone know? With the threat of SAMs, terrorists could paralyze travel and commerce and capture world attention indefinitely.

The grand jury in Manhattan swiftly indicted Kassar and Al Ghazi. Milione and Brown delivered a warrant to the Spanish police, who arrested Kassar as he passed through Madrid on June 7, 2007. The same day, Romanian police arrested Al Ghazi in Bucharest and handed him over to Archer, who ushered him onto a DEA plane bound for New York. Kassar was sentenced to thirty years in prison; Al Ghazi, to twenty-five years in prison. Kassar's palace, bank accounts, and other property were seized.

The Kassar arrest made international headlines that put the DEA Special Operations Division on the map, at a fortuitous moment. Nine months earlier, Representative Henry Hyde, a powerful Illinois Republican, had tacked a provision onto the USA Patriot Act that created a new federal felony, criminalizing the use of drug money collected anywhere in the world to aid international terrorism anywhere in the world. Hyde had been frustrated that Afghan traffickers, having achieved a near monopoly on the world opium supply, were using the profits to sustain the Taliban, kill American and allied troops and civilians, and prolong the war in Afghanistan. The Afghan cartel's heroin and opium trafficking did not violate U.S. laws of the time because those laws were aimed at stopping drugs from entering the United States. Afghan heroin was marketed mostly in Europe, Iran, and Russia. Most of the heroin sold in the United States was made from opium poppies cultivated in Mexico and Colombia.

The Hyde provision gave the DEA sweeping new extraterritorial authority that was not limited to the Afghanistan war zone. It was a ticket to everywhere, so long as the DEA didn't screw it up by overreaching. One scandal, anything that looked like abuse of power, and the law, and maybe the agency itself, could be swept away, its jurisdiction assigned to the FBI, a more hidebound, risk-averse bureaucracy.

DEA leaders decided that this audacious, inevitably controversial statute should be invoked only by the Special Operations Division, and within it, only by a small, handpicked, closely supervised team of seasoned agents. No cowboys, no showboaters. The chosen few were organized into the Bilateral Investigations Unit, successor to the old untouchables group. The new unit came to be known as the 960 Group, after the section of the U.S. legal code where the Hyde Amendment landed.

Milione was a natural choice to run the new group. He had proved he could walk the line between dauntless and wild-ass crazy. Under his leadership, the 960 Group, housed on the corner of the second floor of the SOD building, came to exude an almost mystical aura, something like Skull and Bones at Yale. The 960 Group was not for anyone who needed structure or hated flying. It attracted agents who yearned to go to places they didn't know existed. The most successful were never in the building long enough to set a yellow legal pad on a laminate desk. Milione's view was, agents who weren't out talking to sources weren't doing their jobs.

In April 2007, Milione was briefing Juan Zarate, President George W. Bush's deputy national security advisor, about the Kassar investigation when Zarate pulled out a news clip. "Here's a guy you ought to take a crack at," he said. The piece described a Russian named Viktor Bout, who was to the arms trade what Wal-Mart was to retailing—high-volume, cheap, and unstoppable. Bout was even bigger than Kassar. He owned an air cargo fleet and was delivering massive quantities of weapons to militants in many countries, including Angola, the Democratic Republic of the Congo, Liberia, Rwanda, Sierra Leone, Sudan, and the FARC in Colombia. By one U.S. government estimate, he had made $50 million supplying arms to the Taliban during its rule in Kabul. Zarate wanted him stopped because he was supplying Charles Taylor, who had led a rebel army in Liberia and Sierra Leone, drugged and recruited children as soldiers, and imprisoned women as sex slaves.

As assistant secretary of the Treasury for terrorist financing and financial crimes, Zarate had used his authority to blacklist the Russian from the international banking system, but the sanctions did not seem to have impeded him. Bout appeared to enjoy the active protection of the Kremlin. Zarate was disappointed that the intelligence agencies didn't go after Bout. Some in the intelligence community even did business with him because he provided a service they couldn't get elsewhere—a sort of FedEx service for clandestine lethal aid. The Pentagon, the British government, NATO, and UN had used Bout and his front companies at one time or another to ship weapons to groups they supported.

Zarate didn't think that Bout was directly involved in the drug trade. He sold guns to anybody—*anybody*—who wanted them, including drug traffickers. Zarate turned to the DEA agents because he wanted Bout shut down for good, and he thought DEA agents would do the job. Zarate had spent a lot of time with DEA agents and knew he could count on them to jump out of their lane, display ingenuity, take chances, and piss off some people at the State Department, the CIA, and a few foreign capitals. One of the DEA's unofficial mottos was "Better to ask forgiveness than permission."

So when Zarate asked Milione if he could do something about Bout, Milione said, "Sure." He and Brown put together a scenario they called Operation Relentless. They used roughly the same template they had devised for the Kassar case—an oblique approach using an associate of Bout to get close to the man himself and to entice him to Bangkok with the promise of a mega-deal.

On March 6, 2008, in a meeting in a DEA-bugged hotel conference room in Bangkok, Bout offered everything the "FARC representatives"— actually DEA informants—wanted and more—20,000 to 30,000 AK-47 machine guns, five tons of C-4 military explosive, antiaircraft cannons, sniper rifles with night vision scopes, drones, ultralight aircraft armed with grenade launchers, and 700 to 800 SAMs, enough to wreak havoc at airfields across the world. Bout boasted that the SAMs could knock down U.S. helicopters and American military pilots working with the Colombian police to search out FARC cocaine labs. With extras, he calculated the price for the first phase of the deal at around $20 million.

The Thai police appeared with handcuffs, with Milione, Brown, and other DEA agents a few steps behind them. Bout didn't try to talk his way out. He had talked too much already. "You have all the cards," he told Milione.

By the time the LeRoux investigation was on, the 960 Group had hoodwinked and handcuffed a dozen or more drugs and arms kingpins, all without violence and without losing a single case in court. "The power of treachery," Milione said, was always underestimated.

The unit had been expanded to four teams of agents and intelligence analysts, one team for each continent. Milione had been promoted to assistant special agent in charge of the Special Operations Division. As the case agents for LeRoux, Cindric and Stouch called on the agents on their own Africa team, then borrowed people from the Asia and Europe teams and from DEA posts overseas.

Pat Picciano, a Thai-speaking agent assigned to the DEA Bangkok contingent, served as liaison to Colonel Chokchai, the on-scene commander for the Thai government. On Takedown Day, Picciano relayed messages between Chokchai, who was all over Phuket with his raiding party, and Cindric and Stouch in the honeymoon cottage/command center.

After finding Hunter's safe house empty, Picciano and some of the Thai cops plunged into a thicket of banana trees and scrub in the yard. Picciano's mind clicked through the possibilities: *Maybe Hunter spotted the cops on the road to the house. Maybe he saw cops on the street. Maybe he got word from the neighbors. Maybe he was hiding in the bushes. Maybe he was up one of the trails.*

The hillside, rising 1,200 feet above sea level, was laced with footpaths, dirt driveways, and more banana trees and scrub. Hunter could be hiding anywhere around there. Picciano climbed back in his Toyota and floored it, tires flinging up gravel and sand and sending chickens and lizards scattering. Some of the Thai cops peeled off to other trails. The hill disappeared into a cloud of dust and giant flying insects.

No Hunter. This was very, very bad.

Cindric looked at Stouch. "Fuck, we gotta launch Estonia." It was midmorning in Tallinn.

Stouch nodded. He called Steve Casey, a 960 Group agent who had flown to Tallinn with his partner, Matt Keller, to coordinate the arrests of the mercenaries Michael Filter and Slawomir Soborski. Stouch found Casey and Keller with Toomas Loho, chief of the Estonian narcotics unit, and Rene Kanniste, head of the organized crime bureau. Chris Urben and Ryan Rapaszky from the DEA Copenhagen office were with them. They often shared trafficking intelligence with Kanniste and Loho, who were struggling to contain Tallinn's opioid epidemic, caused by a tsunami of cheap Afghan heroin and even cheaper Chinese fentanyl. The Estonian cops were glad to return the favor by arresting Filter and Soborski.

"Time to launch," Stouch told Casey.

"We got it," Casey said, giving a thumbs-up to Loho.

Casey and Loho raced out of the building and down a short alley to the Estonian SWAT hut.

"It's a go!" they shouted at the SWAT commander.

Sixteen Estonian SWAT cops filed out of the hut. They were on the big side of huge in street clothes. In black tactical helmets and matte black body armor that covered everything except their eyes, they looked like giant mutants. Still, a good sniper could shoot through an eyehole or armpit.

Casey had briefed the SWAT cops to prepare for anything. Filter and Soborski had been unarmed when they walked off their flight at Tallinn International on September 21, but by September 25, Takedown Day, they could have acquired a small arsenal or even a large one. Tallinn, a Baltic port just 120 miles from the Russian border, was known as the Silicon Valley of Europe for its thriving information technology industry, but it was also a major crossroads for transnational organized crime and drug traffickers. In the local underground, native Estonian mobsters mingled and sparred with Russian, Chechen, Ukrainian, and Belarusian criminal networks, any of which would gladly sell weapons to visiting gunmen. Filter and Soborski knew this part of the world and might have set up an arms delivery to their hotel before they left Phuket.

"They're mercenaries," Casey told the Estonian policemen. "Assume they're going to have guns, assume they're going to have knives, assume they're going to fight. That's what these guys have been doing for years. That's what they're paid for."

Filter had been a German army sniper deployed to a remote base in northern Afghanistan. Though he was just twenty-eight and his service record was thin, it was doubtful his commander would have trusted him to defend against Taliban ambushes if he weren't an excellent sharpshooter, reliable and hypervigilant.

Soborski, forty-one, was even more competent. He had spent thirteen years in the Polish military, eight of them in the elite counterintelligence unit JW GROM, whose motto was "Unseen and silent." Besides being a seasoned sniper, he had gone through extensive training in close-quarter combat, explosives, karate, and other offensive and defensive techniques.

As an operator on the Polish police hostage rescue team and president's protection detail, Soborski had trained with, among others, the FBI Hostage Rescue Team and its counterparts in the Czech Republic, Germany, Spain, and Belarus. He spent five years on a protection detail for the president of Poland and had guarded President George W. Bush and Pope John Paul II on visits to his country. After leaving active military service, he worked as a contractor in Afghanistan, Haiti, Eastern Europe, and Dubai and in maritime security missions, protecting merchant ships against pirates in the Indian Ocean and Persian Gulf.

Georges had developed a sort of grudging respect for Soborski, one maverick to another, especially when he overheard Soborski telling Hunter to fuck off, that he had hired on for traditional protection work, not contract hits. Everybody, including Georges, wanted to tell Hunter to fuck off, but the Pole was the only one who actually did it.

Still, Soborski hadn't quit when he heard that the job involved killing, so he would have to pay the price. Georges warned the DEA agents to tread carefully around him. "He's poison," the Frenchman said.

Casey took Georges's words to heart and passed them on to Loho and Kanniste and then to the SWAT team. "Be. Very. Careful." He said it over and over.

The Estonians listened politely, but they had that look Casey recognized, because he had worn it himself. The look was confident, edging toward cocky, and a little impatient. *We've got this,* the look said. *Listen, we know our job. Don't worry about it.*

Casey worried. He feared that the Estonians were underestimating the lethal potential of the two mercenaries. Was he sending them to their deaths? As the SWAT cops piled into their van, Casey approached the nearest SWAT operator, who was about the size of a restaurant refrigerator, and tried to drive the point home, again.

"You guys, just be safe," he pleaded. "Let's all come home tonight."

The big cop roared with laughter. "Don't you worry, I be safe," he said. "And we have fun later."

By fun, he meant vodka.

By 11 a.m. on Takedown Day, Loho, Casey, Keller, Urben, and Rapaszky were standing on the sidewalk outside the hotel, staring at the mix of medieval and Soviet-era architecture. It was gray and cold. The agents shivered and shifted from foot to foot in the frigid wind blasting across the Baltic, but they couldn't go inside the hotel because Estonian law barred foreigners from being on the scene of arrests. The SWAT team filed into the hotel and up the stairs. A few minutes later, one of the SWAT cops emerged and told them that the SWAT leader had knocked on the door and *boom,* both mercenaries were on the floor face down before the door stopped vibrating. Textbook. By 11:34 a.m., Casey called Cindric and Stouch to say that Soborski and Filter were in custody.

Casey went into the hotel and saw Filter slumped on his narrow bed, wrists cuffed behind his back, eyes downcast, as the cops searched his belongings. An Estonian prosecutor was there, laboriously documenting the search and the evidence. Filter was a visibly broken man.

Soborski was standing in the hallway, also cuffed, with three SWAT cops around him. He was watching the search of his duffel. Unlike Filter, he was standing tall and dead calm, and his eyes were alert, flicking left and right, scanning the doors and hallway.

"Okay, this guy's going to run," Casey thought. "He's going to try to do something. He's looking for an opening, for someone's guard to be down." Casey's shoulders and legs tightened involuntarily, bracing for a chase.

The police took both men to the station and put them in separate holding cells. Loho and a couple of his cops went into the cell with Soborski. Casey waited just outside. Loho emerged in a few minutes, looking shaken. Soborski had tossed Loho the handcuffs that had bound his wrists behind his back and sneered, "Here, you'll be needing these."

How did he do that? Casey had no clue, but he pulled out his phone and fired off a warning email to Cindric and Stouch in Phuket: "Just so everyone is aware and to be vigilant. Soborski was transported back to Estonian HQ and put in a room. He then proceeded to undo his handcuffs from behind his back and handed them to the Estonian cops."

Outside the holding cell, Loho said something to the SWAT cops in Estonian, then escorted Casey to another room and said, "I'll be back."

Loho returned in forty-five minutes and said, "Everything is taken care of. They are processed now."

Casey went back to his hotel room to do paperwork. He never did get that vodka with the SWAT cop. There was too much to do. The next day, Loho phoned him with some strange news. Shortly after the handcuffs incident and the DEA agents' departure from the police station, Soborski had been rushed to the hospital with a medical emergency. Something in his abdomen had ruptured—an appendix or a spleen—and he had had surgery. Soborski was lucky he had gotten arrested, Loho said, so he could get medical treatment. It was a surprising development, but the Americans had no choice but to take the Estonians' version of events.

Back in Phuket, Takedown Day was not going as well. It was mid-afternoon there, and Rambo Hunter was still missing. Cindric and Stouch were burning through their cell phone batteries, pleading with Chokchai to get some cops to the airport, the port, anywhere Hunter might be found if he were trying to flee the island. Milione said very little, but every now and then he shot them an encouraging smile or brushed off a problem with a flick of his hand.

Picciano and Grace were sitting glumly in Picciano's Toyota SUV on the hilltop above the safe house, looking at the dust settling on the trail they had just ripped up, trying to figure out what to do next, when Bee, Picciano's Thai helper and translator, called from a Thai cop car. He had good news, maybe. Bee had just remembered that he had the cell phone number of the maid who cleaned the safe house. He had met and sweet-talked her when he was helping the Thai cops bug the place. He had just called her to find out if she knew where Hunter might be.

"He moved out a month ago," she said. "He's staying with his girl-friend."

She said she had cleaned his new place, which was a cottage next to the Loch Palm golf course, just over the hill.

Picciano and Grace called Stouch, who brightened. "The golf course," he said. "Remember those pings? Wasn't there a golf course right there?"

"Yeah," Cindric nodded, grinning. "There. Fucking. Was."

The flip phone's signals from the golf course might not be gremlins after all. He checked the system again. The flip phone's emissions from that spot were growing a little stronger.

He shouted into his cell phone: "Jimmy, how far are you from the fucking golf course? We're getting long pings."

Grace shouted back that they were close.

"Are there houses there?"

"Yes!"

There was a small, gated community of vacation houses, the Garden Villas, on the rear perimeter of the golf course.

Picciano pulled up to the golf course just as Chokchai and his men converged on the place.

A few plainclothes Thai cops stationed themselves on the road and at the entrances, watching for approaching motorists. Others walked across the grounds, asking people if they had seen a pale American with a really shiny, bald head.

As Picciano walked toward the golf club bar and office, he spotted a Harley-Davidson in the parking lot, and in the bar, a bald American, back to the street, tapping on a laptop. Picciano gave Chokchai a thumbs-up and trotted inside. When he got close enough to see the face of the man who had been riding the Harley, he realized he wasn't Hunter. He was another bald, muscular American. Obviously, there was more than one Vin Diesel wannabe in Phuket. Hell, there might be several hundred.

"False alarm," Picciano radioed Chokchai.

The Thai cops questioned the golf club staff and guests. Somebody pointed out a vacation house. A neighbor said that the renter looked like an American. He had left on a motorbike with a young woman.

Grace phoned Cindric. "He's not here."

"Jimmy, are you fucking with me?"

"No."

Cindric gripped his stomach, stared at Stouch, and let fly with more F-bombs.

The Thai cops fanned out, interviewing more people, showing them photos of Hunter. Some people thought they had seen him, but these *farang*—foreigners—looked a lot alike.

A Thai cop posted near the road and golf course entrance radioed that a man and woman were heading toward the house on a motorbike.

Picciano and Grace, who were standing on the roadside, heard the bike before they saw it. Then the faces of the riders came into view.

"That's him!" Picciano shouted into his phone to Chokchai. "That's Hunter coming!"

Chokchai and his men steered their cars right behind Hunter and pulled into the gated community. Picciano, driving his Toyota, fell in behind them. His heart was pounding so hard he could barely hear. When he got a closer look at the man's face, he grinned. That was Hunter, for sure. The woman was his Filipino wife.

Hunter's smartphone was inside the house, turned off, with the battery removed. That's why Cindric's satellite cell phone tracker hadn't found it.

Grace called Cindric in the command center.

"We got 'em!"

It was 5:05 p.m. local time. Cindric, Stouch, and Milione stood up and gripped one another in an awkward three-way hug that knocked off Milione's glasses.

"Thank God," Milione said, and exhaled, finally.

Chokchai's team rushed to a local hotel to make the next round of arrests, LeRoux's five-man arms-and-drugs crew.

Three of them were about to pull up at the hotel. They were Scott Stammers and Philip Shackels, the British traffickers who worked for LeRoux, buying and selling meth, cocaine, drug precursor chemicals, and small arms, and their local muscle, Adrian Valkovic, a Slovak who was sergeant-at-arms of the Bangkok branch of the Outlaws Motorcycle Club, a worldwide organization noted for violence, gun-running and manufacturing and distributing meth. The Thai cops surprised the three after they climbed out of their car and handcuffed them. The last two were arrested in their hotel room. They were Kelly Reyes Peralta, LeRoux's Filipino meth dealer, and his supplier, Lim Ye Tiong Tan, the Manila representative of a Hong Kong–based Chinese Triad organized crime group.

Once the Thai cops had all five secured, Grace called Cindric. "Got 'em."

Cindric and Stouch were elated. The Brits, the biker, and the dealer were good catches. The arrest of Lim was best of all. He was the Pyongyang connection. Bald and scrawny, he affected the look of a Brooklyn hipster—black shirt, black jacket, beige cashmere scarf draped around his reedy neck, and of-the-moment combat boots laced up over skinny black pants. He was pure Chinese underground. He knew exactly how the North Korean meth pipeline worked. If he chose, he could expose a lot of it—the meth manufacturing plants, middlemen, bank accounts, shipping routes, business fronts, all of great interest to the American national security community, which was scrambling to find a way to deny Kim Jong Un the funds he needed to accelerate his nuclear weapons and ballistic missiles programs. Lim might also expose Chinese government complicity in Triad smuggling operations that moved meth and other contraband out of North Korea and cash back to Pyongyang.

Murphy's law had one more shot at blowing up the whole plan, and it was a strong one. Gögel and Vamvakias were still up in the air. If they got away, the conspiracy case would be hollowed out, and the other eight suspects might walk. LeRoux had given his mercenary team more target packages, military-speak for directives to conduct targeted killings. It was conceivable that the mercenaries could try to fulfill those missions to collect the cash they were promised.

Kenya Airlines flight 508 bearing Gögel and Vamvakias, and unbeknownst to them, Brown, was supposed to land at Accra at 12:10 p.m. local time and depart an hour later. If, during their time on the ground in Accra, the pair got a text or some other signal from Hunter, their mates in Tallinn or some other accomplice the agents didn't know about, Gögel and Vamvakias might bolt into Accra, disappearing into the jumble of open air markets and side streets. Brown deplaned at Accra, intending to watch the ramp closely. He hoped that if the worst happened, he could find some Ghanaian police to tackle the pair on their way into the pandemonium. It wasn't a great plan, but it was all he could think of.

Milione, Cindric, and Stouch crouched in their honeymoon cottage/command center, the air humid with their sweat, waited for a message from Brown, and watched the clock. "The curveballs are going to come," Milione said soothingly. Everything was going to be okay.

The younger men weren't so sure. Gögel and Vamvakias had to be taken down, soon. "We needed them, 100 percent, no question about it," Stouch said. "We could not fail. There wasn't any room for failure."

They would know for certain that they hadn't failed when flight 508 took off for Monrovia. Once it was in the air, Gögel and Vamvakias would have no way out. The flight's departure was scheduled for 1:10 p.m. Accra time—which would be 8:10 p.m. Phuket time. Brown was supposed to let Cindric and Stouch know when the plane went wheels up.

At 8:10 p.m. in Phuket, Cindric and Stouch waited. And waited. Brown didn't call. The agents were determined not to panic. They'd been through the Accra airport many times. It wasn't Zurich. Delays were the rule, not the exception. Still, their hearts were pounding like bongos.

Ten minutes passed. Then another ten. Then another ten. The honeymoon cottage went silent. Cindric and Stouch stared at their phones and laptops, willing them to light up. Milione watched them, seeing anguish, channeling calm. When this play worked—not if, but when, he thought, because his faith was absolutely unshakable—they'd get that blast of pure joy. He had experienced it when he got Kassar, and when he got Bout, and when he got those Afghan kingpins with the unpronounceable names, and when he got a whole bunch of second-string scumbags.

"That's where it becomes fun," Milione said later. "Now you're scrambling. You're overcome by an event or an unexpected thing, or the bad guy surprises you. That's where you separate the men from the mice." Some agents froze. Others got sharper and more determined. He classified Cindric and Stouch as the second type. "When it looks like the whole thing is going to go to shit," he said, "they go, 'Fuck it, we're going to *get* this guy.'"

At 8:52 p.m. Phuket time—forty-two long minutes after the mercenaries were supposed to have taken off from Accra—they heard three electronic pings. An email from Brown had just landed in all three men's mailboxes. "FYI Kenya air flight departed," Brown had written. "The big guy is sitting in 12G and the shorter guy is in 27C. See you in Liberia."

The agents' eyes met. They'd done it! They didn't need to say it out loud, but that note from Brown was like dropping a ninety-pound backpack.

The next message came in at 10:50 p.m.: "Got 'em."

That meant the Liberian police had Gögel and Vamvakias in custody. All ten arrests were in the bag, not a shot fired. Cindric and Stouch whooped and looked at Milione.

"Fucking GREAT," Milione beamed and stepped backward. So did the two agents. Nobody wanted to try another group hug.

Cindric cracked open a Thai beer. It was shitty, because he liked shitty beer, and it was so cold it made his eyes ache. As soon as he learned that the DEA plane had landed in Westchester County, he would text Jack, their undercover operative, who had spent eight harrowing months inside LeRoux's organization, wearing a wire and reporting everything he heard and saw. LeRoux had given Hunter a contract to kill Jack. Jack was in the United States, hiding out and praying that the agents would get Hunter before Hunter got him. Cindric's message to Jack was going to be cryptic: "Look at the doj.gov website." Jack would know what that meant—that U.S. attorney Preet Bharara of Manhattan had just announced the arrest of Hunter and the other mercenaries, declaring that "an international hit team has been neutralized by agents working on four continents."

Jack loathed Hunter. For a time, he had lived in a group house with the Kentuckian and the other mercenaries employed by LeRoux. They all knew that LeRoux was a tyrant, capricious and paranoid, who suspected everybody around him of stealing from him. Sooner or later he would order one of them to kill another for some imagined offense. They made a pact that the designated gunman would stage a fake hit with fake photos of a fake blood-smeared corpse—who would open his eyes, get up, wash off the grisly proof of death, and get himself another job, someplace LeRoux would never look.

Hunter didn't join in the mercenaries' covenant. He followed LeRoux's orders blindly, no matter what. When it came Jack's turn to feel LeRoux's wrath, for the usual trumped-up charge of embezzling, Hunter got his gun and started stalking Jack. "Hunter broke the pact and was as loyal as a weasel," Jack said. "He did everything LeRoux wanted, as long he got paid for it."

When Jack got Cindric's text and realized that Hunter was behind bars, he called his fiancée, Anya, who was on the other side of the world. They were safe, for now.

Maybe.

CHAPTER THREE

THE RHODESIAN

"I DON'T WANT TO SIT ON A SOFA," LEROUX SAID. "I WANT TO SIT ON PILES of boxes full of hundred dollar bills and five hundred euro notes. That's what I want."

It was a sultry evening in Manila in the fall of 2009. LeRoux gestured around his glass-and-steel penthouse in the Salcedo Park Twin Towers, one of Manila's swankiest addresses. The living room, the size of a small ballroom, offered a commanding view of Makati, the glittering international finance center of greater Manila. Manila Bay, inky blue at this hour, was just beyond.

As founder, CEO, COO, and CTO of a highly profitable global e-commerce pharmaceutical business, LeRoux could stack cartons of currency to the ceiling of his penthouse and his many other hideaways around the South Pacific and Africa. Nobody but LeRoux knew how many tens and hundreds of millions of dollars, euros, and gold he had stashed in banking havens such as Hong Kong, Shanghai, and Dubai.

Yet he *needed* so much more.

Jack, a European navy veteran who had worked for LeRoux for the past year and a half, felt a chill go up his spine. The Boss, as LeRoux insisted on being called, wasn't content with being the world's biggest Internet pill peddler.

Jack could sense that he had his mind set on becoming some fusion of Pablo Escobar, onetime king of the international drug underworld; Viktor Bout, the world's most hated and feared arms merchant until his arrest in March 2008, and something else altogether. Something new and terrible. LeRoux, said Jack, "was convinced he was going to be the biggest, and, if he ever would be caught, it would be in the history books." He was intent on generating awe. Stunned silence, sheer terror—*awe*! If his mark on history was a big bloody gash, well, the world deserved it.

Jack didn't know anything about LeRoux' origins or why he seemed so angry. Was he seeking vengeance? Vengeance for what? He didn't explain, and Jack dared not ask. Nor did Jack think of using the words "no," "can't," "stop," or "bad idea" around LeRoux. He was just a hired hand. As far as he could tell, LeRoux didn't have an adult friend who could play the part of *consigliere*. The Boss seemed to be on his own, his head full of rampaging thoughts, with no boundaries and no brakes.

Jack was one of the few people LeRoux trusted to come to the penthouse and talk business face-to-face. LeRoux made an exception for him because he was *capable*.

LeRoux needed Jack's eclectic set of skills to fulfill his latest vision, which was to create a new kind of criminal enterprise—a digitally powered, high-volume warehousing and delivery operation for drugs and arms. Call it black-market Amazon, or Amazon-for-arms. If he succeeded, LeRoux would be Escobar plus Bout *plus* Jeff Bezos.

The vision required extensive physical facilities, including an airstrip to accommodate cargo planes, a seaport to handle cargo containers, staff quarters, latrines, kitchens, barricades, sentry towers, and, to defend it all, a private army, very *Apocalypse Now*, with anti-aircraft emplacements on all sides. LeRoux gave Jack an architect's rendering that was based on a U.S. Army firebase in Vietnam. Every staple, every plank, every rebar, and every roll of concertina wire had to be brought in and assembled from the ground up. LeRoux wanted to locate it on a stretch of arid Somalian badlands populated by gunmen, Islamists, and goatherds.

LeRoux sensed when he interviewed Jack that he was the man for the job. He had run his own construction company in northern Europe, so he could read architectural plans. He had spent time in war zones. He could shoot, apply a tourniquet, and bed down on a scorpion-infested patch of desert like the rest of LeRoux's mercenaries. With his pleasantly craggy face, deep bass voice, and self-effacing manner, he could put on a tie and talk wine vintages with a government minister while slipping him an envelope of bills. He could walk into a bank and wire ten thousand euros to Hong Kong, without raising suspicion.

"My golden boy!" LeRoux dubbed him. The Boss lavished as much warmth as he could muster on his new favorite. It wasn't much but it was better than anything Jack had gotten from his own father, an abusive alcoholic who, to his dying day, wouldn't concede that his son did anything right. Jack liked to hear the Boss say "golden boy." And, of course, there was the money.

Jack was in way over his head. He hadn't seen this scheme for a cyber-enabled black-market megastore coming until he was caught up in it, and now he didn't know how to get out of it.

Too late, he realized that LeRoux's pharmaceutical business and real estate investments were just covers for his more malign plans, which he was pursuing along multiple tracks.

His latest brainstorm was to expand his portfolio from conventional small arms to large weapons systems and weapons of mass destruction. He had recently made a deal with Iran's Defense Industries Organization to develop key components for the DIO's program to build advanced, precision-guided rockets and missiles—"smart rockets" was the jargon in the military-industrial complex. Determined to amplify its power across the Middle East, Iran was stockpiling rockets and conventional missiles and supplying hundreds of thousands of them to its proxies, including Hezbollah, the Shi'a militant group that controlled much of Lebanon, the Houthi rebels in Yemen, Shi'a militants in Iraq, and other militants around the Middle East and South Asia. Iranian missile factories would soon start cropping up in Hezbollah territory in Lebanon and parts of Syria controlled by Iran's ally, the Syrian dictator

Bashar Al-Assad. Whenever Iran's unguided rockets and missiles were lobbed at Israel, they did little damage because they lacked up-to-the-minute navigation systems, due to effective international sanctions. The situation would be very different if LeRoux succeeded. He had sent emissaries to Tehran to meet with the head of the DIO and offer to help Iran craft navigation systems that would make ordinary rockets and missiles "smart," meaning, capable of crippling strategically vital targets, including military command and control centers, communications nodes, airport control towers, ministries, and critical infrastructure such as water systems. Such fearsome weapons, small enough to be transported by bands of militants, could alter the skylines of Jerusalem and Tel Aviv. Once he cinched a deal with Iran to pursue the missile guidance project, for which he expected to be paid $100 million, he assembled a team of scientists and engineers, mostly from Romania, and set them up in a clandestine research lab in Manila, with testing facilities and bunkers in the countryside.

To obtain chemicals for the project and to deliver parts to Iran without being detected by intelligence services, LeRoux assigned several of his engineers to designing a small diesel-powered submarine. He had already completed construction of a docking facility for the sub at a yacht maintenance yard he owned on the coast of Batangas Province, south of Manila.

He created a separate business to buy and sell North Korean methamphetamine, through a Chinese Triad group. The Triad was offering as much as six tons of pure crystal meth a month, for the asking price of $360 million. On the street, that much high-quality dope would bring somewhere around $1 billion. To LeRoux, it was just another opportunity with nice upside potential. He didn't care that a transaction of that magnitude would put a big chunk of hard currency in Kim Jong Un's pocket, greatly enhancing his ability to menace the United States and its allies with the threat of nuclear-tipped missiles. North Korean engineers were working steadily to extend the range of the regime's ballistic missiles to reach the continental United States. It was possible, even likely that some of the millions generated by the meth would underwrite the North Korean arms race.

What Jack didn't see, when he first met LeRoux, was his ravening, insatiable thirst for money and control. Like most people, Jack had preconceived notions about how world-class international criminal leaders behaved. To date, most of the stereotypes had been true, and for good reason. Without exception, Colombian and Mexican cartel bosses used their jewel-encrusted guns and girls, dressage horses, private zoos, torture chambers, and over-the-top muscle cars to brand themselves winners. Swagger was marketing. The Kardashians knew that. So did Pablo Escobar, El Chapo Guzman, and all the rest of the crime lords who had achieved tabloid/clickbait status.

LeRoux defied categorization. He lived austerely and reclusively, indifferent to most creature comforts. The penthouse where LeRoux always met Jack was starkly furnished. It looked like the inside of a new refrigerator, with Ikea-white walls, a three-cushion couch, the biggest flat-screen TV on the market, and a table with four uncomfortable straight chairs. Even as he confided his desire to wallow in currency, LeRoux perched on one of the straight chairs, his lumpy backside hanging over the seat. Jack sat across from him on a second straight chair.

LeRoux had seven or eight other luxury properties around Manila and Subic Bay, plus places scattered from Hong Kong to northern Europe, but Jack had the impression that the penthouse was the place where he spent most days, making business deals via text, email, and voice-over-Internet systems. He used outdated hardware and software that he had studied inside and out, to assure himself that his computer and messaging systems didn't have trapdoors that foreign spies could enter.

In the penthouse kitchen, two bored cooks hung about, gossiping with the bodyguards. LeRoux kept the cooks and a maid on duty around the clock, even though he usually sent out for his favorite foods:

Big Macs, pizzas, and Kentucky Fried Chicken wings. If fast food was good enough for Warren Buffett, who was famous for eating breakfast at McDonald's every single morning of his frugal life, it was good enough for LeRoux. But the Sage of Omaha, closing in on his eighth decade, looked as if he might live forever, while LeRoux, at thirty-six, was bloated and ungainly. That's probably why he mainlined Diet Coke and Coke Zero by the case, in the futile hope of containing his spreading belly. LeRoux didn't drink alcohol. His strange big brain was his instrument, the fount of all his wealth, and had to be kept clear and clean. No bling, blonds, or clubbing. His vice was prostitutes, sometimes in multiples. He ordered in. Cindy Cayanan, LeRoux's regular girlfriend, accountant, mother of two of LeRoux's children, and, at home, his feisty Dragon Lady, kept to one of the other residences, sometimes raging about his sessions with hookers, which he called "raves," but mostly acquiescent. He was the money in the relationship. It appeared that they both enjoyed a good fight, almost as much as a fuck.

There was a bed in the master bedroom and in a second bedroom, a pile of U.S. Army M4 assault rifles and some body armor. No art. No décor. No mementos. He didn't want to possess anything he couldn't throw in a suitcase. He was in a constant state of readiness to vanish.

"He always had a backup plan ready," Jack said. "He paid top dollar for the most exclusive homes but inside was barely nothing. He never showed off. He lived very minimalistically and always was prepared to move."

Running an organized-crime business required complete mobility and the absence of sentiment. As indelibly, quintessentially Rhodesian to his core, LeRoux was well suited to the role. He had spent his first dozen years in a society, now dispersed, of extraordinary privilege intertwined with unremitting tension. White colonists in politically isolated Rhodesia believed in taking what they wanted and depending on themselves. They fought hard and dirty and almost to the bitter end.

Almost, because they made sure they had a way of escape. And then they slipped back, if they could, because they never really belonged anyplace but Rhodesia.

Paul Calder LeRoux was born on Christmas Eve 1972 in Bulawayo, Rhodesia's gritty, vibrant second city. He was the illegitimate son of a young white woman and her lover, both of British descent. A married white Rhodesian couple, Paul and Judith LeRoux, adopted him. Two years later, a daughter—Paul's little sister—arrived.

Today, only 17,000 people of European extraction live in Zimbabwe, a landlocked nation of 150,000 square miles wedged between South Africa, Mozambique, Botswana, and Zambia. At the time of LeRoux's birth, some 260,000 whites resided there, ruthlessly dominating, exploiting, and fearing the country's 4.8 million blacks. Bulawayo, a precolonial tribal capital whose name meant "place of slaughter," had blossomed into an industrial powerhouse and processing center for the region's abundant metal ores, cattle, cotton, tobacco, and maize. The colony's wealth cushioned it from international sanctions meant to force Prime Minister Ian Smith, an unyielding champion of white rule, to agree to a transition to majority—black—rule.

But the black nationalist movement was gaining strength. Three days before LeRoux was born, the colony's long-simmering racial and economic disparities ignited into what whites called the Bush War and blacks called the War of Liberation.

At exactly three o'clock on the morning of December 21, 1972, black nationalist guerrillas, backed by the People's Republic of China, attacked a tobacco farm owned by a Belgian émigré hated for his cruelty to black laborers. Sporadic guerrilla raids on other white farms followed. The Rhodesian security forces, among them a shadowy clandestine unit known as the Selous Scouts, counterattacked ferociously. The civil war escalated as both sides engaged in hideous atrocities. The British historian Piers Brendon, in his 2008 book, *The Decline and Fall of the British Empire,* wrote:

Cities such as Salisbury and Bulawayo, where most Europeans lived, were hardly affected by the bloodshed. But guerrillas, some backed by China and others by Russia, crossed the frontier from Mozambique and Zambia to attack remote farmsteads, railways and roads. Rural whites turned their houses into fortresses, protected by sandbags, searchlights, barbed wire and guard dogs. The guerrillas tried to enlist the native population, using terror tactics against anyone who resisted. Chiefs were regularly tortured and murdered. Schoolteachers were raped. Villages were looted and burned. Counter-insurgency measures were no less savage. They included collective punishments, the closure of schools and clinics, the establishment of free-fire zones and protected villages similar to concentration camps. African cattle were seized or deliberately infected with anthrax. Captured combatants were given electric shocks, dragged through the bush by Land Rovers or "hung upside down from a tree and beaten." One District Commissioner engaged in "stamping on them" said that he had "never had so much fun in my life." The Selous Scouts committed the worst atrocities, especially during cross-border raids and hot pursuits. . . . By 1974, though, more insurgents were being recruited than killed.

By 1978, Rhodesia was in a weakened position. Its only ally, South Africa, was staggering under international sanctions because of its own apartheid policies. Under pressure from the United Nations, Great Britain, and the United States, Smith reluctantly held elections. On March 4, 1980, guerrilla leader Robert Mugabe's party won in a landslide. The colony of Rhodesia disappeared from the map, replaced by the independent nation of Zimbabwe.

Liberation brought no peace. Mugabe launched a dirty war against tribal and political rivals. He created a 5,000-man Fifth Brigade, had it trained and equipped by North Korea, and dispatched it into the countryside to pillage, rape, torture, and slaughter. Between 20,000 and 80,000 people, mostly civilians, died.

The LeRoux family would have avoided witnessing the worst of the violence if it is true, as has been reported, that they lived in the mining town of Mashaba (also spelled Mashava), about 150 miles east of Bulawayo, where Paul LeRoux the elder was reportedly a supervisor of underground asbestos mining in the enormous Shabanie and Mashaba asbestos mining complex, one of the largest and most hazardous mining operations in the world at the time. Available accounts of the period indicate that Mashaba was a relatively quiet company town, meting out misery and early death to black asbestos miners, but it would have afforded an uneventful childhood to the son of a white overseer.

White privilege couldn't survive Mugabe's financial mismanagement, which launched the Zimbabwean economy into a tailspin and sent white professionals fleeing. For many white Rhodesians, returning to the British motherland was not an option. Rhodesians labored under a stigma dating back to the colony's early days. "Kenya was advertised as a rich man's playground, a sportsman's paradise, the officer's mess as opposed to the Rhodesian sergeant's mess," British historian Brendon wrote. In modern times, British intellectuals dismissed white Rhodesians as thuggish, dull-witted, entitled hicks who couldn't make a go of life in the real world. "One is struck in Salisbury by the startling incompetence of the Europeans," British journalist Richard West observed in his 1965 book, *The White Tribes of Africa*. "The rude, lazy hotel staff, the shop girls who cannot add, the airline staff, who misread your ticket, are all incompetent even by African standards. But they retain their jobs because customers prefer to be served by whites and because there are few Africans qualified to replace them. The whites make sure of that." Robert Blake, a British historian who wrote the well-regarded *A History of Rhodesia,* described the colony as a "cultural desert" that "never threw up as a by-product any sign of intellectual, literary or artistic life."

Some Rhodesian intellectuals agreed with these condemnations. Foreshadowing American progressives who regarded Donald Trump's base as rednecks and, as Hillary Clinton famously sniped, "deplorables," Frank Clements, a white Rhodesian reformer and journalist who served as mayor of Salisbury in the early 1960s, complained in his 1969 book, *Rhodesia: The Course to Collision,* that the Rhodesian whites who put Ian Smith in power were "the misfits of British society" who "had decided that they themselves were not equipped to succeed at home. In no field of activity, from accountancy to welding, from journalism to selling, did Rhodesia offer inducements to the successful or the conspicuously talented."

Even for the best and brightest of the white Rhodesians, job prospects were bleak in Britain and Western Europe, then in the grip of a severe recession and mass unemployment. Most white Rhodesians chose to resettle just over the border to South Africa.

The LeRoux family joined the white exodus in 1984 and landed in the grimy South African mining town of Krugersdorp, 540 miles to the south of Bulawayo. LeRoux's father reportedly parlayed his knowledge of mining into work as a consultant to South African coal mines.

South Africa offered the newcomers a marginal living and little peace. In 1984, Afrikaner hard-liners enacted a new constitution that guaranteed whites control of parliament, gave Indians and "coloureds" a minority share and excluded blacks altogether. When black nationalists launched protests, the white government decreed a state of emergency and suspended civil rights, drawing international condemnation and tougher trade sanctions that cratered an economy already beset by years of drought.

Krugersdorp did not escape civil unrest. Its neighboring black townships joined the protests and bombed government buildings. In 1990, Nelson Mandela, the leader of the black nationalist movement and head of the African National Congress, was freed after twenty-seven years in prison. Four years later, apartheid was abolished, the first multiracial elections were held, and Mandela became South Africa's first democratically elected president.

During the years of political isolation and recession, Krugersdorp, like other West Rand towns, saw the rise of squatter camps populated by down-at-the-heels whites, as John Grobler, an investigative journalist in southern Africa, put it, "mostly Afrikaners, mostly poor and, as result, quite a criminal element coming from that area." With a legal system in survival mode, enforcing laws harshly or not at all, South Africans, white, colored, and black, did what they could to survive.

What actually went on in the LeRoux household remains a mystery. From time to time, LeRoux hinted to acquaintances that his childhood, though not physically impoverished, was emotionally arid, that his mother was frail and his father had left the family. He also claimed that his father developed an off-the-books sideline as a diamond smuggler and introduced his son to figures in the South African underworld. It has not been possible to verify details of LeRoux's childhood and teenage years. By the accounts of several people who have known him over the years, LeRoux was an able manipulator and fabulist who said whatever served his purpose at the moment. Though he wasn't a habitual complainer, he wasn't averse to portraying himself as Oliver Twist or Horatio Alger if it got him what he wanted.

This much is beyond question. The teenage years are the worst time to be an outsider and LeRoux was one in every respect—an English-speaking Rhodie among mostly Afrikaans-speaking whites, a white in a population that was 85 percent black and Asian. Whites were at the top of the economic and social heap in South Africa, but LeRoux, chunky and socially awkward, was no good at any of the sports his schoolmates worshipped and didn't fit in with the cool kids.

He buried himself in his computer. He studied programming at a South African technical school, soon outstripped his classmates and his teacher, and learned new techniques on his own.

In 1992, when he was twenty, he snagged his first job, working at a London-based information technology consultancy called BEI International, which provided document management systems to law firms and other clients. He coded network security and records management systems for corporations, banks, law firms, and government ministries. He presciently made a point to develop a specialty in the young field of cybersecurity, hardening computers and computer networks. The field would soon double and redouble, as businesses, intelligence services, identity thieves, and malicious hackers carved increasingly ingenious electronic pathways into computers that held sensitive data.

For a young man of no connections and no prospects, this was an interesting and possibly ingenious choice. When he landed in London, it was as an orphan—friendless, feckless, and scruffy, with no family or friends to guide him into the circles where businessmen and women exercise power and make money. The corner suites and private clubs were still the domain of men, and a few women, who graduated from Ivy League institutions or Oxbridge. An unkempt, poorly credentialed white southern African like LeRoux would never be invited to bloviate over martinis and coconut shrimp at the World Economic Forum at Davos.

But as a cybersecurity expert, he could spend as much time as he liked roaming around inside the digital brains of great institutions and tinkering with servers and network connections. He would be welcomed into the electronic nerve centers of banks, corporations, law offices, and government ministries. He would be routinely ignored and taken for granted, but an enterprising IT security guy could learn a lot by observing how big powerful institutions worked at their most fundamental level.

LeRoux could have used his powers to search out and destroy immense quantities of data. He didn't. He was no troll. He was destined to be an innovator.

In London, he met and married a young Australian woman. He followed her to Sydney in 1994 and joined a firm called New Era of

Networks—NEON for short. The marriage didn't last, but he got Australian citizenship and an Australian passport out of it. Later, he often introduced himself to people as either Rhodesian or Australian, but usually not South African, though he carried a South African passport. There may have been something about the intrepid Crocodile-Dundee-this-is-a-knife Australian identity that appealed to him.

After the divorce, he resumed his rootless life as a security geek for hire. He jumped from NEON to a firm called Crypto Solutions and bounced around between London, Hong Kong, Virginia, and Seattle.

LeRoux would later make the uncheckable but plausible assertion that while in Britain, he consulted for GCHQ, the legendary British signals intelligence agency celebrated for cracking the Nazi codes during World War II. It had moved from the original Bletchley Park grounds to technocratic digs in Cheltenham, but the aura of romance and mystery lingered. To call LeRoux a rogue spy would be a stretch, but if it is true that he did a stint inside the supersecret GCHQ compound, he would have gained invaluable lessons from the engine room of Britain's spy services.

In 1997, during one of his interludes in London, LeRoux met a young man who would inadvertently show him his destiny—Wilfried Hafner, a pioneering entrepreneur with a cybersecurity and electronics consulting company in Munich. Slim, dapper, bespectacled, and bald as an egg, Hafner was twenty-five, just seven months older than LeRoux, and he was a former hacker of considerable skill and notoriety, but he had switched sides and was now running several companies and advising governments and corporations on how to shield their data from industrial spies and saboteurs. He had rich and respectable investors and a network of business contacts stretching from Hong Kong to Rio. He looked the part of the suave cosmopolite. At their first encounter, LeRoux was impressed by Hafner's crisp manner and impeccably tailored suit. The Rhodesian had never wanted a suit, but he wanted that one. Its dark wool said gravitas and the fit, draping beautifully from shoulder to hem, said money for a tailor. "Well, you're a guy who knows how to dress," LeRoux said.

Hafner saw a hefty twenty-four-year-old, wearing the standard bro-grammer uniform, a baggy T-shirt and cargo pants. Divorced and on his own, LeRoux was subsisting on junk food, struggling to make rent, and trying to figure out how he was ever going to escape IT-guy ser-vitude. "He was unhappy because he had no money," Hafner recalled. "He did not have a real life."

But Hafner knew that LeRoux had something else, something that at that moment was absolutely vital to Hafner's next product line. LeRoux was a bare metal code ninja. He could talk to machines. In addition to more advanced and modern programming languages, he had chosen to master ancient computer languages technically known as "low-level programming," also called "assembly programming" and "machine code." These older languages used strings of letters, numbers, and symbols devised by mathematicians and electronic hardware de-signers in the 1940s, '50s, and early '60s, at the dawn of the computer era. They communicated with a computer's raw hardware—the silicon chip itself and the other moving parts—before the operating system kicked in. The esoteric craft of low-level programming was known in the geek world as "bare metal," or "writing close to the metal." Few pro-grammers bothered to learn it. Web design, image display, and other common tasks that made things look pretty in pixels used modern "high-level" programming languages, whose commands were written in English and which were relatively easy to navigate.

Hafner's engineers, writing code to encrypt his clients' sensitive data, had encountered a gnarly problem that required knowledge of low-level programming. Hafner asked around and was referred to Le-Roux, who did not disappoint. In a few days, he had banged out a solution.

Two years later, Hafner returned to LeRoux with an offer no bud-ding entrepreneur could refuse—a big title—chief technical officer—

more money, and, most important, a place at the table, meaning a full partnership in the venture. Hafner wanted to launch a new company to pioneer a next-generation encryption technique called "full disk encryption" or "whole disk encryption." The practice, then common, of encrypting email and text messages one at a time was not only laborious but inadequate. As banks, businesses, and agencies moved from paper to digital storage and as the capacity of hard drives expanded, people were storing ever larger quantities of sensitive information on their laptops, carrying them around and sometimes forgetting them in taxis, subways, and cafes. Sometimes these machines were surreptitiously targeted and downloaded by spies breaking into offices and hotel rooms and by officials at border checkpoints in repressive nations such as Russia, China, and Iran. The only way to secure an entire machine and prevent the theft of its intellectual property was to wrap it inside an unbreakable multilayered coding system. The technical difficulties were daunting.

"You can find programmers out there like sand at the beach, but only few—less than one percent—with the skills for developing full disk encryption," Hafner said. LeRoux was in that golden one percent, not only because of his knowledge of low-level programming but also because of his adroitness in solving many other types of problems. Any programmer could copy what somebody else had done. Innovation required someone who could imagine how to do things that had never been done, and then do them.

"Paul proved to be a brilliant programmer," Hafner said. "He is one of the smartest and most consequential technical person I know. Many people may have cool ideas, but Paul also knows or finds a way to transform those ideas into reality. He also follows through where many give up."

But to become a full partner, he would have to give up his vagabond ways, park his butt in a chair, glue his fingers to a keyboard, and spend two or three years tapping out magical little cybersymphonies that only machines could hear. To press the point home, Hafner picked up LeRoux in his Mercedes 500 SL, swept him away to his villa in Cap d'Antibes, the Cote d'Azur's most exclusive enclave, and started showing him the opulence that could be his if the company caught fire.

Hafner found LeRoux a hard man to inspire. He was indifferent to the iconic sights—the cerulean sky and sea that had transfixed, among others, Claude Monet, Henri Matisse, Pablo Picasso, Edith Wharton, Somerset Maugham, Graham Greene, F. Scott and Zelda Fitzgerald, Cole Porter, Rudolf Valentino, Alfred Hitchcock, Bono, and Mick Jagger; the spot where Fitzgerald finished *The Great Gatsby* and started *Tender Is the Night;* the musky cafes of St. Tropez, where Brigitte Bardot danced barefoot in *And God Created Woman*; the cliff where Jean Seberg played at goading Deborah Kerr to her death in *Bonjour Tristesse.* He didn't want to go to the Picasso museum. He declined Hafner's offer of a lavish lobster dinner at the rococo Hotel Carlton in Cannes, the film festival watering hole where Alfred Hitchcock had filmed Grace Kelly and Cary Grant flirting in *To Catch a Thief.* LeRoux, clinging to his T-shirt, shorts, and flip-flops, complained that all those movie stars hanging about the Carlton's marbled terrace made him uncomfortable. A beachside fish-and-chips joint was fine, thank you.

The vision of extreme wealth struck him like a *coup de foudre* when they went to at the International Yacht Club and the Quai des Milliardaires, Billionaires' Cay, in Antibes. French locals called it the Cove of False Money. Bobbing in the sparkling blue water was a fleet of superyachts owned by Russian oligarchs, Greek shipping tycoons, and Persian Gulf sheiks. The sleek leviathans had perks that would make a James Bond villain gasp with envy—one, sometimes two, helicopters and helipads, pools and sport courts with jet-skis and other toys. Armed guards, big pale Russians and Ukrainians toting M4s or Uzis, stood at the ready. The deck chairs were decorated with stunning young women, or girls, adjusting Chanel sunglasses to hide black eyes dealt out by their cranky lovers/keepers/masters. LeRoux's eyes lit up like a slot machine that just landed on three cherries. Inside his head, a switch had just flipped. In retrospect, it seemed as if this was the moment when an unknown young programmer became LEROUX.

"He said, I want to get to this," Hafner recalled. "It's not that he *needed* to have a yacht, but he wanted to have the money to be able to *buy* a yacht. He started calculating. If somebody has the money to buy a yacht, which is $100 million or more, first what he's doing is buying a house, then a second house, buying his car, buying his helicopter, and at the last, buying his yacht. He said, if his yacht cost $100 million, this guy must have much, much more. And just the cost of the people that are cleaning it all day all year, and so on. He was thinking, how much money these people must have, and that is where he wants to be."

He wanted the full Russian oligarch package, not only the super-yacht, but also the party girls with cat-eye makeup, thongs, and thigh-high black boots, the cliffside villa on shore, the townhouse in London and apartments in Hong Kong and Paris, the Ferrari, the strapping, heavily muscled bodyguards, and much, much more.

His lust for opulence swelled when they strolled into the gilded Casino de Monte Carlo. For the occasion, he waived his no-tie rule and allowed Hafner to drape him in a shirt and suit borrowed from a portly oil executive, with Hafner's own silk cravat wrapped around his thick neck. Hafner bought him a stack of chips to wager at the high-stakes roulette table. LeRoux was dazzled. The Russians were there, consuming liters of vodka and pawing gorgeous women dressed in stilettos, a few spangles, and not much else. They were laughing and clinking glasses as they lost great stacks of chips and bills. Hafner could see that LeRoux was interested in gamblers. They were addicts, and addicts of any kind were very reliable customers. To think of the money the casino was raking in! The house couldn't lose. This was an insight Le-Roux filed away for future reference.

LeRoux agreed to join Hafner, and for two years things went well. LeRoux lived in Rotterdam and teleworked, collaborating with Hafner and others in the company via the Internet. Hafner noticed that Le-Roux had a perverse streak. He couldn't resist messing with people. He lied when he didn't need to. He liked to brag to Hafner how he had played somebody. He would lie to a colleague, then tell Hafner what he had done and laugh about it.

"He's a good actor, in telling a story that was completely made up, to achieve something else," Hafner said.

He was a user. "He often found the solution by getting someone to do something for him," Hafner said. "He would go on the Internet and find someone who did." He got a lot of free help from other computer geeks, picking their brains for knowledge that they would ordinarily charge for.

His demeanor was usually calm, but occasionally he exhibited flashes of rage and contempt for others. Once while talking to Hafner on the phone, LeRoux belittled some favor Hafner had done him. Hafner hung up. LeRoux called him back, weeping and groveling. Hafner said Le-Roux had offended and insulted him by not appreciating what Hafner was doing for him.

Hafner's voice went stony. "I. Did. Not. Have. To. Do. This." Le-Roux wept anew and apologized again. They called a truce.

Hafner formally launched the new company, SecurStar, in 2001 and put the product, a security software package called DriveCrypt, on the market in November of that year. They were on their way!

Until they weren't, because LeRoux's mood turned inexplicably dark. In 2002, a few months after the launch, LeRoux told Hafner he was unhappy with the pace the company was setting and with his pay. "I'm ambitious," he complained. "I'm in need of money." LeRoux said he wanted to live in luxury. Plus, he had recently remarried, to a Taiwanese expatriate named Lillian. They had a baby son, the first of the four children they would have together.

"Encryption software is a niche market," Hafner told him. "You're in the wrong business." The company would pay off eventually, but not as spectacularly nor as quickly as LeRoux wanted. He offered to introduce LeRoux to people in the online casino business in Costa Rica. They probably needed a good programmer.

LeRoux perked up. He hadn't forgotten that night at the Monte Carlo casino—those gambling junkies flinging bills around like confetti at a political convention, the gold, the cars, the women. The drawback, Hafner said, was that LeRoux would have to move to Costa Rica to pursue the casino opportunity. What about his little son? Hafner could hear the baby, about five months old, crying in the background. What about Lillian?

"I'll dump my wife and the kid, no problem," LeRoux said with a laugh. "I've heard South American women are prettier."

Hafner was appalled. How could a man joke about abandoning his family? He was growing increasingly uneasy about his collaborator's character. A few months earlier, LeRoux had mentioned that he was adopted and said of his biological father, "I don't give a shit about him." Hafner was shocked. How could he speak ill of his own father? Where Hafner came from, people didn't disrespect their parents, not even in jest.

Then Hafner discovered that LeRoux had stolen from the company. He had gotten his hands on a valuable string of code proprietary to SecurStar and had sold it out the back door to a British company. Another team of engineers within the company had written the code, which drove a security device called a crypto-key. Because it was extremely difficult to write, that string of code was worth $100,000, and maybe more on the black market.

When Hafner confronted him, LeRoux didn't deny pilfering the code. He made some lame excuses. Hafner fired him, but he was baffled. For the chief technical officer to cheat his own colleagues was beyond his belief. And for what? LeRoux did not need to steal. He had just blown the opportunity to be made a full partner in SecurStar. As the company grew, so would his share of the profits. He would have made far more than $100,000 if he had had a little patience. He lost something beyond price—his relationship with Hafner, his mentor. It was as close to a real friendship with a person his age as he had ever had or ever would have.

Except for a brief unresolved dispute in 2004 over the ownership of some software, LeRoux disappeared from Hafner's life. Then one day in 2008, a message popped up in Hafner's old Yahoo email account. "Hi, how are you doing?" It was LeRoux. Hafner's temper had cooled, and anyway, in business, he made it a practice to hold his cards close and not to make lasting enemies. They talked. LeRoux seemed excited to reconnect, friendly and polite as always, but more grown-up. As an aside, Hafner mentioned to LeRoux that to satisfy demand from military and other government clients, he was developing software to prevent telephone calls from being intercepted. He was going to call it PhoneCrypt. The venture would be off and running as soon as he raised the last $3 million.

"I made over $20 Million U.S., and I want to invest the money," LeRoux said. "I would be happy to invest in SecurStar."

Hafner didn't want to let LeRoux back into his life, and the next line cinched it. "I feel that we can make the company the next Microsoft," LeRoux said airily. "Send me over your business plan."

LeRoux came on way too strong, all alpha, and his high-handed remark—"send me your business plan"—was downright rude. Hafner listened politely and incredulously. LeRoux should have known that Hafner's investors were his personal friends of long standing. They didn't demand elaborate business plans. Hafner told them about a project, and they liked it and invested, or they didn't. Hafner thought that LeRoux was trying to rewrite the narrative, casting his old boss as the supplicant and himself as the rich angel investor who needed to be pitched.

Hafner concluded that LeRoux was running some kind of con job, or maybe fishing for intelligence about Hafner's next business moves.

Hafner did not believe that LeRoux had made anything like $20 million. When he told the story to a colleague at the company, they both concluded that LeRoux was just a strange needy guy who self-destructed.

"I still don't understand what happened to Paul," the colleague said. "He was the most brilliant guy I ever worked with. Could have gone to the very top. It's really insane."

They did not know—they could not know—that LeRoux *was* on top. He had a lot more than $20 million. He had created the biggest black-market e-commerce pharmaceutical company on the planet. He had boxes full of hundred-dollar bills and 500 euro notes, but since narcissists never get enough, he had to have more.

At that point, he was fully committed to what filmmaker John Huston called, in his film noir masterpiece *The Asphalt Jungle,* the "left-handed form of human endeavor." He had felt a vocation to entrepreneurship, in the mold of his contemporaries—Musk, a South African a year and a half older than LeRoux, and already disrupting the mainstream economy in various ways, large and small, and Bezos, six years older than LeRoux, also from modest means, who had founded Amazon in 1994 and was on his way to building an online retailing juggernaut that by 2018 would make him the world's richest man. Both Musk and Bezos were launching space exploration ventures, a radical departure direction from their original businesses, digital maps and books, respectively.

LeRoux's innovations were always on the dark side. He was sampling many different kinds of crime, bland and shocking, cerebral and violent.

Through them all, he fell back on a mind-set he must have absorbed in Rhodesia—dig in hard, don't spare the bullets, and be ready to move.

"He knew if somebody was going to catch him, it was going to be the Americans," Jack said. "He didn't know what place would be safe. He needed a lot of bolt holes in a lot of places." Eventually, LeRoux would try and fail to bribe the king of Swaziland to give him diplomatic status that would protect him from extradition. Sanctuary in Iran would become another option to consider. LeRoux believed that because of his work with the Iranian Defense Industries Organization, Tehran would grant him political asylum, should he need it. The drawback was that, in Iran, an enormous white guy would be highly visible. Also, a society tightly controlled by religious fanatics and the Iranian Revolutionary Guard Corps wasn't an appealing destination for a freewheeling, irreligious war profiteer and lover of women.

The Rhodesian in LeRoux kept tugging at him to return to the place he was born. In 2007 and 2008, LeRoux paid $12 million to Israeli arms dealer Ari Ben-Menashe, who was reputed to be close to Robert Mugabe, then the president of Zimbabwe. LeRoux wanted to lease a large parcel of land confiscated from white farmers during land reforms Mugabe ordered in the year 2000. LeRoux didn't get what he wanted. He got no plantation, and he got no money back.

LeRoux tried another tack. Several times in 2009, he sent Jack to travel around the Zimbabwean countryside to scout out possible safe houses. He gave Jack very specific instructions: search out a colonial-era villa with white, plantation-style columns, some acreage, and a "big, curvy driveway." The description suggested a nostalgic fantasy harking back to a bygone era when white gentlemen planters enjoyed a life of ease in the green hills of southern Africa. The more languorous characters were called "verandah farmers," a term meant to evoke idle days and debauched nights, sipping cool drinks on the broad front porches, observing from a distance the toils of the black farmhands, then toddling off at dusk for dinner and an orgy with other planters' bored wives.

That was not the way Paul and Judith and their children lived, but LeRoux might have seen colonial mansions and harbored romantic notions about the glory days when a white man could stroll into the mahogany-paneled Bulawayo Club bar and order the "boy" to fetch him a gin and tonic.

As a child in a whites-only school, he would have been told the so-called Pioneers Myth, about intrepid English settlers taming the verdant, empty plain and carving out a civilization. It is highly doubtful he would have been told that white Rhodesia was founded on and sustained by blood and lies. As British journalist Richard West wrote in 1965 in his classic book *The White Tribes of Africa,* "Rhodesia began with a swindle." West chronicled how diamond magnate Cecil Rhodes and his British South Africa Company claimed the territory for Britain in 1890, lured by reports of vast deposits of diamonds, gemstones, gold, silver, copper, chrome, iron, and other valuable minerals. They went to Bulawayo and tricked the king into signing away the tribe's metal and mineral rights for £100 a month, plus the promise of guns and a boat that they did not deliver.

When the indigenous people rebelled in 1896, British troops and Rhodes's militiamen exterminated them. Historian Brendon described scenes of horrific cruelty: British soldiers and settlers putting villages, grain stores crops to the torch; slaughtering men, women and children; collecting trophy ears; and making their victims' skin into tobacco pouches. In the famine that resulted, people were reduced to eating roots, monkeys, and plague-ridden cattle corpses. The streets of Bulawayo filled with emaciated refugees trying to escape to South Africa.

LeRoux wasn't interested in his homeland's shameful imperial history. He just wanted what he wanted—the plantation, the Landcruiser, the Range Rover, obsequious servants, women.

Zimbabwe "was home for him," Jack said. "But maybe also his narcissistic mind wanted to get the land back from Mugabe. He definitely had a thing with Zimbabwe. It was about getting what he wanted, and if he had to do business with an evil person like Mugabe, then so be it, as long as he got his part off the deal. He didn't care about the people. They were all monkeys to him. But getting a part of his country back somehow seemed important to him."

CHAPTER FOUR

BLACK CLOUD

LEROUX LAUNCHED RX LIMITED IN 2004.

He moved to Manila and set up his base of operations there because it offered cheap labor for his call centers, which took orders and pushed sales. As important, the Philippines' legal system was rife with corruption. He could buy silence.

He registered a long list of Internet domains—acmemeds.com, all-the-best-rx.com, cheaprxmeds.com, allpharmmeds.com, BuyMeds Cheap.com, my-online-drugstore.com, preapprovedrx.com, matrixmeds .com, your-pills.com, speedyrxdrugs.com, 123onlinepharmacy.com, epropecia.com, and fioricetdosage.com. He set up a hand-crafted black cloud of his own websites and multiple servers. A few sessions at his keyboard and he was a founder! In the New Economy, founders were rock stars. No factory, no staff, no board, no business plan—no problem. In the tech age, all anyone needed to start a company was a good idea, and LeRoux had one.

Pills.

Little pastel bits of feel-good and fuck-off were going to make him rich enough to curl up on a sofa made of currency. They were going to get him boats, cars, villas, airplanes, long-legged girls—freedom.

Exactly how this stroke of genius came to him isn't clear, but genius it was. Later, he accused his old boss Hafner of leading him into the underground pill trade, but his account is not credible for several reasons. It is more likely that someone in the Costa Rican online casino game mentioned the prescription drug gambit to LeRoux.

Whatever the case, LeRoux's timing was spot-on. He was perfectly positioned to ride the crest of a wave—a tsunami, really—that the established drug cartels didn't see coming. In the United States, the world's largest market for drugs, both legal and illegal, "dirty" street drugs peddled by the likes of Pablo Escobar and El Chapo were on their way out. Pills that looked like Willy Wonka made them were in.

In 2004, according to an annual U.S. government survey, 7.2 million Americans regularly abused pharmaceuticals by obtaining them through nonmedical channels ranging from friends' and relatives' medicine cabinets to "pill mills" run by unscrupulous medical professionals to street drug dealers. That number was roughly double the 3.7 million Americans who habitually abused cocaine, heroin, methamphetamine, and hallucinogens combined. The only substance that outpolled pills was marijuana, with 14.6 million regular users in 2004. Plummeting demand for cocaine was a striking trend, from 5.8 million regular users in 1985, at the height of the crack cocaine epidemic, to 2 million in 2004. Other street drugs had also lost their luster. According to the survey estimates, by 2004, some 166,000 Americans were using heroin regularly; 583,000, methamphetamine; and 929,000, hallucinogens. (By 2017, cocaine use had declined further, to 1.9 million habitual users, but heroin use had tripled, to 475,000 people, many of whom switched to the cheap, plentiful street drug after falling victim to the epidemic of prescription opioids abuse.)

The numbers translated to a very appealing business opportunity. There were at least 7 million very loyal potential pill buyers in the United States and probably almost as many in the rest of the world. The black market was a tiny fraction of the global pharmaceutical market, whose revenues exceeded $1 trillion in 2014, but it was big enough to generate some serious money. It was a niche, but exactly the kind of niche LeRoux was seeking—not yet saturated and plenty of room for growth.

Even better, LeRoux didn't have to spend a dime on marketing.

The pharmaceutical industry had been shaping the image of pills over many decades, lavishing many billions of dollars on ads and other promotions. (One estimate put Big Pharma ad spending at $33 billion in 2004.) Pharma ads invariably showed the product being manufactured in pristine labs and dispensed by physicians in white coats. Healers! Nobody argued with healers.

LeRoux's websites piggybacked on those themes. His your-pills.com website of May 14, 2005, featured a photo of a man and a woman, both in the white coats of physicians, both fair-skinned, apparently American archetypes. It promised, "Our U.S. Licensed Physicians will review your order and issue your prescription. Next, our U.S. Licensed Pharmacies will dispense, and FedEx your order discreetly using next day delivery."

LeRoux's matrixmeds.com website for September 1, 2005, featured a photo of a movie-star-handsome man in surgical scrubs, rattling off a lot of very good reasons to buy online: "Why put up with the waiting rooms, the time off of work, the traffic, the embarrassment, and the long lines when you don't have to! With our unrivaled system, you can have your prescription delivered tomorrow. No wonder we were voted Number 1. Decide for yourself. You don't need to suffer from ailments that are preventable. Live life to its fullest! Get the medication you need to start a better life today." It added, "With MatrixMeds.com, you get USA Prescriptions. MatrixMeds.com is NOT a Canadian online pharmacy. MatrixMeds.com is NOT a UK online pharmacy. MatrixMeds.com is NOT a Mexican online pharmacy." All true. It was completely illegal, existing in cyberspace by a South African citizen living in Manila.

LeRoux's cheaprxmeds.com website took a different tack, playing on Americans' dissatisfaction with astronomical prices of pharmaceuticals in the United States, compared to lower prices in neighboring Canada. The site claimed to be a Canadian business employing "qualified, licensed Canadian physicians and filled directly by a licensed mail order Canadian pharmacy."

All of this was hype, but there was truth to it. Unlike other e-commerce pill peddlers, LeRoux did not buy pills wholesale from poorly regulated third-world sources and dispatch them to American buyers. He realized that the front-end costs for purchasing, maintaining inventory, packaging, shipping, and getting past U.S. border controls were substantial. That method needed a lot of hands and incurred a lot of risk.

Instead, he recruited a network of physicians and pharmacies inside the United States. He remained offshore as the unseen digital middleman somewhere in a cybercloud. A prospective customer went online and filled out a questionnaire that was assigned to a bona fide doctor or, in some cases, to someone posing as a doctor. Either way, the person who read the questionnaire and wrote a digital prescription was paid by RX Limited. LeRoux created an algorithm to distribute the questionnaires among real and fake doctors in the network, so that each participant's queue would contain about the same number of "patients." The resulting prescriptions were forwarded to participating pharmacies that shipped the pills to customers, using a FedEx account set up by RX Limited. LeRoux's call centers collected credit card payments and paid the real or fake physicians and the pharmacies.

Ethical standards for American pharmacies required a pharmacist to know that a prescription came from a physician who had personally seen the patient. But, as LeRoux was well aware, the pharmacists' code of conduct was voluntary, not a legally binding regulation. Doctors also had ethical standards, but not every person with a license to practice medicine obeyed them. LeRoux sent representatives to the United States to recruit doctors and pharmacists who needed money and were willing to ignore ethical issues to be part of the network.

The system raised the risks that a customer would get access to too many pills or to medications that were dangerous when mixed. Since repeat customers were assigned randomly to various doctors, no single doctor knew about any particular customer's purchases. The physicians were paid only when they wrote prescriptions. A doctor who reviewed a questionnaire and rejected a purchase got nothing. Consequently, an RX Limited customer was always right. Anyone who ordered pills got pills. RX Limited usually had about five to ten doctors on duty every day, each approving between 50 and 300 prescriptions per day.

In addition to its own marketing websites, RX Limited used marketing affiliates, paying commissions to independent marketers whose websites would splash ads for RX Limited. According to the testimony of Jonathan Wall, who helped LeRoux manage the business, people who worked in a Manila-based call center called Global I-Net were essentially telemarketers who telephoned individuals who had already bought drugs from RX Limited and pushed them to buy more. A separate Manila call center, Dial Magic, handled customer complaints and questions about shipping and other matters.

To manage risk, LeRoux consulted an American lawyer who knew pharmaceutical regulation. The lawyer warned him against selling any drugs on the federal Controlled Substances Act list. That list included opioids, steroids, and other potent pharmaceuticals, as well as street drugs such as heroin, methamphetamine, cocaine, marijuana, LSD, and so-called club drugs. Selling from the Controlled Substances list violated the federal narcotics laws, which gave the DEA clear jurisdiction over a case and a likely win in court.

On the other hand, selling a pharmaceutical *not* on the Controlled List without a valid prescription fell under the legal rubric of "misbranding," a violation of the federal Food, Drug and Cosmetic Act, enforced by the U.S. Food and Drug Administration. The Justice Department could seek fines or, in aggravated cases, criminal penalties, but it rarely did. U.S. attorneys had to conserve resources for hard-core crime. They were generally unwilling to spend time and effort to bring prosecutions or even civil cases against proprietors of websites that flouted FDA regulations but did not sell demonstrably dangerous opioids, which Americans held responsible for an epidemic of addiction and deaths.

LeRoux followed the lawyer's advice and restricted RX Limited sales to milder pharmaceuticals. He was not motivated by concern for his customers but rather by avoiding any activity that could give the DEA a reason to go after him. He figured he could make plenty of money selling popular uncontrolled pharmaceuticals, such as the pain relievers Tramadol, Fioricet, and Soma; Viagra, the drug that helped men maintain erections; and Propecia, which promised to slow hair loss and baldness. (Tramadol, a mild opioid pain-killer that won FDA approval for the U.S. market in 1995, proved to be prone to abuse and was elevated to the Control Substances Act list in 2014.)

As extra insulation from legal jeopardy, he instructed his call centers to sell pharmaceuticals only to people who lived in states that treated off-prescription sales of uncontrolled drugs as civil or administrative violations but not criminal acts. RX Limited did not fulfill prescriptions in Florida, Tennessee, Kentucky, and Nevada, where it was a state crime to sell prescription drugs online without a visit to a doctor.

He scattered his credit card processing arrangements far and wide, so that no single financial institution would see the whole picture. Most were in countries not known as money laundering havens.

LeRoux's business style was a combination of what he learned working for Hafner and his own intuition. Hafner showed him focus, passion, and tenacity, but he had no need to cloak his business activities and identity. LeRoux did. He improvised a series of clever ruses that enabled him to play ghost—to vanish from the sight of routine law enforcement. These gambits weren't perfect, but they were good enough for some years, until he accumulated enough wealth to buy his way out of trouble in most places.

Remarkably, on his own, far from anyplace New Economy entrepreneurs gathered to exchange ideas, LeRoux developed an approach to business that looked a lot like the methodology that, in a few years, would be all the rage in Silicon Valley. Author Eric Ries gave it a name in a blog post in 2008 and elaborated on the concept in his bestselling 2011 book, *The Lean Startup*.

Ries held that the twenty-first-century business world was moving too fast for the traditional MBA-school playbook, involving years of product development, investment banking, board cultivation, executive hiring, and marketing. Instead, Ries said, entrepreneurs had to move swiftly and with agility, using trial and error to find a niche that assured solid returns. "Lean in the sense of low-burn," Ries wrote in 2008. "Of course, many startups are capital efficient and generally frugal. But by taking advantage of open source, agile software, and iterative development, lean startups can operate with much less waste."

By unlocking creativity, harnessing cheap or free technology, spending minimally and acting adroitly, the entrepreneur should produce a "minimum viable product," test the market, and move ahead only after finding objective proof that the concept was right.

Forget romantic notions about vision and dreams, Ries argued. What mattered was numbers. If the first returns are solid, scale up fast. If not, pivot, and redirect your passion and energy to finding the next big idea. Failing was no shame. To the contrary, failure, redefined as pivoting smartly away from a loser, saved time and money.

"It is really about—*Try a little, learn a lot*," said Eric Hellweg, managing director of digital strategy for the Harvard Business Review. "A lot of what lean start-up says is, stay scrappy until what you're thinking works—until it really does resonate and you see some market validation."

According to federal court proceedings in Minneapolis, in 2005, working through an Israeli associate, LeRoux hired an Israeli citizen named Moran Oz to serve as the day-to-day manager of RX Limited. According to his lawyer, when he took the job, Oz thought the business was legitimate, even altruistic; he claimed that he was told RX Limited aimed to give Americans without health insurance access to affordable prescription drugs. Oz worked out of executive offices in Jerusalem. LeRoux scaled up rapidly. By 2007, according to Oz's lawyer, the Jerusalem office had 30 employees and a call center in Tel Aviv had 150 people. More call center workers were in Manila, where LeRoux was living much of the time, and Costa Rica, where LeRoux still had a finger in an online casino business. In Manila and Jerusalem, LeRoux made it a practice to put Israelis in back-office jobs involving substantial sums of money. He thought they took care of business well, had connections all over the world through the Jewish diaspora, and, unlike Arabs, traveled anywhere they wanted without attracting the kind of attention that landed them on counterterrorism no-fly lists.

LeRoux found he had more worries from business competitors than from law enforcement. The black market in pills was cutthroat, with rivals hacking one another's servers, stealing customer lists, and sabotaging software. LeRoux was well equipped to win these skirmishes. He applied his cybersecurity skills to creating elaborate defensive measures. He set up more than fifty servers in various nations, including the Philippines, Israel, and Costa Rica, and rotated them daily. When one server detected an attempted intrusion, it automatically shut down, and the traffic rotated to another server.

In 2008, just as RX Limited hit cruising speed, the business environment for Internet pharmaceutical sales started to change. In the United States, policy makers and lawmakers were beginning to recognize that abuse of prescription drugs had become a serious public health problem. In October of that year, Congress enacted the Ryan Haight Online Pharmacy Consumer Protection Act, named for a teenager who died after taking Vicodin, the trade name for a pharmaceutical containing hydrocodone, a prescription opioid painkiller. An Internet pharmacy had sold the youth the pills that killed him. The legislation in his name strengthened the federal Controlled Substances Act by making it a felony to distribute a controlled substance across the Internet without a valid prescription.

The Haight Act put pressure on the Visa network to bring some accountability to the payment system and to force its member banks to scrutinize online transactions and curtail questionable sales of prescription drugs. Visa officials responded by assigning a special code to pharmaceutical transactions to highlight them and by auditing some member banks. LeRoux's e-commerce sites were collecting money using the Visa network, with payments processed through banks in Mauritius, the Netherlands, Israel, and Iceland. LeRoux considered issuing his own Visa credit card through banks in a country with lax regulation.

The Haight Act put a crimp in his plans. Although RX Limited was not selling controlled substances, the new spotlight on Internet pharmacies threatened to raise questions about RX Limited's commercial relationships with banks that processed its credit card payments and with shipping companies.

LeRoux tried to head off deeper inquiries by carpet-bombing the banking system with subterfuges. He sent the banks fake paperwork and set up fake websites that appeared to meet the letter of the new law. When American Express and Discover demanded that online pharmaceutical sellers have valid pharmacy licenses, LeRoux signed up licensed pharmacists to front for him.

Amazingly, he managed to outsmart the Google algorithm. Google executives were trying to do their part to curb prescription drug abuse by barring questionable online pharmacies from buying keywords for the Google AdWords program, which caused advertisers' names to pop to the top of search results. LeRoux solved this problem by identifying the IP addresses Google was using to collect information about RX Limited. He then redirected the Google probes to fake websites that omitted information that would have disqualified RX Limited from buying keywords.

RX Limited's success was starting to leave tracks. The traces were faint, but they were ineradicable, if someone with good detective skills could find them and read them.

In September 2007, a few DEA agents in Minneapolis stumbled onto a suspicious cache of records from a Chicago pharmacy. The records showed that the pharmacy had sent a large volume of prescription drugs to various individuals, using a single FedEx account.

The agents followed the paper trail back to the FedEx account and, back further, to the pharmacies using it. They found no fewer than one hundred pharmacies scattered around the United States in a network linked to the account's owner, RX Limited.

The agents took a hard look at the identities of some of the signatures on the prescriptions. Some were doctors, but some weren't. A single individual falsely claiming to be a physician had authorized about 150,000 drug orders between September 2005 and April 2008. Another prescriber was a dentist. The Minneapolis agents didn't know what they were looking at, and they didn't know if they had a federal case, but they knew this much: RX Limited stunk. They decided to try to get to the bottom of it. They went online and made undercover buys of prescription drugs from RX Limited. They found and interviewed a physician who admitted participating in the RX Limited network and approving large numbers of pharmaceutical orders, without even reading the customers' questionnaires.

Before long, they had identified Moran Oz as the man in charge of RX Limited. They obtained search warrants for his email accounts. Over many months, they pierced his communications and identified his possible superior: an individual named Paul LeRoux, with an address in Manila. Following DEA's standard operating procedure, they sent inquiries to authorities in the Philippines, asking for information on LeRoux.

The investigation promptly leaked back to LeRoux. He had set up an early warning system, by putting an official in the Philippines Department of Foreign Affairs on his payroll. LeRoux knew the man only by a code name—"Dragnet Man." For a large fee, Dragnet Man purloined U.S. and Australian law enforcement reports sent to the Philippines police, as well as files on American law enforcement personnel and diplomats posted to Manila. He provided these documents to LeRoux.

By 2009, LeRoux was confident that his defensive measures were adequate, and he doubled down on his expansion plans. He had to feed the beast—the narcissism and need that drove him. He had to go bigger and badder.

The solution, he decided, was to diversify, found more companies, buy more protection, erect more walls. Have a Plan B, and Plans C and D and E. Hire more front men. Get fake passports, like a stack of playing cards. Get more. Keep moving.

The agents in Minneapolis learned a great deal more about the inner workings of RX Limited when they got onto the trail of Jonathan Wall, a dual U.S. and Israeli citizen who lived in Kentucky and made purchases for LeRoux. Wall was eventually charged with 23 counts of violating U.S. pharmaceutical laws and mail fraud. In December 2015 Wall would agree to cooperate with federal prosecutors and would plead guilty to one count of violating the federal Food, Drug, and Cosmetics Act.

Wall was born in Louisville, Kentucky, and for a period made a living as a federally licensed firearms dealer there. In 2012, as agents of the federal Bureau of Alcohol, Tobacco, Firearms and Explosives were conducting a routine inspection of his gun sales records, he told them that he had lived in Israel, had served in the Israeli military, and had married an Israeli citizen whose father worked for an Israeli firearms company. When he returned to Louisville, he imported guns from his father-in-law's company.

His story to the ATF agents sounded straightforward, but, it turned out, he had another line of work. Delving deeper, the DEA agents found that in 2007, between Israel and Louisville, he made a detour to Manila and took a $3,000-a-month job as manager of one of LeRoux's call centers. (He later testified that he got the job because he had gained experience in a shady Israeli call center that sold fake diplomas.) The employees working under Wall were essentially telemarketers. Their job was to telephone people who had already bought drugs from RX Limited and push them to buy more. A separate call center handled customer complaints and questions about shipping and other matters. If a particularly vexing problem came up, Wall later testified, it was referred to Moran Oz and other senior figures at what he called the "brain center" in Jerusalem.

Wall did something that annoyed LeRoux. In a fit of pique, LeRoux fired him from the call center after a few months. But then LeRoux reconsidered and rehired him at another of his business locations in Manila. He used Wall to do all sorts of odd jobs, including as a courier to carry cash to Hong Kong, where another LeRoux associate banked it. Wall was assigned to buy equipment and handle paperwork involving lawsuits about business properties.

It occurred to LeRoux that Wall could be very useful as a straw man back in the States. As an American citizen, Wall could buy things that would have attracted unwanted attention if a foreigner had tried to acquire them. LeRoux told Wall to move back to Kentucky in June 2008 and raised his salary to $3,500 a month, which was paid via a wire transfer from Hong Kong.

In his new role as LeRoux's purchasing agent, Wall acquired cars, boats, computers, and dive equipment for RX Limited. When LeRoux decided he wanted his own jet, Wall bought it for him. It was a 1982 Westwind manufactured by Israel Aircraft Industries. The plane, tail number N127PT, was registered on October 17, 2008, in the name of the Bank of Utah, listed as trustee. Between that time and 2012, the jet was recorded landing at such diverse destinations as Brussels, Bangkok, Sendai, Japan, and Sabah, Malaysia. (LeRoux himself was seldom aboard. Playing the ghost required self-discipline. "He traveled most of the times in economy class, as he had the idea he would blend in among the common people," Jack said.)

In Kentucky, Wall established a shipping company called Phalanx Trading to facilitate his shipments of goods to LeRoux overseas. According to Wall's plea agreement and testimony in Minnesota, LeRoux told him set up a wholesale pharmacy operation to supply RXL's grow-

ing network of American pharmacists. The move was designed to maxi-
mize RXL's profits. He obtained Kentucky wholesale pharmacy licenses
under the fake names Jesse Merced and Wayne Hatfield. Building on
these bogus credentials, he got wholesale pharmacy or drug distributor
permits from several states. In 2010 or 2011, he applied to the DEA
for a controlled substances registration under the name Wall Wholesale. This permit would have allowed him to handle pharmaceuticals
on Schedule V, the least restrictive section of the federal Controlled
Substances Act list. The DEA turned down his application in 2011. "I
knew that it was illegal," Wall later testified of the wholesale pharmacy
idea. He said he dragged his feet so it would not become reality. Why
didn't he quit LeRoux outright? "I needed the job, and I needed the
money," he testified. "This was at a time when there were not jobs. It
was the middle of this recession."

Wall worked for LeRoux until sometime in 2012. The DEA agents
in Minneapolis calculated that between 2008 and 2012, he personally
received at least $1.9 million from LeRoux-controlled bank accounts,
all wire-transferred from Hong Kong.

In his plea agreement and testimony in federal court in Minneapolis, he admitted that he had carried out duties relating to pharmacy
business and had made purchases vaguely described as "hard goods."

The story LeRoux would tell was considerably more interesting. Le-
Roux said he gave Wall a shopping list of hardware and technology items
which his engineers needed to develop items and technologies requested
by the Iranian Defense Industries Organization. LeRoux later claimed
he didn't know the purpose behind the list. The reason the Iranians
wanted some items were obvious. The DIO requests for Honeywell jet
engines, X-plane flight simulator software and certain electronic and
mechanical components for aircraft made sense. Obstructed by trade
sanction, Iranian engineers had been struggling for decades to develop
an indigenous industry to make aircraft parts to maintain and modernize Iran's fleet of aircraft, both commercial and military.

The purpose of other electronic, mechanical and chemical items had to be inferred. For instance, what did the DIO want with potassium perchlorate? The chemical is a powerful oxidizer that makes fireworks flash and supplies the thrust that propels rockets and missiles skyward.

In short, the list was trouble, but whose trouble? Who wanted this stuff? Why? Wall didn't know.

"The longer I worked for Mr. Le Roux, the more aware I became of, you know, how illegal everything he was doing was and how much disregard for the law he had," Wall would later testify. For instance, he said, "he was having me ship him things without licenses." The U.S. government requires exports of technology classified as "munitions" to have a license from the U.S. State Department. Exports of items classified as "dual-use," meaning that they can be used either for military or civilian purposes, must be licensed by the U.S. Commerce Department. By his own account, Wall suspected that at least some of the things LeRoux was ordering him to ship abroad should have been disclosed to government regulators and license applications submitted. He didn't do so.

He didn't ask LeRoux if the shipments were problematic. LeRoux didn't put up with questions or backtalk. Everyone who worked for him had to call him Boss, with a capital B.

"He was a bad boss," Wall later testified. ". . . He would ask for kind of unrealistic things. He had me fire people, good employees, for no reason." But he stayed on. "I needed the job," he explained, more than once.

As RX Limited prospered, acting through Wall and other brokers and middlemen, LeRoux bought several yachts, both motor yachts and sailboats. They were normal fifty-footers, not the super- or mega-variety. He had yet to achieve the Triple Commas Club and full Russian oligarch status. He was fine with that, for the moment anyway. His empire on the dark side was in the building stage. It was wise to blend in.

CHAPTER FIVE

MAGIC!

SOMETIMES LEROUX ACTED AS IF HE HAD SUPERNATURAL POWERS. WHEN-ever he made a new business connection or scored a deal, even the purchase of a few barrels of chemicals, he chuckled and exclaimed to anybody who was around, "Magic!"

Maybe it started out as an offhand remark, but he kept it up. There was something hypnotic about the way he planted subliminal hints that he had special powers. He managed to convince his subordinates and interested outsiders that he was all-seeing and all-powerful, so he kept doing it.

For a long time, LeRoux's incantation—magic!—beguiled Jack. It was probably why he took a job and stayed on even after he realized that a lot of people who worked for LeRoux ended up dead. When Jack first traveled to the Philippines in 2007, he intended to take a brief holi-day to recuperate after a bruising divorce and a burnout work schedule. He had sold his construction company, so he had a little money in his pocket. He had been a diver and deminer for his nation's navy, and be-fore that, a swimming champion, so he went to Subic Bay to do some diving, catch some sun, catch his breath, and figure out his next move.

Once he saw Subic, he cashed in his return ticket. The Pacific Rim was what he'd been missing all his life! Those reefs! All those ship-wrecks! Such history! Glorious islands and bright blue water! Golden girls! Even the city markets and pubs were vibrant and full of laughter. He decided to stick around awhile longer, freelancing as a dive bum—a diving instructor paid by tourists.

He met a lithe young Filipina, simple and willing, nothing like his uptight ex-wife and the other tweed-encased women back home. Only problem was, dive-bumming wasn't enough to cover the bills for two. In June 2008, as he was pondering where to find an extra paying job, he happened to run into Leo, an acquaintance from back home. Leo had served in the military, then drifted around the Far East and Africa, doing security gigs. The mercenary Facebook led him to Manila and a job as one of LeRoux's enforcers.

Leo thought Jack was the Boss's type—ex-military, extremely fit and disciplined. He wasn't into the rough stuff, as Leo was, but there might be something for him. Leo took Jack to the LeRoux security team hangout, Sid's Sports Bar, a dimly lit Irish-style pub on Jupiter Street in Makati, the upscale financial district in metropolitan Manila. It was a short walk from LeRoux's RX Limited office in the Cityland building, an address favored by international corporations.

The bar didn't advertise, but expats working in the city center— English, Irish, Australian, American, and Western European—heard about it and drifted in. A homesick bloke could sit down with a Guinness and a nice pile of bangers and mash or shepherd's pie, watch football—soccer, to the Americans—on the flat-screen TVs and play pool on the table in one end of the place. It was relatively quiet on weekdays—no hookers, no K-pop to jangle hungover nerves. On weekends, there was live music and women stopped by.

Leo introduced Jack to his boss, Dave Smith, an Englishman who claimed to have served in the British military. In his younger days, Smith had taught weapons and tactics classes in the U.S. and probably elsewhere, but when Jack met him, he was not a pretty sight. Probably because of his meth, coke, and whiskey habits, his cheeks were caved in, his skin was rough and grayish, and his teeth were just awful. He held court at Sid's, pretending he owned the place. The bar really belonged to LeRoux. LeRoux always operated through front men, and at that moment, Smith was the ranking front man. He was also LeRoux's bagman and "chief of security," a euphemism for head enforcer.

LeRoux had hired Smith in 2005, on the recommendation of a lawyer at the Philippines Department of Justice who was on LeRoux's payoff list. Smith told LeRoux that the lawyer "was responsible for arranging non-judicial killings for the Philippines government." The phrase "non-judicial killings" was a euphemism for the acts of government death squads. Smith boasted that he had been involved in many murders and as many as five hundred rapes meted out as punishment for angering government officials. Could that be true? How? LeRoux didn't care. He liked the idea that Smith was brutal in the extreme.

"Dave Smith said he had a group of mercenaries available who enjoyed killing and torturing and beating and those mercenaries were available for me for any projects I had in mind," LeRoux said later. Smith named the security team Echelon Associates. It was a company with one client, no independence and no assets. LeRoux owned Smith's house and the houses and condos where he housed his several girlfriends. Smith joked that the stress of keeping five or six women sashaying around Manila in diamond necklaces and designer pocketbooks was killing him.

As LeRoux grew to trust Smith, he expanded his role as a front man for LeRoux's growing business empire. He put Smith's name on deeds, permits, licenses, and other documents pertaining to ownership of businesses, real estate, boats, and cars. Smith became LeRoux's public face.

When Jack met him, Smith was driving around Manila with a million dollars in cash in suitcases in the back of his Infinity SUV, just in case LeRoux needed him to pay someone. All of LeRoux's workers' salaries came out of the trunk of Smith's Infiniti, which was Smith's workaday car. Smith's weekend rides were a Lamborghini and the highest-end Mercedes, worth $300,000. His special joy was his MV Agusta motorcycle, a gorgeous Italian job that set him back at least $50,000.

Jack found it bizarre that LeRoux entrusted a dissolute creep like Smith with so much money and property, but then, everything about LeRoux was inscrutable. All Jack could figure was, Smith was not only LeRoux's alter ego but also his lightning rod. Smith attracted all the attention. If anything bad happened, it was easy to believe that this central-casting bad guy was the guilty one. Nobody seemed to ask who was behind him.

Over a beer or two, Smith satisfied himself that Jack was who he said he was. In a couple of days, he decided it was time for Jack to meet the Boss.

But not at Sid's. Never at Sid's. LeRoux never darkened the doors of the pub. For one thing, he didn't drink. "His brain had to stay clear all the time," Jack said. For another, he didn't like to socialize. Smith, Leo, and the other mercenaries who frequented the place were just hired hands—tools. Their conversation, about tits, sausages, and guns, was too basic to interest LeRoux.

Smith escorted Jack to LeRoux's penthouse for the job interview. At the door, Smith handed Jack off to three Filipino bodyguards who searched him for weapons and wires and ushered him into the cavernous living room.

LeRoux lumbered in, lowered himself onto one of the straight-backed chairs, pulled it up to the square table, and motioned for Jack to sit across from him. He didn't offer his guest as much as a cup of tea.

When he walked into the penthouse, Jack assumed that LeRoux was a fat tech mogul with a boatload of cash and an itch to do something more colorful. A nerd. But when the big man began to speak, Jack changed his mind. This guy was no nerd, and he wasn't soft. He was a force of nature, like a big wave that bowled you over if you resisted but floated you upward if you gave in. He expressed himself clearly, in complete sentences, no "uhs," "ums," "y'knows," "likes," or the dreaded "Know what I'm sayin'?" His supremely confident attitude was overpowering. He clearly knew what he wanted and where he was going to get it. When Jack was in LeRoux's presence, it didn't occur to him not to obey.

LeRoux saw that Jack wasn't a mercenary, which he later defined as "a trained person with military experience with an aggressive posture who will beat, intimidate, threaten, shoot and/or kill anyone on instruction." Jack obviously had no appetite for muscling people around. LeRoux was looking for someone to oversee a major construction project in a shithole without asking too many questions. He saw that Jack had a head for figures, knew how to read and execute architectural plans, and could get on with people, even black Africans, whom LeRoux regarded as beasts of burden, useful if managed. He didn't tell Jack that. Instead, he flattered the newcomer.

"LeRoux, I think, saw in me that when I loved something and put my head to it, I could get anything done," Jack said. "I had a great historical and cultural knowledge, good people skills, and, for some reason, I'm a trustworthy and likable person. He saw someone who could do more for his business and crazy ideas. For me, the adventure came first."

LeRoux read Jack like a big-print kid's book. He offered him all the adventure travel he could manage. He gave Jack a list of places in the South Pacific and Africa and sent him to check out luxury real estate and villas that might serve as safe houses for LeRoux. Jack's itinerary was straight out of a Somerset Maugham novella—Madang and Port Moresby, Papua New Guinea; Hai Phong, Vietnam; Krong Kampot, Cambodia; Phuket, Thailand; Jakarta, Indonesia; Chinde and Maputo, Mozambique; Dar es Salaam, Tanzania; Nairobi and Mombasa, Kenya; Pretoria and Nelspruit, South Africa; Addis Ababa, Ethiopia; Djibouti; Accra, Ghana; Lome, Togo; Cap Ternay, Seychelles, and the Comoro islands.

It was on these all-expense-paid jaunts that Jack began to wonder if he had been a little naïve and the Boss had something to hide. Many of the spots he visited weren't for jet-setters. When Jack got to Port

Moresby, the capital of Papua New Guinea, a dirty, expensive city with a pricey yacht basin, shantytowns, and roving bands of muggers and pickpockets, he said to himself, "Bloody hell. Who the fuck am I working for? Why would you need a house here?"

But Jack was having too much fun to quit. His next task for LeRoux was as a bagman. "He divided his money over multiple accounts all over the world, preferable in countries with no tax and no questions asked," Jack said. "He invested large amounts in gold. The rest he used to fund other ventures. I believe his trick was to wire by bank and send money by Western Union or money exchange houses, in small amounts and always from different names. Most of the time it was sent to countries where they ask few questions about anything. I remember receiving $8,000 through Dahabshiil, [a money exchange house in] Nairobi. I just walked in and said, 'This person sent 8K from that place.' They paid me without showing any ID or signature. In Asia and Africa, it's so easy to hide anything you spend or have."

LeRoux's money-moving procedures were so convoluted that neither Jack nor any other underling had a way to see the Boss's entire financial picture. "He had so many fake and real companies that for most it was impossible to track," Jack said. "LeRoux confused everyone except himself, as he knew every single dollar he had out there."

Jack moved from his little apartment in Subic Bay to one of LeRoux's properties that served as a safe house for Hunter and other mercenaries on the "security team." Located in an upscale, gated community in Manila, it had five bedrooms, five baths, and a big kitchen. It had no pool or other flashy stuff. LeRoux thought that ostentation encouraged the local political hacks and police cops to demand higher bribes.

It was at the mercenaries' safe house that Jack learned that the worst hazard working for LeRoux wasn't street criminals in Port Moresby or Bulawayo but right there in Manila. One night, Leo let Jack in on the secret to survival in LeRoux's world. He explained that LeRoux sometimes had fits of temper, accused various employees of theft or treachery, and ordered one of the mercenaries to kill the accused. Most of those he suspected worked for the pharmaceutical operation or some other branch of LeRoux's empire, but LeRoux had been known to tell one mercenary to kill another.

The mercenaries made a pact, Leo said. If ordered to kill a comrade, they would go through the motions and fake some photos of the "deceased," who would make himself scarce. "There was daily gossip about everything LeRoux did, crazy stuff, ideas about people who died, everything," Jack said.

Even then, Jack stayed on, rationalizing that since he knew all LeRoux's gunmen, he would be a step ahead. The mercenaries and office workers made the same decision, staying on with LeRoux, even though they all heard the gossip. The pay was good, and, as LeRoux instinctively knew, money can buy a lot of denial.

After three months of bro time with the mercenaries, Jack, ever the romantic, decided to marry the hot girl from Subic Bay. He asked Hunter to help them find a place to live. Hunter handed Jack the keys to yet another penthouse, this one on the fortieth floor of a skyscraper.

"Here, it's yours as long as you need it," Hunter said. This one was empty. Jack and his girl bought new furniture and enjoyed the view.

Whenever Jack reported to LeRoux, it was always at the Boss's nearly bare white penthouse atop Tower 2 of the forty-five-story Salcedo Park Twin Towers in Makati City. He owned an identical and completely empty penthouse atop Tower 1. Jack learned that he had bought both penthouses and registered the Tower 1 penthouse as his official residence, though he actually worked in the Tower 2 penthouse, because he figured that if the cops or business enemies showed up to raid his place and arrest him or shake him down, he would see them going into Tower 1 and have time to make his escape from Tower 2.

As far as Jack could tell, LeRoux owned five or six other houses, condos, and hideaways around Manila alone, and more places in the

Philippines countryside. He had a colonial-style beach house on the coast near Manila and another beach house in Subic Bay.

At least one residence was for Cindy Cayanan, his mistress and their children. Others were places where he could indulge his sexual fantasies. He liked freaky. LeRoux ordered up prostitutes, sometimes three or four at a time. LeRoux bragged—*bragged*—to Jack that he had become enraged at a young woman for not performing a sex act the way he wanted, so he beat her with a baseball bat, sending her to the hospital. When her father, an official, complained, LeRoux told Jack that he paid the man $2 million in hush money on the spot, then added him to his payroll for regular bribes. The episode turned out to be a win-win for the men. Jack never found out what happened to the poor woman.

"I think he had a few complexes considering his body or maybe because of his inability to have a normal social conversation with a woman," Jack said. "Of course, being in the Philippines and having all that power, and with women easy to get, I believe whatever frustration he had, it was easy to work out on those women. It was a way to dominate and abuse women to polish his ego."

Jack noticed that LeRoux had a small boy's fascination with gear, especially firearms, but no mechanical aptitude whatsoever. That fact became apparent one day when LeRoux showed Jack a stack of M4 assault rifles, the kind carried by U.S. Army infantry soldiers. "My new tools," he said proudly.

Jack took one and broke it down in a routine "clear-disassemble-reassemble" drill that took twenty seconds or so, a normal time for those in his navy unit. He was looking to see whether the serial numbers of the parts matched. If they didn't, that meant that LeRoux had been ripped off with a mess of random parts. But the numbers matched. The guns were new, as advertised. He smiled and told LeRoux that the guns were the real deal.

LeRoux quivered with delight. Seeing a man slap and click the steel parts of an assault rifle together seemed to be close to an erotic experience for him. It occurred to Jack that he must have fantasized about being a soldier, which is why he surrounded himself with warriors and their tools.

LeRoux showed off what he knew about the M4—all the specifications, where every component was made. He had obviously gone online and memorized the data. "He knew about every single weapon on this planet, from a small gun to missile systems," Jack said.

But his knowledge stopped at book learning. "There is a big difference between knowing the theoretical parts of a machine and the practical part of actually using it in combat," Jack said. "Only by being in real-life situations you learn how a gun performs, not by reading it online. But it's freaking impressive that he knew so much detailed information about *everything*."

When it came to hand-eye coordination, LeRoux was missing something. That's probably why he had to hire hit men. He knew all about guns on paper, but hand him a loaded one and he couldn't hit a cardboard target, much less a moving one.

His sense of proportion was all out of whack. While they were playing with the M4, LeRoux decided to reward Jack for a job well done, so he reached into a closet and extracted a brand-new bulletproof vest, one of a batch he had ordered custom-made in Sweden for his bodyguards. "Here, keep that with you for when you go into dangerous places," he beamed.

Jack suppressed a laugh. The Filipino bodyguards were diminutive. Two of them could almost fit into one of Jack's shirts. Jack thanked LeRoux diplomatically, took the tiny vest back to his place, and threw it into the bottom of a closet.

Late in 2008, LeRoux revealed the real reason for his interest in Jack. He was going to create a stronghold—his own small kingdom—in a part of Somalia that he judged was far off the radar of the Great Powers.

"My objective in Somalia was to obtain a small territory and set myself up as a warlord, using whatever violence was necessary," LeRoux said later. But he didn't tell Jack that.

Instead, he cheerfully informed Jack that he was going to start up a commercial fishing business in the Indian Ocean. He had his eye on a place called Galmudug, on the Somali coast. It was an autonomous area with its own president and the beginnings of a governing body of tribal leaders. Nobody important wanted that scrap of territory, not the warlords in Mogadishu and only occasionally the al-Shabaab militants to the south. The tribal leaders of Galmudug disdained al-Shabaab's fractured Islamism and, LeRoux thought, would probably welcome help in keeping them out of the territory.

Hunched over the dining table, LeRoux showed Jack satellite images he had commissioned, detecting abundant schools of tuna in the Indian Ocean right off the Galmudug coast. The bounty of the sea was a gold mine! Demand for tuna in Hong Kong and China was nonstop. They would erect a tuna cannery on the coast. They would also harvest and sell shark fin in China and lobster in the Gulf Arab states. They would make a fortune and spread the wealth—well, a bit of it—to Somalis who would be lucky to see a handful of euros in a year.

Working through one of his proxies, a South African businessman named Edgar Van Tonder, LeRoux had already registered a corporation called Southern Ace Limited in Hong Kong. Southern Ace was a front for acquiring gold and timber receive and laundering pharmaceutical company proceeds. He told Jack they would use Southern Ace to set up a base for the Galmudug fishing business. Jack would supervise construction and operation of the new base. He would be the face and voice and hands-on leader of the venture. LeRoux would be the silent partner, using the alias Bernard John Bowlins, a white Zimbabwean.

To get a fake Zimbabwean passport and national identity papers for "Bowlins," Jack would have to make a side trip to Zimbabwe and bribe somebody.

Jack was flattered by LeRoux's confidence and praise. In retrospect, he would see that it was all a manipulation. By all objective measures, LeRoux was a textbook narcissist and possibly a psychopath. He had no interest in others. Every conversation was all about LeRoux—his desires, his needs, his whims, and his beloved projects. What saved him from being insufferable was that he had something of the aura of Steve Jobs, whose aides invented a term for the Apple founder's way of driving subordinates to deliver on his visions. Jobs, they said, had a "reality distortion field," and everybody who entered it got caught up in it.

LeRoux used his piercing eyes, authoritative manner, imperturbable smile, and exclamations of "magic" to cast a spell. He hypnotized Jack into believing that he could get it all done—and do it in Somalia, one of the most chaotic places in the world. Jack let LeRoux's reality distortion field wrap around him like a blanket. What was left of his better judgment wafted away.

"All I have to do," Jack rationalized, "is get on the ground, assess the situation, and arrange the level of security I need to stay alive." Crossing the street in Manhattan was dangerous, too. And look at the upside. As a man who loved two things, adventure and working with his hands, what could be better than building a company, maybe even a new industry, in a forgotten corner of the world? This was probably exactly how Cecil Rhodes and his pioneers felt. Jack suddenly understood imperial exuberance.

The first thing he had to do was talk the local leaders into giving Southern Ace permission to do anything LeRoux wanted. LeRoux had sent two emissaries to negotiate with them in 2008. They got nowhere. In January 2009, Jack went to Nairobi to try again. He met with the president of Galmudug, Mohamed Warsame Ali, a politician and diplomat who went by the nickname Kiimiko. Jack promised that the Southern Ace tuna fishing business would create hundreds of jobs. He pledged to build housing for workers, a water pumping station, a school for the workers' children, a mosque for their worship, and more. When that didn't seal the deal, he handed out LeRoux's cash.

After four months of negotiations, Jack returned to Manila in triumph, with a signed agreement and big plans.

When he landed, his life turned upside down. His Filipina wife met him at the airport, looking cadaverous. When they walked into the borrowed penthouse, Jack peered around and saw—nothing. It looked the same as when they moved in. She wasn't living there anymore.

She confessed that she had been taking crystal meth, a lot of it. Meth was to Manila what coke was to Manhattan, Miami, and Malibu in the early 1980s—the party drug of choice, money pit, and, for some, a one-way trip to oblivion. She had sold all their furniture and everything else she could find to buy meth for herself and her friends.

Jack felt nailed to the floor. His head was spinning. He called LeRoux, who sent his lawyer to reprimand the building management for letting a bunch of meth freaks strip the penthouse without intervention from the security guards.

Jack didn't care about the furniture. He was brokenhearted. He filed for divorce, returned to Somalia, and threw himself into the work of constructing the fishing business. He desperately wanted to do something unselfish—"to build something there," he said, "to organize and work with people who have been abused and abandoned by their government for the past twenty years."

And if he and LeRoux got rich in the sushi trade, even better.

LeRoux exploited this twist of fate to his own darker purpose. Holed up in his penthouses and safe houses, he was multitasking—devising bigger and better projects, knowing that Jack, sober and earnest, would do a good job for him in Somalia. Jack would work even harder, he knew, without the annoying distraction of booty calls with a girl jacked on meth.

Very rarely, Jack caught a glimpse of some of the demons that

hounded LeRoux. Once, while they were discussing the fishing business, LeRoux remarked that they needed to do something that was
legally risky.

"Who can we trust?" Jack asked.

On the word "trust," LeRoux whirled to face Jack and exploded.

"If you find out your whole life was a LIE," he shouted, hurling
words like poison darts, "and it was done by the people you call FAM-
ILY, then what is the point of trusting ANYONE? I have NO trust in
my business partners but MORE than in my FAMILY, that's for sure."

Jack was rocked back on his heels. Although he had heard that Le-
Roux blew up at people, this was the first time he had ever witnessed
one of his hissy fits, and it was shocking. LeRoux gave the impression
that the explosion was triggered by his recent discovery that he had
been adopted—and that he couldn't forgive Paul and Judith LeRoux
for not leveling with him.

The rant might have been a play for Jack's pity. LeRoux could have
been angry about being adopted, but that fact wasn't news to him.
Fully a decade earlier, when LeRoux was working at SecurStar, his boss
Wilfried Hafner had witnessed a similar fit, only on the earlier occasion, LeRoux cursed his biological father, not his adoptive parents.

In 2008, LeRoux set out to search for his birth mother. According
to internal DEA documents, he enlisted the help of a cousin's husband, a white businessman who, like LeRoux, had been born in the
colony of Rhodesia and who now lived in South Africa. As the man
later recounted to DEA agents, LeRoux wanted to find his own birth
certificate. The man made a trip to Bulawayo and came up with the
document.

There was no happy reunion. Much later, LeRoux told others that
he thought his birth mother had been abandoned as a child. The impli-
cation was, she had nothing to offer him, so he stopped searching. But
this remark, like other references to his supposedly sad family background, could have been yet another manipulation.

After the no-trust outburst, Jack didn't ask LeRoux about his family or childhood. He didn't want to kick a hornet's nest.

"Most of the time LeRoux just completely avoided the subject of family in such way that I felt something bad had happened," Jack said. "He was locked in his own world. He was cold as a block of ice. You couldn't have emotions or feelings. That was for weak people."

Jack found life much simpler in Somalia. Except for LeRoux, nobody—not ex-wives, not ex-girlfriends—could find him unless he wanted to be found. What guy hasn't had that fantasy?

Jack rented a sixteen-room, two-story concrete blockhouse near the dilapidated airport in Galkayo, the main city in Galmudug. On the outside, the house looked like a big concrete box, but the interior was decorated with tile and hand-carved wooden furniture. It was cool and airy and rather pleasant. It could accommodate forty people. Jack used it as a barracks for his growing entourage of house servants, bodyguards, and construction workers.

Jack organized 250 of the local tribesmen to act as a militia to protect the building and area. He armed them with weapons, equipment, and vehicles acquired in Somalia's bustling arms bazaars. He bought light and heavy machine guns, grenade launchers, and body armor. He acquired two Russian ZU-23 antiaircraft guns—truck-mounted, double-barreled cannons that fired like a machine gun and could knock down a helicopter. Jack had no intention of taking down aircraft but thought these weapons would frighten al-Shabaab scouts. Mounted on trucks, with two thousand rounds of ammunition, they looked like steel dragons rolling down the rutted roads.

Jack spent piles of LeRoux's money. He purchased and installed large diesel generators to power the base. The school and mosque went up, and the water pumping station, as promised. He obtained some fiber optic cable and set up Internet connections.

He spent his evenings studying the Somali and Muslim culture. He wrote a manual for LeRoux's Western employees, with rules on how to live, work, approach, and behave in Somalia. He proudly showed LeRoux how he had mastered nuances of the culture. For instance, he wrote that when you entered a meeting with tribal elders, you should always greet the oldest person in the room first, even if the president were among those present.

"Brilliant," LeRoux said. He promised to circulate his tome to the rest of the staff. He valued Jack's person-to-person diplomacy. He didn't know how to cultivate the tribesmen. He was glad to pay Jack to do it.

Since a contingent of al-Shabaab militants camped nearby, Jack built a concrete wall around the house, topped with a razor-wire fence. He set up three circles of guards and checkpoints around to protect the house. Every night, Jack could hear rounds flying. He slept with a loaded AK-47 in his bed and a light machine gun with an ammunition belt in his room, in case the compound was overrun.

Jack drilled his rookie militiamen to adopt round-the-clock vigilance, testing them constantly. Once, during the night, he climbed out of the house and crept up on the guards who were supposed to be protecting the perimeters. All seven were sleeping. He took their AK-47s away, then walked around to the front door and knocked, to make the point that if a six-foot-three white guy could break out, steal assault rifles from seven guards, and walk to the main gate without being noticed, then they were doing a lousy job and would all be dead if this were the real deal.

"After that night, not even a cat could sneak by," Jack said and laughed.

But al-Shabaab was constantly trying. The camp measured about thirty-one acres of flat desert. Jack ordered the militiamen to make constant patrols in Land Rovers. On one searing day, at about noon, the patrol radioed that eight al-Shabaab fighters had gotten inside the outer perimeter and were making their way toward the compound. Jack ran to his Land Rover and followed, peering through a pair of binoculars. He could see the intruders, almost a mile away. What kind of men would pick this bloody-hot moment to run around the desert? Maybe because they thought most people would be napping?

The al-Shabaab men must not have known they had been spotted. Jack turned on the video of his phone and recorded the militiamen sneaking up behind the attackers. His men were dressed in ragged pants and shirts, sneakers and headscarves, no helmets or proper armor. They had no place to take cover. The ground was flat, gray dust. Several of them were toting heavy rocket-propelled grenade launchers on their shoulders. These were tall as a man and kicked like a mule. They were usually mounted on trucks but the men had to go on foot across the dusty plain.

Once in range, the militiamen shouted *Allahu Akbar!* God is great! They opened up with their machine guns. The desert erupted in explosions and screams. Jack could see his men spraying the landscape with bullets. Their machine guns were jamming because of the fine dust. They switched to rocket-propelled grenade launchers.

When it was over, six al-Shabaab militants lay dead. Two had escaped. The tribesmen so hated the Islamists that they didn't give the bodies a Muslim burial, as they did when they killed traditional enemies. The cadavers were left to dry in the sun. Amazingly, Jack's militiamen suffered only superficial wounds. Jack welcomed them back to the compound with a jug of juice—no alcohol on the premises. He saw a teaching moment. See how the training and vigilance he was demanding paid off? They had the power to keep al-Shabaab from encroaching on their land and kidnapping and killing their families, provided they never let down their guard. They nodded and chattered and resumed their patrols with new enthusiasm.

Jack kept the video on his laptop. "It reminded me that I was safe because of the way I worked with those people," he said. "Things can change any second, and if you have them as an enemy you're done because a human life means nothing there. They had wildlife like ostriches and springboks and they only killed to eat and not more than necessary. They had immense respect for their natural habitat. But when it came to humans they could shoot each other over an argument about a small thing like less sugar in their tea."

This wasn't hypothetical. Jack had been thirty feet away from two men who pulled guns on each other in the local market, just because one put too much sugar in the other's tea. One died. The other survived.

"Crazy," Jack said, "but if you didn't know how to handle people like that you don't survive a day."

When Jack had to fetch supplies from abroad, he took a flight on a small Somali-owned transport service that made runs from Galkayo to Mogadishu and Djibouti with an ancient Russian-made Antonov AN-24. The pilots were Romanians who seemed to survive on vodka-laced coffee. They liked Jack and invited him to sit in the cockpit when they buzzed villages.

"They were always cracking racist jokes, smoking cigarettes in the cockpit, and doing flyovers to show me Mogadishu and Galkayo from above," Jack said. "They were crazy people but the only ones who wanted to fly there. They were old-school, communist, racist, mentally disturbed pilots, and I guess the vodka helped."

The pilots weren't the worst of it, though. "The really crazy guy," Jack said, "was the mechanic walking around with a big hammer just in case something got stuck so he could bang it and get it working again."

Kibitzing afar from Manila or other safe houses, LeRoux communicated with Jack via Skype, puttering and nattering about every step of the construction. Once the Galkayo camp was set up, Jack started on the coastal docking facility for the fishing boats. It was on an empty spot on the coast, seven hours drive from Galkayo. He negotiated with tribal leaders along the road between Galkayo and the coast so he and his men could drive trucks through their territories. He hired fifty workers and another fifty militiamen. He had arms and equipment shipped to the coastal site and started construction.

Every day and every night, LeRoux was on email and on Skype or some other encrypted communications platform. He sent Jack twenty emails a day about instructions, money wires, logistics, financial reports, and development plans. Jack responded with dozens of photos, because LeRoux insisted on seeing everything he was paying for. When the camp Internet went down, LeRoux and Jack continued communicating by satellite phone.

LeRoux ordered ten fishing boats from a boatbuilder in Mogadishu, stocked them in Galkayo, and docked them at the coastal base.

Jack met with leaders of the Somali pirates to negotiate a price so that LeRoux's boats and vehicles could come and go to the coastal camp unmolested.

"It is good you have an opening with them," LeRoux texted Jack after the first meeting. "As u know . . . we are not there just for fishing. u need to become self-sufficient (in terms of money) while we ramp up the fishing and the other areas of business we interested in, that means oil, it means fishing, it means other businesses i will discuss with u in person. What we are doing now is setting the ground work for co-opperation [sic] with all our friends in many profitable areas where we can help each other."

Jack and the pirates closed the deal in good time. "The pirate leaders are businessmen and mostly have families in the UK or Europe where they live a good life," Jack said. "The tribe elders are the true leaders. When you have their grace, nobody will touch you. I had their highest respect and grace and so even the pirates were not able to take me. Daily people came and brought me goats as a way of saying thank you for providing more than 300 families an income and stability. When a Somali pirate or high-ranked politician wanted to come close to me, my locals warned them not to come too close to me or they would be shot, because these guys did not provide them with anything. I am not dead because I respected them and their culture, plus I gave them jobs and income."

Things were going so well that the tribal leaders had an initiation ceremony to induct Jack into the tribe. Jack donned a traditional sarong, which he found refreshing in the heat. The governor of the tribe presented him with a Russian-made, silver-plated pistol and anointed him *Ado Sa'ad,* meaning White Tribesman.

Jack didn't tell LeRoux about the ceremony and honor. "Some things you just didn't mention to him, as he would have seen it as me getting too much power there and maybe tried to remove me," Jack said. LeRoux wanted to be the one and only White Warlord. He didn't intend to share the credit with a hired hand, not even over a campfire on the back side of nowhere.

Jack was constantly trying to persuade him that the villagers' respect and loyalty had to be earned, as Jack had earned it, but LeRoux stayed stony. When dealing with somebody of higher status, the Boss could be superficially charming, but when it came to people he considered inferiors, he dropped the mask and reverted to full Rhodesian. He didn't appear to hate or recoil from people of color. He never used the n-word. He hired plenty of Filipinos and some black Africans. He simply didn't see them as thinking beings equal to himself, and he didn't care about their opinions and needs.

In the summer of 2009, temperatures in Galkayo soared. The little schoolhouse was like an oven. Jack ran a cable from the generators to the school and set up fans. It seemed a small thing, but when he mentioned what he had done to LeRoux, the Boss became enraged and shouted, "Who is paying for those little monkeys?"

"You!!" Jack retorted. It was crucial to the success of Southern Ace that the workers showed up, he said, and they wouldn't if their children were miserable or sick with heatstroke.

"If the people love you and respect you because they feel you genuinely care about them, then they will make sure you stay safe," Jack said. "They understand very well not to bite the hand that feeds them."

If the laborers and their children felt mistreated, the elders would get angry and tell the militiamen to pull out. With no guards to stop them, al-Shabaab militants would overrun the camp. Then where would they be?

LeRoux agreed, grudgingly, but he made it clear he didn't care what the workers thought. He didn't care what Jack thought, either. Jack could see that now. LeRoux was very bright and charismatic, but, now, after months of dealing with the man, Jack sensed there was something terrible and non-human coiled inside him, something with fangs and claws, spitting venom. He could almost hear it scratching to get out. When it did, Jack decided he didn't want to be there. He started to think about how to extricate himself. LeRoux was adding to his responsibilities—talking about moving the base of RX Limited to Somalia, where it would be less prone to American influence than the Philippines. LeRoux was worried that if American diplomats and the DEA leaned hard on the government of the Philippines to stop RX Limited, he could be extradited.

"Basically, he was going to relocate and continue the same pill business," Jack said. "LeRoux wasn't a quitter. He relocated and started again."

He told Jack to obtain a Somali license to import and export pharmaceuticals. He wasn't actually going to ship the drugs through Somalia, which would be tough, given that the only connections to the outside world were either a Humvee or drunken Romanians. He simply needed what looked like legitimate paperwork to show pharmaceutical wholesalers in the United States, Europe, and Asia so they would sell pills to RX Limited representatives anywhere.

"As long as there is a valid license, most companies don't care where it goes," Jack said.

CHAPTER SIX

INVISIBLE CITY

IN SEPTEMBER 2009, LEROUX TEXTED JACK TO GET TO HONG KONG AND meet him at the InterContinental hotel ASAP. They were going to pivot.

Jack rousted out the Romanian flight crew. The mechanic pulled out his hammer and pummeled the Antonov here and there. The pilots had their preflight caffeine-and-hundred-proof breakfast and ran through their checklist.

It was an eighteen-hour, four-airport trip—Galkayo to Djibouti, and from there, on less colorful airlines, to Dubai and then Hong Kong. Jack got to the InterContinental lobby around 10 a.m., ready for a little luxury or at least a shower.

LeRoux wasn't there. The front desk said he hadn't made a reservation for himself or Jack. After about half an hour, LeRoux shambled in, dressed like a slob, as usual, in an oversize polo shirt and a pair of rundown slippers. The InterContinental was a five-star hotel. LeRoux was probably staying at a *pied-à-terre* he kept in the city.

He motioned to Jack to follow him into the hotel restaurant, a white-tablecloth place that looked appealing but wasn't open for lunch. He gestured for Jack to sit down at an empty table in the empty restaurant. No "How was your flight?" No "Are you thirsty? Hungry?" The answer would have been "Starving." Jack noticed, wanly, that there was an inviting breakfast buffet down the hall, designed for the hotel's Western guests. It offered everything he could want, everything he hadn't seen in months—steak, eggs, home fries, smoked salmon, papaya, pineapple, croissants, brioche, Belgian waffles, and so much more.

LeRoux wasn't hungry. He had already had breakfast, probably an Egg McMuffin from McDonald's Hong Kong, which he would have eaten while walking to the five-star hotel. He didn't think about Jack, and he wasn't about to spend thirty dollars on food for an underling.

He got right down to business. How were things going for Southern Ace in Somalia? Jack was puzzled. Like LeRoux didn't know? He had been briefing LeRoux twice a day by encrypted email. But he launched in on a description of the fishing camp's progress.

LeRoux interrupted. "The project in Somalia has to become self-sustainable," he said. "We have to start looking for anything possible to start making money to pay for all the expenses."

There was no fishing business. It would take too long to turn a profit. He had more lucrative sources of income in mind.

First of all, he wanted to sell hard drugs—heroin, cocaine, meth, opioids, and whatever else the market wanted.

Second, LeRoux was going to green-light RX Limited sales of pharmaceutical opioids and start shipping them directly to customers. The call center workers said that customers in the United States were begging for the synthetic opioid, oxycodone, brand name OxyContin. It was the best-selling opioid prescription drug on the United States market, with sales zooming from 12 million pills in 1998 to 70 million in 2008. Hydrocodone, brand name Vicodin, an opioid painkiller, was almost as popular, with sales of 55 million pills in 2008. Both were highly addictive.

LeRoux knew that selling opioids and other pills on the Controlled Substances Act list would give the DEA grounds to go after him. The DEA investigation in Minneapolis could be expanded to include opioids, a much more serious matter.

On the other hand, he'd make a lot more money selling opioids. No customers were as loyal or free-spending as addicts. Pain relief trumped pleasure. Tranquilizers and sleep aids were enjoyable, but people could live without them. Addicts would give their last dollar, literally, for the drugs their bodies had to have, or suffer excruciating pangs of withdrawal.

Routing the paperwork through a Somalia license was one way to keep his new opioid trade under DEA's radar. Just in case the American agents figured out what he was up to, he was upgrading the security of his communications system. Heretofore, he had used a simple Gmail address—Johan588@gmail.com. In around 2009, he set up his own domain, fast-free-email.com, and gave all his men email addresses through his server. He encrypted their communications with two encryption protocols—SSL (Secure Sockets Layer) and PGP (Pretty Good Privacy). LeRoux himself was john@fast-free-email.com. Hunter's email was Rambo@ fast-free-email.com.

LeRoux wanted to cultivate opium, the raw material for heroin; marijuana; and coca, the feedstock for cocaine, in Somalia.

He was going to start up a second, even more ambitious venture for small arms. They were going to take control of Galmudug and, on the coast, build a base for the biggest international arms business ever conceived. LeRoux thought arms were a sure winner. War was money. War was a growth industry.

By definition, the *black* market in small arms was unquantified, but for LeRoux, the prospects were thrilling and irresistible—billions of dollars, doubling and redoubling as militant bands, guerrillas, warlords, death squads, and private militias cropped up like weeds and new conflicts flared up.

At any given time, societies in a couple of dozen countries were locked in life-and-death struggles and would pay for light, portable, lethal goods. The demand from warlord factions and Islamist groups was apparently inexhaustible, and that wasn't all. Wealthy people in places that weren't in active conflict were plagued by robbers, kidnappers, and assassins. They all had to have bodyguards, and the bodyguards had to be equipped. He would be their supplier, no questions asked. Guns were as desirable as crack, crank, and smack. Demand would fluctuate from year to year, but it would never go away, because the postmodern, globalized world had entered an era of never-ending war. Colonial powers and authoritarian rulers had been replaced by chaos as globalization elsewhere left behind certain peoples and regions. Tribes, clans, and communities that weren't engaged in an active conflict but might be drawn into one at any moment, wanted a stockpile of weapons for the defense of their people and territory.

LeRoux was already exploring angles to get into the arms trade. He chartered his first arms dealership in Manila—Red, White and Blue Arms Inc. It was an indoor shooting range and gun club, with a store that sold small arms to collectors, gun enthusiasts, private security forces, and the Philippine National Police. Competitive shooting was a popular sport in the Philippines. A gun club was a good way to cultivate powerful men while sampling the marketplace.

LeRoux observed that guns, like drugs, were addictive. Nobody who fell in love with them could stop at just one. Powerful people wanted rooms full of them, houses full. They would build private armies just to show them off. If a warlord, political power broker or business tycoon already had an army—call it a militia, guerrilla group, gang, or security force—he or she needed to equip it.

People who looked at the arms trade from afar might imagine that it was all about exotic stuff, like nerve gas or anthrax, or big weapons systems, like cruise missiles and Predator drones. Such things showed up in the black market maybe twice a decade, but the workaday gun world was all about small arms, a lot of them. Volume was where the real money was, and LeRoux was determined to lock down a piece of it. He set out to establish sources of inventory, fast—starting locally, expanding globally.

Since there were no small arms manufacturers in the Philippines, LeRoux had to import them from someplace. To do that, he needed authentic end-user certificates issued by the Philippine government, with proper seals and stamps. He was already bribing police officials to protect his e-commerce pharmaceutical business from U.S. investigators. For the new gun business, he paid off more officials, those at the firearms and explosives division of the Philippine National Police, to issue end-user certificates that verified that the department was the official buyer of the arms. When the guns arrived, the police agreed to transfer the arms to LeRoux to sell to the real buyers.

As a test run, LeRoux bought a shipment of SIG Sauer pistols made in New Hampshire. These were fine firearms, but even with a legitimate end-user certificate from the Philippine police, he ran into U.S. government export controls that involved a lot of paperwork. Long guns were practically impossible to export from the United States.

LeRoux looked for less fastidious sources of supply. He compiled a list of countries that manufactured small arms for their military forces and might not be as punctilious about paperwork as the Americans. He started with Indonesia because it was near the Philippines and not too sophisticated.

LeRoux sent Dave Smith to approach the Indonesian-government-owned arms factory, PT Pindad, to arrange a small test purchase—one hundred knockoffs of Israeli Galil SSI assault rifles and ten 9mm handguns, worth less than $100,000.

To make the sale look legitimate, Smith provided Indonesian factory officials with end-user certificates from the Philippine police and the Republic of Mali. LeRoux and Smith had gotten the end-user certificate from Mali by sending Hunter and an Israeli RX Limited employee named Shai Reuven there to bribe a clerk.

To ship the Indonesian arms from Jakarta to the Philippines, Smith hired Bruce Jones, a fifty-something British sea captain who lived in Subic Bay and hung out in the expatriate bars there. Jones went to Istanbul and bought a tramp merchant ship called the *Captain Ufuk* for $800,000. He picked up a crew of thirteen Georgian sailors, sailed from Turkey to Jakarta, collected the arms on August 10, 2009, and arrived at Port of Mariveles on Bataan Peninsula on August 19. Smith sent three of his Echelon mercenaries—Hunter, Chris DeMeyere, and Adam Samia—to join Jones on the last leg of the trip to make sure the guns got where they were supposed to go.

Once the *Captain Ufuk* arrived in Bataan, Smith took one of Le-Roux's yachts, the *Mou Man Tai,* to offload the Indonesian arms. (Here was yet another irony: In Chinese, *Mou Man Tai* means "No Problem" or "Relax.") When about half the rifles had been moved from the Ufuk to the yacht, Smith and the offloading crew called it a day. Jones's Filipino wife, who had made the journey with him, was pregnant and feeling ill. The couple climbed aboard the yacht with Smith and departed. The rifles were taken to Dave Smith's beach house and then moved to the house of his friend Herbert Chu.

The next day, before Smith could return for the rest of the rifles, the Philippine Coast Guard showed up. Guardsmen boarded the Ufuk, discovered the other fifty rifles, plus forty-five bayonets, and detained the crew for gun-running.

It wasn't a large seizure, by international standards, but it blew up into a scandal that made news across Asia. Jones and Smith were arrested. LeRoux bailed them out. He spent at least $1.2 million in bribes to make the Philippine government investigation go away and keep his name out of the press.

American diplomats posted to the U.S. embassy in Jakarta gave the Indonesian government a stern lecture about not selling arms to strangers who might turn out to be extremists. Indonesian authorities needed little convincing. Since the late 1980s, they had been fighting their indigenous Islamist terror group Jemaah Islamiyah, which had staged a series of attacks in Indonesia, notably the bombings of two Bali nightclubs in October 2002 that killed 202 and injured another 209, and most recently, on July 17, 2009, an attack on two U.S.-owned luxury hotels in Jakarta, the Ritz-Carlton and JW Marriott, which killed nine and wounded at least fifty. In the wake of the *Captain Ufuk* scandal, the Indonesian Parliament and Defense Ministry enacted tighter arms export controls.

LeRoux scratched Indonesia off his list of potential suppliers. There were other prospects, especially since the opportunities for an upstart gun-runner had suddenly proliferated. Since Viktor Bout had been arrested in March 2008, there was room at the top for a new arms mega-merchant. In his Manila lair, LeRoux read about Bout's arrest and learned from the older man's mistakes. "The guy should have known better and been more protective for his person," LeRoux scoffed to Jack. The Russian, LeRoux said, was past his prime—vain, sloppy, and a publicity hound besides. The Americans had even gotten their hands on home movies Bout had made of himself, cavorting naked in the snow, dancing in a karaoke bar, hanging out with butchers and tyrants. (In 2012, Bout would be sentenced to twenty-five years in federal prison for his conviction on four felony counts, including conspiring to kill Americans and conspiring to provide material support to terrorists.)

LeRoux shared Bout's hunger for extreme wealth and the power that went with it. He planned to exercise his influence behind the scenes, without the flamboyance that Bout displayed, and without depending on a nation-state. Bout had had the backing of the Kremlin, but it could disappear in a blink of Vladimir Putin's eye. LeRoux preferred to go it alone, shielding himself with his own strict rules for operational security: never show up to do a deal in person, communicate virtually, never use your real name on any transaction, and deal strictly in cash or gold exchanged by surrogates.

LeRoux told Jack he wanted to stir up more small wars. "It's good if countries get trouble and civil wars," he told Jack. "It's good for business."

Sitting in the restaurant, hungry and dehydrated, Jack labored to grasp the awful implications of LeRoux's vision.

"On the coast we would build almost a small city that was completely independent of anything and anyone," Jack said, "with warehouses, housing for staff, a high security camp to keep us safe and to stock all arms and ammunition, a mosque, water wells to use locally, an airstrip, livestock and so on." There would be an impregnable fortress in the center, and around it, simple huts for workers and guards. The place would function as a fulfillment center for arms shipments to combatants engaged in small wars and secular conflicts anywhere. As more personnel were needed, the complex would expand.

LeRoux's new city would be almost invisible. He had chosen the coast of Galmudug as the building site because it was without strategic value. There were no radical Islamists and no commerce except for goat herding and subsistence farming. It was of little interest to international intelligence and law enforcement. If the Big Powers didn't care what went on there, his presence—his *control*—wouldn't show up on their radar.

In the first phase of the project, LeRoux said, they were going to take control of the major arms bazaars in Somalia. They would attract customers from many places, across not only Africa but also South Asia, Southeast Asia, East Asia, and the Pacific Islands. The demand from warlord factions and Islamist groups was virtually inexhaustible. "Once you have warehouses full of arms in Somalia, you can easily take over the trade on the continent," Jack said.

For the next phase, LeRoux had already engaged a Manila architect to draw up blueprints for a large, self-contained arms receiving and shipping facility with modules so that it was expandable as volume demanded. It was labeled "Forward Base Site Development Plan." There were spaces for offices, bunkrooms, shower rooms, kitchens, and arsenals.

Connected to the Somali base would be a private port, outfitted with landing craft to load and unload arms and other goods and supplies from merchant ships and bring them ashore, unseen by airport and waterfront snitches on whom intelligence services traditionally relied.

Near the port, LeRoux wanted an airstrip that was at least 6,500 feet long, to accommodate big cargo planes coming in from Europe, the Middle East, North Africa, and Asia. LeRoux had already bought an Antonov AN-12 medium-range military transport, which he parked on the tarmac at the Galkayo airport. It was not in good working order, but it could be fixed, probably. LeRoux's plan emulated Viktor Bout's MO of using old clunkers to deliver arms to militia bands in the countryside. If a plane crashed due to mechanical difficulties or attack, or if it were seized by the authorities, the enterprise would not suffer a ruinous loss. Aircrews were expendable. LeRoux intended to buy a whole fleet of old Russian and Ukrainian Antonov cargo planes. These, he said, would deliver arms from Eastern Europe and building equipment from the United Arab Emirates.

Though the coastal site was going to be the moneymaker, LeRoux intended to retain Jack's original compound in Galkayo, to use as a base for sending orders and receiving supplies, either by truck from the port of Bosaso or by plane at the Galkayo airport. The airport wasn't much to brag about. LeRoux had recently negotiated a deal with some Ukrainian arms smugglers, but when the ring's pilots found out their destination was Galkayo, they refused the mission. But LeRoux was sure it could be improved to serve his needs.

One major drawback in both Galkayo and the nameless coastal site was the lack of water.

LeRoux explained to Jack that he had figured out how to solve that problem. He had purchased desalination equipment. He wanted Jack to erect a desalination facility and run 300 kilometers, or 186 miles, of pipe from the coastal site to Galkayo in the interior. Because al-Shabaab was likely to try to sabotage the water pipeline, Jack would have to devise a way to oversee and protect nearly two hundred miles of pipeline. "It would blow everybody's mind in Somalia that we actually were willing to do that," Jack said. "It was LeRoux's way to please the locals. In fact he didn't give a shit about them, but he needed them. It was actually madness."

Jack was too worn-out to protest. He stared at LeRoux dully, trying to jog himself awake by scribbling notes on the back of his airplane ticket. Eighty minutes into the meeting, Jack could see the cooks in full prep for lunch service. He poured himself some water from a carafe on the table. It was free.

A waiter came over to take their lunch order. Jack was desperate for a steak. The cuisine in Galmudug was goat, goat, goat, and flatbread. He was sick of goat.

"We don't want to eat here," LeRoux said, waving the waiter away. "We're finished meeting anyway."

Jack's spirits sagged. He was embarrassed to be drinking the free water and not ordering anything. He felt lightheaded with hunger.

"What time is your return flight?" LeRoux said. It wasn't a question. "I need you to get back and start working on the new plan."

Jack was stunned and confused. "You cheap Charlie prick," he muttered to himself in his old navy slang. "How can you expect me to fly all the way back the same day? Not even a shower?"

But he answered that his flight back to Somalia was in a few hours. He flagged down a cab and dragged himself back to the airport.

Up to now, LeRoux had been pretty good to him. Why this harsh treatment? Why now? Maybe it was just the way powerful men acted. After enduring his father's alcoholic rages for twenty-four years, he could put up with a lot, and he'd been proud of himself for doing it. But now anger pumped enough adrenaline into his system to give him an idea. He strode up to the Cathay Pacific desk. "When is the next flight to Addis? Or Nairobi?" he asked.

"The Nairobi flight leaves in four hours, sir," the reservationist said.

"That prick," Jack said to himself. "Fuck it."

He turned to the reservationist.

"I'd like to upgrade to business class." He handed over a credit card LeRoux had given him. Business class cost $3,000 extra. LeRoux could have saved $2,800 by shelling out for a $200 room at a two-star hotel in Hong Kong. But it never seemed to occur to him that other humans had needs, or if he noticed, he didn't care.

Jack found the Cathay Pacific business-class lounge and took a long steamy shower in a private bath suite. The food in the lounge didn't look that great, so he went out, found a restaurant, and ordered the biggest steak on the menu. Back in the lounge, he enjoyed a nice glass of wine and dessert. Upon boarding, he discovered to his delight that he was the only passenger in business class. He pulled off his boots, reclined his seat, stretched out his lanky frame to full length, and slept sweetly for hours. He landed in Nairobi to find there were no flights going to Somalia for several days. He took his R&R break there. He would rather have done it in Hong Kong, but he didn't have the nerve. He was relieved when LeRoux paid his expense report without complaint.

But once he had caught up on his sleep, Jack had to face a terrible reality. LeRoux was plotting to become the most powerful black-market drugs and arms dealer alive, and he had made Jack his co-conspirator. LeRoux wanted superstardom in the dark world.

Up until that point, Jack had been on the legal side of LeRoux's empire, but now LeRoux was setting him up to run the criminal enterprises, too. He was going to front for LeRoux's narcotics and arms ventures, and worse. How could he get away? *Could* he get away?

Jack didn't get much time or space to think. LeRoux's orders were pounding down like shells from a Maxim gun. He was having brainstorms that he fired at Jack with manic zeal.

He wanted to take over the khat trade, unknown in the West but worth millions of dollars in East Africa. The khat mafia, composed mainly of Somalis, ran the trade out of Kenya, flying small planes loaded with product out of the Nairobi airport. LeRoux had sent a couple of his mercenaries to take a proposition to the khat mafia, offering to become their partner and expand the reach of their network, in exchange for a piece of the action.

The khat mafia leaders turned LeRoux's men down. "You can't just walk up to these people and expect them to hand over a three-million-dollar-a-month trade to some strangers," Jack said.

The next idea was even more ambitious: mount a coup in the Seychelles Islands—some 115 islands located in the Indian Ocean, ranging between three hundred and a thousand miles from the East African mainland. LeRoux said that Dave Smith introduced him to a man who claimed to be a relative of President James Alix Michel of the Seychelles. The man offered him $300 million and a diplomatic passport from the Seychelles if he and his Echelon mercenaries deposed Michel and installed the man in Michel's place. LeRoux gave the idea of mounting a coup serious consideration. The money was attractive, and he had been looking around for diplomatic status in Africa, in case things got too hot for him in the Philippines. He told Smith to send Hunter to the Seychelles to survey the situation.

Hunter returned with an optimistic assessment. "Hunter reported that approximately thirty mercenaries would be required, thirty Echelon mercenaries . . . to take over the government, basically to defeat any resistance in the Seychelles," LeRoux said later.

He reluctantly demurred. "I responded to Smith that I believed that the project was not viable," he said, "because, although the Echelon mercenaries being trained killers and well-trained and capable of initially overrunning the country and taking over the government, it would not be sustainable in the long-term, because the country had allies in the region . . . the neighboring countries such as Tanzania would intervene."

LeRoux focused on other money-making projects that he could carry out inside his safe haven in Somalia. He had greenhouses and agricultural equipment shipped to the Galkayo camp so that he and Jack could explore the idea of cultivating opium, coca, and marijuana. The water from the planned desalination plant could be used to irrigate the illicit crops. He dispatched a horticulturalist from the Philippines. The poor guy stayed with Jack for several months, trembling behind concrete block walls. So did the Filipino accountant LeRoux sent to run the numbers. Jack noticed that the frightened bean counter went to bed every night clutching a teddy bear.

The horticulturalist did a study of the agricultural conditions and advised LeRoux that growing contraband crops wasn't likely to make money anytime soon. Even with an assured supply of fresh water, planting, cultivating and harvesting were labor-intensive and subject to the vagaries of weather. Marijuana was a grass that grew easily. But opium and coca couldn't be grown in the Somalian desert.

LeRoux pivoted to methamphetamine manufacture. It was entirely synthetic and needed only a couple of lab workers and some barrels of chemicals from China or India. He told Jack they would set up a large methamphetamine production facility at the camp near the airport, using chemicals acquired for fertilizer as feedstock for crystal meth. They could make a finished product to rival the North Koreans.

Jack countered, acutely unhappy now, with a proposal for a legitimate business, oil production. A local tribal leader had led Jack to an abandoned oil-drilling site in Galmudug, cemented over years earlier by an American oil exploration mission. Jack urged LeRoux to approach a major international oil company and offer to broker a deal with the local strongmen so the company could drill in peace.

LeRoux listened, briefly, but then turned off the discussion. He didn't want to play junior partner to an American oil company. Too visible, and it didn't fit his image of himself as a lonely genius, like Elon Musk or Steve Jobs. His reality distortion field was getting stronger. He told Jack he wanted to do everything himself. He ordered drilling equipment from China and drilled down 600 to 800 feet. He found nothing. It turned out that the well needed to be 2,000 feet deep.

Jack estimated that LeRoux would need to spend $10 million in capital costs to drill the well to 2,000 feet. He thought LeRoux could easily afford it. He figured LeRoux had many times that amount in cash in Hong Kong. LeRoux lost interest. The oil-drilling project would require a couple of years of investment in infrastructure before it would turn a profit. Jack was crestfallen.

"With the oil and tuna, he could be a very wealthy man, but he wanted it fast," Jack said. "It had to be fast and it had to be dirty. He wanted to go one hundred percent rogue. That was more exciting for him. His problem was impatience. If he waited and gave us the time to build that airstrip at the coast and develop the fishing factory, which would be a great cover for the arms to fly in from Eastern Europe, he would be a seriously powerful man and even more dangerous than he already was. He wanted all to be built in a day, figuratively speaking, and that was impossible."

LeRoux's kaleidoscope of proposed ventures baffled Jack, whose ideas about business were very traditional and linear. Start small, get bigger, and bigger. Build up or build out, but connect all the parts logically, like building a house. The twenty-first century way of doing business advocated exactly what LeRoux was doing—hopscotching from venture to venture in seemingly unrelated fields until something started to catch fire. LeRoux had a toe in projects all over the world so he could sample markets and assess the likelihood of government intervention. For example, around the same time he was brainstorming plots in Somalia, he was also experimenting with an online gambling start-up in Costa Rica, which he called the Betting Machine.

Professor Howard Stevenson, who founded the discipline of entrepreneurship studies at the Harvard Business School in the 1980s, famously defined the concept as "pursuit of opportunity beyond resources controlled." He meant that entrepreneurs were individuals or small groups with more vision, guts, and drive than money and without the patience for the traditional corporate-style product development umbrella, without all the checks, balances, imposed conformity, and timidity of groupthink.

It was no accident, Stevenson said, that many famous entrepreneurs were penniless when they set out. "They see an opportunity and don't feel constrained from pursuing it because they lack resources," Stevenson explained to *Inc.* magazine in 2012. "They're used to making do without resources." What they had was obsessive focus, a need for speed, a try-anything-once attitude, inexplicable self-confidence, a high tolerance for risk, a hide like a rhino, and an all-consuming urge to rip the systems apart. As Mark Zuckerberg, the cofounder of Facebook, told his developers, "Move fast and break things. Unless you are breaking stuff, you are not moving fast enough."

LeRoux fully embraced the Silicon Valley playbook—experimenting, staying loose, making snap judgments, persevering when something looked promising, pivoting when he smelled a loser. All these qualities cast him as textbook entrepreneur. "He thinks big," said Jeff Reid, a business professor at Georgetown University and founding director of the university's Entrepreneurship Initiative. "He looks for unique angles. He tries new things. If there's a market there, sounds like he's going to find a way to get it."

If LeRoux had only managed to come off as less cold-blooded, even if he had to fake it, he could have been putting down avocado toast and bacon jam with tech titans in San Francisco's Pacific Heights, nicknamed Billionaires Row. But people didn't exhilarate him. He was happiest alone, plotting his schemes in his sterile penthouse.

Jack obeyed him, grudgingly but diligently until the summer of 2010, when an IED planted by al-Shabaab blew up near one of the Land Rovers Jack's militia used for patrolling the Galkayo camp perimeter. Five militiamen suffered burst eardrums and wounds from flying glass. There was no medical facility nearby. Jack contacted LeRoux and asked what he should do.

"Bury them in the desert," LeRoux said and laughed.

What did he mean? Bury them alive? Or let them bleed out, then kick sand over them?

Either way, Jack was shocked. This was callousness even for Le-Roux. Jack threw all five of his men into a Land Rover, got them to an airstrip, and persuaded some khat smugglers with a beat-up plane to take the wounded men to the hospital in Djibouti. As it turned out, one of the wounded men was a cousin of the president of Djibouti. (Some 60 percent of the Djibouti population consisted of ethnic Somalis, including the tiny nation's chief executive.) The Djibouti leader saw to it that all the wounded men were treated well. All survived their wounds and were never billed for their hospital stays.

When Jack related the happy outcome, LeRoux was unimpressed. The militiamen were *marginals*. He really couldn't understand why Jack had bothered.

Late that summer, LeRoux faced a threat to his own security. Bruce Jones, the captain of the tramp merchant steamer *Captain Ufuk,* had started giving interviews about the gun-running deal. Jones had contacted a reporter for the *Manila Bulletin* and was talking about what he called the "Bataan smuggling syndicate." He named, among others, Dave Smith. He didn't name LeRoux, but LeRoux was only one step from Smith.

On September 21, 2010, Jones and his wife, Maricel Aramay, were driving through Angeles City when two men on motorbikes pulled up next to their Toyota SUV and shot them. Jones died of multiple wounds from a .45-caliber handgun. Aramay was wounded but survived. Although they staged the ambush in broad daylight on a busy city street, the gunmen were not identified or charged.

According to court records, LeRoux eventually admitted that he ordered Smith to have Jones killed. Later, he said, Smith told him that Jones would not be a problem anymore.

Shortly after the Jones murder, LeRoux sent an email to Jack. "I need to talk to you. Take the first plane to Hong Kong."

Jack obeyed, but he was as frightened as he had never been, confronting al-Shabaab or random gunmen in the marketplace. Working for LeRoux was like trying to sleep with a bad-tempered black mamba in the house. You just never knew when you put a foot on the floor whether a venomous snake was curled up under your cot and would choose that moment to strike.

No doubt about it, LeRoux was frustrated and angry that Jack didn't have the landing strip and warehouses up and running. He didn't understand—didn't want to understand—the logistics of moving heavy equipment, steel girders, rebar, and the rest of what it took to make a port and transit zone work.

Never having spent time in the field, LeRoux thought all the building equipment he ordered would appear at the construction site in a matter of weeks after he ordered it. He didn't count on the time it took to haul the stuff overland from Djibouti.

"It was a complete logistical nightmare," Jack said.

LeRoux decided he should buy landing craft and send the building materials and equipment by cargo ship.

Jack had negotiated a deal with the pirates to land equipment and arms on the shore. But there were still waves, weather, and boulders to contend with. The conditions made transit and landing difficult, requiring many hands.

Fact was, Jack wasn't exactly dragging his feet, but he wasn't pushing hard, either. He had been hoping that LeRoux would reconsider the tuna fishing business, but realistically, he knew that the fish story was just that, a fable meant to lure him into LeRoux's web.

"He was talking to me about taking over countries!" Jack said. "Establishing his own state. Taking over an island!"

Jack had stayed on, fearful of and resenting LeRoux but taking his orders. He knew that he was now deeply enmeshed in LeRoux's conspiracies involving drug trafficking, gun-running, kidnapping, and maybe a coup. If LeRoux's people got caught, he would be culpable, too. He could wind up in a stinking cell with a beast like Dave Smith. LeRoux would vanish. He always did. And when the coast was clear, he'd start up a new business, and he'd get another Jack.

To make matters worse, just before he landed in Hong Kong, Jack read about the assassination of Bruce Jones. The Manila newspapers, which were online, were playing it as a sensational murder mystery. Jack had met the affable Jones in the bars in Subic Bay. He guessed, correctly, that Dave Smith had tagged the *Captain Ufuk* debacle on the happy-go-lucky Englishman and then, when things went wrong, LeRoux had Jones terminated.

LeRoux confirmed as much when they met in an empty restaurant in a luxury hotel in Hong Kong. Again, LeRoux refused to order food. Again, he expected Jack to fly straight back to Africa.

This time, Jack poured himself a glass of free water and got right to the point. "What happened to Bruce?"

"Ah, when you play with fire, this is what happens," LeRoux said with a smirk. "This is what happens when you screw with the company."

"He thought so much of himself, that he was so powerful, he could make you disappear, no matter who you were," Jack thought. "This was lunacy."

Jack had heard tell of other violent deaths of people associated with LeRoux, RX Limited, and the *Captain Ufuk*. He didn't know names and details, but having lived with Hunter and his mercenary team, he didn't think they were getting paid for simple strong-arm duty.

Jack resolved to break away. He had been thinking about it for a while. It was like a terrible marriage. He had gotten hooked on the adrenaline rush of the daily drama. LeRoux had seemed to sense this. He stood frozen, a deer in the headlights.

A woman jolted him into action.

Jack had met Anya in October 2009 on one of his supply-buying trips to Djibouti and Dubai. The thunderbolt struck him. She was a woman, not a girl, educated, refined, with a responsible job with an international corporation.

After a string of failed relationships, and because he was working in the Somali desert, he wasn't looking for romance. But it struck like a thunderbolt. When they started talking on a long flight to Addis Ababa, he was drawn to her killer smile, and she seemed to like his dry sarcastic humor. Feeling shy, he screwed up his courage and offered his email address. To his amazement, she took it. A couple of weeks later, when he was back in Somalia, his email pinged with a message from her. They made a date in Dubai. They strolled around, peered in shops, and parted. The next day, they met on the beach and talked for hours, and Jack told her his rambling life story.

Which went like this: His father dumped him in the pool when he was five. By fifteen, he was a national champion. It was an isolating sport, not like football or even tennis. When other boys his age were goofing around, breaking arms and legs, jumping off walls and out of windows, chasing girls, learning to drive, and generally learning about life, he was in a lap lane, hearing nothing but the water and his coach and father shouting.

He hated every cold dawn in the chlorine haze, every practice, every stroke. He was furious with his parents for dragging him to swim practice. He especially resented and feared his father, an engineer, nuclear plant safety inspector, and, on the side, a wine connoisseur with a collection of 1,500 bottles. Behind closed doors, his father was a drinker and chain-smoker who wouldn't tolerate disagreement from his four sons, particularly the rebellious Jack. When Jack balked at the daily trip to the pool, his father beat him, kicked him, stubbed cigarettes out on his back, and once waved a gun and threatened to shoot him.

When Jack turned eighteen, he did what young men do—he ran away to sea. He joined the navy of his nation and became a diver in a unit that searched for unexploded World War II–era mines in the North Sea and the English Channel. For an adrenaline junkie, there was nothing like the thrill of plunging into the murky depths and bumping up against a Nazi bomb. Jack and his mates found at least two a month.

In 1990 and 1991, during the Persian Gulf War, Jack worked in a joint operation with the U.S. Navy's Mine Countermeasures force in the Gulf, searching for mines planted by Saddam Hussein's forces and helping the U.S. Navy SEALs.

He kept up his training while in the navy and made the national swim team for the 1992 Olympics in Barcelona. He didn't get much practice time and was out of the competition after the first heats, but he could always say he was an Olympian.

Soon after he left active duty, his father was diagnosed with cancer. Jack, at that point twenty-four, slept next to him for six weeks, watching over him, bathing and changing him day and night until his body gave out. He yearned to hear his father say, just once, "I love you." That never happened. Jack wasn't sorry for his vigil. He believed in filial duty. He forgave his father. "I was the son who said no to certain things, and oh boy, did I pay the price, but hey, it made me what I am today," he said.

Jack used his father's modest bequest to start a construction company. He loved building and found he was good at it. He worked seventeen hours a day to keep the company in the black in a tax system that was close to confiscatory. He married a pretty gymnast who turned out to be a perfectionist. After he filed for divorce, his nerves shot, he was done. He sold the company and took off for the Philippines, intending to explore the world. And he did. It had been an education, but not the kind he had expected.

Jack figured Anya would run away. She was smart, frugal, independent, and beautiful. She had a bright future. What did she want with a guy like Jack? But she stayed. They went to his hotel, talked deep into the night, shared a chaste embrace, and fell asleep.

After that, he left his *Lord of the Flies*–style encampment in Galmudug and met her in Dubai. They did not make love for three months,
but when they finally did, there were more thunderbolts. As he put it
later, "I experienced the virtues of the Kama Sutra."

He confided in her about everything—about the pirates, smugglers,
his divorces, and LeRoux. "I'm working for a genius sociopath," he
confessed.

They met in Dubai, and he filled her on the meeting with LeRoux
in Hong Kong. She listened for a while, then said gravely, "You have a
decision to make. You can have a decent life and explore the world with
me. Or you can have a life of extremes without a guarantee of what the
next day will bring."

"She made me see reality," Jack said. "I always knew what he was
and what I had gotten into, in a way, but you're stuck in it and you only
deal with people in the business. It was very boxed-in at times, as there
you are, in the desert, with a few foreigners telling their life stories and
two hundred fifty Somalis who have had nothing for twenty years. She
did great by talking sense into me and making me realize there is much
more in life."

In October 2010, Jack got himself to Djibouti and caught a ride on a
UN relief flight to Dubai. Anya met him there. He told her that he was
finished with LeRoux. They went out on the balcony of the short-term
flat they had rented and had a little ceremony. They lit candles, poured
glasses of good red wine, and burned all the forged passports Jack had
collected from various African and Asian countries while working for
LeRoux. They let the ashes drop on the cement floor and blow away.

From Dubai, Jack emailed LeRoux that he was quitting. He didn't
tell him much, only that he wanted no part of the drug trade and that
he was going to take advantages of opportunities in legitimate business
elsewhere.

Once he got a little psychological distance from LeRoux, he realized that he was very angry and bruised. He did something out of

character. He went on the CIA website, found the "Contact" page, and fired off an email, saying that if somebody in the CIA was interested in LeRoux, he had a few things to say.

When he cooled down, he realized that ratting out LeRoux probably wasn't good for his health. He was somewhat relieved when he didn't hear from the CIA. LeRoux evidently wasn't a priority for American intelligence.

Jack found a job in Dubai, although he didn't like the place because, underneath the façade of conservatism and piety, Dubai had replaced Switzerland and the Caymans as the world money-laundering capital. "All the biggest criminals in the world can do whatever they want there," he said. "They all use the system—Paks, Afghans, Somalis."

When LeRoux got Jack's email resigning, he was livid. He sent two men to replace Jack in Galmudug—a white South African mercenary named Shaun Wright and Mischeck Dzichaunya, a black Zimbabwean who had been a senior police officer in the Mugabe regime and who helped LeRoux with his yachts and ran his boat repair yard.

They didn't get along with the Somali leaders, and they neglected to pay the Galmudug militiamen, so all of them took off, leaving the Galkayo base unprotected. The coastal base was barely started. With the venture collapsing, LeRoux was losing his entire investment of about $3 million to date.

LeRoux blamed Jack. After a month had passed, Jack got a message from Leo that LeRoux had put out a hit on him. That very day, Hunter was in Dubai stalking him. Jack pictured himself staring down the barrel of Hunter's gun, with LeRoux standing nearby or listening via Skype, savoring the sound of Jack's head cracking like a melon.

Jack knew that Hunter was a follower, not a leader. If LeRoux had told Hunter to kill him, there was no way Jack could talk Hunter out of it. Jack had to fix things with LeRoux.

Jack telephoned LeRoux and asked him to call Hunter off. The conversation didn't go the way Jack had hoped.

"You can walk away, but you cannot hide, you're going to die," Le-Roux snapped. "If people cheat me, then I make them disappear. You know you can't hide from me. I'll find you anywhere in the world. You know you're going to die."

"But I didn't cheat you," Jack protested. "If you put a hit out on me, I'll take you down."

"If I go down, you go down," LeRoux snarled, and hung up.

Toward Christmas 2010, Jack decided to try again to make amends. He didn't want LeRoux as an enemy for life. He didn't want to spend the rest of his life looking over his shoulder for Hunter or worrying about an attack on Anya.

He emailed LeRoux copies of his financial records for the Galmu-dug operation. They were meticulous and proved he could account for every penny of LeRoux's expenditures.

A couple of weeks after that, LeRoux called. He wanted Jack back. He was sorry.

"I know you didn't do anything wrong," he said. "Anytime you want a job, call me. I can always use good guys like you. I need people I can trust."

Sorry? Jack was touched. He had never known LeRoux to apol-ogize about anything. LeRoux habitually shifted the blame for any-thing bad to somebody else. He regretted his decisions, sometimes, and changed his mind, but sorry? This was the first time Jack had heard the word out of his mouth.

Trust? That was even stranger. Jack remembered very well that Le-Roux had declared he could trust no one.

In his next breath, LeRoux blamed Dave Smith. He said that he had caught Dave Smith telling a lot of lies about Jack. Smith had been jealous of his access to LeRoux. Smith liked to control everything, but LeRoux hadn't let him control Jack.

"The gray pigeon who was behind all the stealing has been taken care of," LeRoux said, with his mirthless chuckle. "He won't be driving a fancy motorbike again." He referred to Smith's beloved Italian-made MV Agusta.

Jack assumed that by "taken care of," LeRoux meant that Smith was dead. He guessed right. Later, he got the details.

As LeRoux later told the story, he suspected that Smith had double-crossed him by stealing $5 million worth of gold bars from him. Smith was supposed to collect the gold and hide it, but he never told LeRoux where he put it.

Instead of asking Smith directly, LeRoux started playing detective. He questioned a girl Smith had dumped. She told him that Smith had stolen the gold and, not only that, he had also been plotting to kidnap LeRoux, torture him, squeeze him for cash, then kill him.

LeRoux, white-hot angry, fixated on Smith's associate, Henry Chu. LeRoux knew that it was Chu who was in charge of hiding the guns Smith had unloaded from the *Captain Ufuk*. LeRoux thought that Chu might have hidden the gold for Smith. Or he would know where it was.

LeRoux asked Chu to come to one of his houses in Batangas Province on the Philippines coast. While they were talking, LeRoux shocked Chu with a Taser gun. Marius, a white South African, threw Chu into the water. Marius was a big guy with a dark thatch of hair and white mustache and beard. He had once been a South African cop and was now a biker who advertised on LinkedIn as a "risk manager" offering "protection services." In other words, he was a professional goon.

Bobbing in the surf, trying to catch his breath from the Taser shock, pleading for his life, Chu screamed that Smith's friend Chito had helped Smith hide the gold. Marius fished Chu out, handcuffed him, then shot and killed him. He attached the body to an anchor and sank both.

Chito met a similar end. Confronted by LeRoux and Marius, Chito gasped that Smith had sold the gold through a broker. LeRoux and Marius took Chito to Batangas, threw him in a small boat, headed out to sea, stunned him with a Taser, and threw him in. As he begged for his life, Marius shot Chito dead and sank his body with an anchor. LeRoux and Marius celebrated with a beer or two on the beach.

LeRoux told Smith, still unsuspecting, to meet him and Marius at the safe house in Batangas. The pretext was that they had to dig a hole and bury a safe loaded with $2 million in ill-gotten gains that belonged to a "friend." The story didn't make a lot of sense. Who would bury an entire safe? If you did it, how would you hoist it out of the hole later? Gravity wasn't going to be on your side. Besides, what was wrong with a secret bank account in Hong Kong or Macao?

Smith didn't question LeRoux. He started digging. While he was down in the hole, sweating in the muggy heat, Marius pulled out a 9mm pistol and shot him in the head. Smith, confused but still conscious, waved his arms, and shouted, "Why? Why? Why?" Finally, he dropped to the ground. Marius shot him several more times, until his gun jammed. Then LeRoux stepped up and shot Smith with his MP5 machine gun. As Marius whacked his gun, a pack of dogs approached, evidently drawn by the smell of warm blood. LeRoux chased the dogs away and grabbed Marius's gun, slapping it to unjam it. Marius grabbed it back, jiggled it, worked the slide, and finally cleared the spent shell casing from the ejection port. He shot Smith five or six times more in the head. LeRoux pulled out a MP5 submachine gun and fired more rounds into Smith's corpse.

The experience didn't improve LeRoux's marksmanship, but he learned something about himself. He *liked* shooting. He *liked* killing. He took pleasure in thinking about Smith lying there in the hole, bleeding out, with feral dogs circling what was left of him. LeRoux wanted more.

LeRoux and Marius wrapped Smith's body in a canvas tarp, hauled it onto a dinghy, motored into deep water, and dumped the body. Only, it floated. The tarp was holding air. LeRoux leapt into the water with a knife and stabbed holes in the canvas.

The body still wouldn't sink. Marius grabbed the dinghy's small

Yamaha outboard motor and tied it to the body, which finally sank. LeRoux and Marius drove back into town and had a beer or two.

Just in case someone pulled up Smith's corpse and the boat motor and traced the serial number, LeRoux filed a police report claiming that the motor had been stolen. His action betrayed his ignorance. As anybody who has ever seen a cop show knows, a good homicide investigator wouldn't need the serial number of the motor to link the dead man to LeRoux. There were a dozen more ways to connect the dots, and plenty of witnesses. There were people who knew LeRoux and Smith and were aware of their odd working relationship. There were official documents such as boat and car registrations and real estate records. There were Sid's regulars, who would notice that Smith wasn't at his usual post at the bar. There were people who had done business with LeRoux or worked for him at RX Limited and now feared him.

There were Smith's family and friends. LeRoux had repossessed Smith's house, confiscated cars, clothing, jewelry, weapons, and other personal possessions, and interrogated Smith's widow and Smith's girlfriends. Women who had lost everything might be tempted to talk.

What LeRoux had never grasped was that he couldn't unplug people, disconnect their memory chips, and toss them in a recycle bin. For all his cunning, vision, and prescience as an entrepreneur, he hadn't learned what most kids know by third grade. What goes around comes around.

CHAPTER SEVEN

PAC-MAN AND IRONMAN

JUST BEFORE CHRISTMAS 2011, DEA AGENT TOM CINDRIC FOUND HIMSELF leafing through a 417-page white paper from the United Nations Security Council about violations of the international ban on arms sales to warring factions in Somalia.

He wasn't sure what he was looking for. The tome had come to him from a friend of his supervisor, Wim Brown, who was leading the 960 Group's Africa team and applying to transfer to the DEA post in East Africa. The friend was Rudy Atallah, a retired U.S. Air Force lieutenant colonel and pilot who had been stationed in Africa for the Defense Intelligence Agency and had also served as the Pentagon's senior expert on terrorism in Africa.

Atallah was now a corporate security consultant specializing in Somalia and the Horn of Africa. He maintained his relationships with the Pentagon and State Department and sometimes helped negotiate with Somali pirates for the release of hostages, among others, Richard Phillips, whose rescue would inspire the Tom Hanks film *Captain Phillips*.

Things had settled down a little since the worst days of the warlords. Atallah didn't want to see Somalia blow up again or become even more inviting to jihadists. Also, helping the Somalis had become a personal mission for Atallah, a native of Lebanon who had fled to the United States with his family during his country's long civil war. "Because Somalia was lawless for twenty-two years, I wanted to understand how people survive in an environment like that," he said. "It reminded me of my childhood. I grew up in Lebanon during the civil war and saw a lot of bad things. Somalia was similar."

When Atallah read the UN Security Council report, he sat bolt upright. It said that a mysterious company named Southern Ace had built a base in Galmudug, formed a militia of local men, and brought in tons of weapons. It said that the nominal head of Southern Ace was one Edgar Van Tonder, who had established the company in Hong Kong in 2007 for the "import and export of logging trucks and trailers and their spare parts," but that "Paul Calder LeRoux also known as Bernard John Bowlins is a 'silent partner' in the company, and believed by law enforcement officials concerned by the company's operations to be the actual owner." (The reference to "law enforcement officials" was attributed to "a military source," but the report did not identify which police and military units were supposedly "concerned.")

For Atallah, the question was obvious: why did this LeRoux, or Bowlins, or whoever he was, want a base in Galmudug? Why would anyone try to get into a place that everybody else was trying to get out of? He figured that whatever Southern Ace was doing, it was up to no good. It sure as hell wasn't logging. Galmudug had no trees. It was all desert.

"Paul Calder LeRoux's name was always a mystery," he said, "so I couldn't let go."

It frustrated him that the CIA and DIA didn't seem to know much about LeRoux and didn't seem to be doing anything about him. Atallah couldn't find out much from the open sources, but he was sure about this: because LeRoux was moving arms, he contributed to the expansion of corruption and instability in the region. "He needed to be removed," Atallah said.

But removed how? Not incinerated by a drone. As Atallah well knew, U.S. military and NATO rules of engagement forbade summary executions of noncombatants, including bomb makers, weapons traffickers, and other common criminals. The military called individuals who were in the webs of corruption underlying wars "malign actors." Under the U.S. military Code of Conduct, they had to be remanded to the custody of civilian law enforcement officials and prosecuted in civilian courts in their countries or in the United States. Trying anyone in Somalia was not an option.

What about the DEA? Atallah had met Brown and Milione when they were investigating Viktor Bout. He was impressed by their adroit work in the cases of Bout and terror financier Monzer al-Kassar. Not only had the agents located the arms merchants, but they had also mounted complex undercover operations to gather enough evidence to indict, apprehend, and bring them to trial in an American court, where they were convicted and sentenced to long prison terms.

Maybe, Atallah thought, the 960 Group was the right bunch to take LeRoux down. "When they [DEA agents] go after someone, they don't hold back," Atallah said. "Other organizations like the [Central Intelligence] Agency have too many layers of bureaucracy to go through."

Brown introduced Atallah to Cindric and Stouch. They were between cases and looking for something involving drugs, arms, and terror. Atallah said he might have something for them. Why not take a crack at this strange dude LeRoux? He emailed the Security Council report to Cindric.

When Cindric got to page 267, he saw what Atallah was driving at and started underlining. It said that Southern Ace, backed by Paul LeRoux, was trying to use Somalia as a production and transshipment hub for drugs and arms. The company, financed by a Manila outfit called La Plata Trading, was trying to develop strains of "hallucinogenic plants, including opium, coca and cannabis" that would grow in Africa. No one had ever succeeded in growing coca suitable for cocaine production outside certain defined elevations and climatic conditions in the Andes. But if anyone could, he could cut out the Colombians and Mexicans and make a play for the cocaine market in Europe, the Middle East, Australia, and Japan, where cocaine commanded sky-high prices. He could disrupt a big segment of the transnational underground economy. Adding heroin and hashish to the mix would not be difficult, since they were made from the processed resin of opium poppies and cannabis, two crops that could adapt to more climates and terrain and could be grown in greenhouses.

The Security Council report said that in early 2011, as suddenly as they had appeared, the Southern Ace bases closed down and its militia disbanded.

Cindric emailed the Security Council report and the results of a quick Google search to Eric Stouch. He wanted Stouch to drop everything and jump on this find. He fished his cell phone out of his khakis and hit his partner's number.

"If half the stuff I've sent you is true, he's a real bad guy," he said happily. "He's a real fucking bad guy. Paul LeRoux is a target. He is a righteous target!"

"I'll read it," Stouch said peevishly. "Okay? I'll read it."

Cindric could almost hear Stouch's eyes rolling. Stouch's motto was "No wasted motion." He was never sure Cindric wasn't squandering time and energy on some interesting but distracting tangent. But in a few moments, he called Cindric back, and his tone had softened. "Okay, okay, you're right," he said. "If half of this is true, he's a target."

"He's in!" Cindric said to himself. "Score!"

Stouch was coldly analytical, stoic, hard to read, hard to rile, and impossible to impress. His friends called him Ironman because he was a fanatical triathlete. Once he locked on to a target, he didn't let go, a habit he picked up helping his dad, a farmer in Pennsylvania Dutch country. Nobody worked longer hours in worse weather for less money, and loved doing it, than a farmer.

Stouch played football for his small college, where he studied psychology. He thought about becoming a sports psychologist or a teacher until he took a criminology course. The curriculum included ridealongs. He spent a night in a Philadelphia graveyard, hanging out with cops hunting a parole violator amid gunfire, heroin deals, and hookers and johns having stand-up, shoulders-to-gravestone sex.

"It was madness and I loved it," he said. "I loved the action and wanted more of it and, of course, I thought I could be doing something admirable."

Stouch started out as a cop in Baltimore, the heroin capital of the States, with 360 or so homicides a year. He loved detective work—investigating murders, rolling around stairwells and corner stores with guys with guns, getting shot at, punched, spit on, and called names. He was fascinated with the process of solving a crime like a picture puzzle, by reconstructing the facts and trying to understand what drove someone to take another's life or sell himself or herself for fast cash.

He signed on with the DEA in 1999, was assigned to Baltimore, and, because of his experience on the streets, went to an inner-city drug task force in the Baltimore-Washington corridor. There he met a man he called "this lunatic agent Tom Cindric." The chemistry was instant.

Cindric was a talkative charmer, except when he lost his temper and got scary. Unlike his partner, who had little patience for information he didn't need to know, Cindric genuinely wanted to know everything—*everything*. He could quiz people for hours about how to shoe a horse or build a barn or make stuffed cabbage or whether kettle bells were better than free weights and who made the best barbecue. One minute, he was talking about how to field-dress a deer. The next, he was praising Martha Stewart's recipe for blueberry jam. ("No pectin!")

Cindric's father, Thomas Cindric Sr., had been a mathematician and master code-breaker with the National Security Agency. His early promise was spotted by none other than Branch Rickey, the same man who, as president and general manager of the Brooklyn Dodgers, had broken Major League Baseball's color line by fielding Jackie Robinson. Rickey had moved on to the Pittsburgh Pirates and in the 1950s met

Cindric Sr., then a penniless math prodigy at the University of Pittsburgh. (The family patriarch, Cindric Sr.'s dad, was a tough-as-nails
émigré from Croatia, living in rural Pennsylvania and scraping by with
whatever work he could get, including bootlegging.) Rickey gave Cindric Sr. a part-time job that helped him pay tuition. To finance the rest
of his undergraduate studies, the young mathematician joined the U.S.
Air Force ROTC program, became an air force officer, earned a graduate degree in advanced math at the American University in Washington, and in 1965 went to work for the National Security Agency, the
supersecret spy agency that intercepted the communications of foreign
governments and people of interest.

Senior NSA officials moved Cindric Sr. up fast. He culminated
his career as dean of the National Cryptologic School, which trained
intelligence officers in the art and science of cracking Soviet codes.
The responsibility of preventing Armageddon weighed heavily on him.
Throughout the Cold War, he labored into the night and over weekends, chain-smoking and pacing, consumed with intercepting the messages of the nation's enemies, especially the Soviets. He fretted over
how many secrets were being missed by all those fabulously expensive
electronic listening posts and eyes in the sky that captured Soviet signals intelligence and relayed them to NSA antennas inside Fort Meade
in rural Maryland.

Tom Cindric Sr. died of a heart attack in 1987, at the age of forty-
seven. He left a widow, Mary Cindric, an NSA administrative assistant,
and three children, the eldest of whom, Tom Jr., was a twenty-year-old
student at the University of Maryland.

Tom Cindric Jr. didn't inherit the math gene, but his father left him
some of the qualities that went with it—curiosity, skepticism, nervous
energy, and discontent. Whenever he was working a criminal investigation, Cindric could hear his dad's voice in his head, admonishing,
"Believing means nothing! Feeling means nothing! What are your

FACTS? To understand what the other side is doing, you have to have the FACTS. Don't believe everything you hear. Triangulate. Don't assume. Probe. Question yourself and everybody else. Facts are all that matter."

The paradox was that you never get all the facts. Like the old story about the blind men and the elephant, you could come up with a theoretical picture that made perfect sense but was dead wrong. The solution was to work harder and get more facts. Not more theories—more facts.

Cindric boiled all this down to a mantra: "There's what you believe, what you know, and what you can prove." Proving anything took a tremendous act of will and commitment of time. That was why he didn't sleep much.

In college, Cindric was all testosterone and anger, which the football coach at Maryland channeled into a fearsome outside linebacker for the Terps.

After he graduated, he thought about going to law school, but who he really wanted to be was *Miami Vice*'s Sonny Crockett, an undercover narcotics detective who'd been around and had the scars to show for it. He had spent his high school years watching *Miami Vice* and emulating Crockett's style. He even bought a white sport coat, though it wasn't Armani like Crockett's. And he couldn't find South Beach pink T-shirts like Crockett's, and he didn't have Don Johnson's cheekbones and hard-ass stubble.

But he could fight. He took a job as a bar bouncer. He got into more than a few brawls. When he straggled home with a split lip and bloody hand, his mother wept. "I didn't raise you like this," she said, grabbing peroxide and gauze. Then she told him to get a real job. A neighbor who was a cop helped him apply to the District of Columbia police force in 1990.

Despite the fights, he had a clean police record and, if there's anything the D.C. cops needed during the worst of the crack epidemic, it was a guy who could take care of himself in the bleak projects of Southeast Washington.

The local drug dealers nicknamed him Pac-Man, after the mean, reckless rookie played by Sean Penn in the 1988 police drama *Colors.*

His sergeant, Rick Clearwater, saw his potential as an investigator and took him in hand. "You need to learn how to talk to people," Clearwater said. "That's your next step." Clearwater took him to a convenience store, where he grabbed three bottles of grape Nehi and some packaged snacks.

"You never go wrong with grape," Clearwater said. "That's how you get them to talk."

"I gotta buy them myself?" Cindric gasped.

"Worth every penny," Clearwater said with a nod.

They drove to the district police station and settled down at an interview table with a scrawny young man who had just been arrested.

"Hey, we got you something," Clearwater said.

"I got nothing to say to you," the youth said to Clearwater, then turned to Cindric. "Fuck you, Pac-Man."

Cindric started to say, "Fuck you," but a look from Clearwater stopped him. The sergeant gave the young suspect his best fatherly smile, all the while watching him with keen eyes. Clearwater's hobby was making custom rifles, a craft that demanded careful attention to detail. He brought the same attentiveness to his appraisals of petty crooks. "You don't have to be like that," he said sweetly.

"Yeah, I do."

"Don't be like that; all we want to know is stash locations."

"I ain't telling you shit."

"You look a little thirsty. I got some grape Nehi here."

The kid looked doubtful but thirsty.

"Come on, man, ain't nobody gonna know. It's just for us to know."

"Gimme that Nehi."

The kid took a gulp.

"Deaf Jojo is slinging big dope."

The kid finished off the soda and ate a sugary snack and told them all about Jojo—the crack dealer—his stash locations and how he operated. When he was done, he asked, "What's gonna happen to me?"

"We'll no-paper you," Clearwater said. "You spend the night in jail tonight, we cut you lose tomorrow." This meant that Clearwater would not file formal charges against the kid. The record would look as if the arrest never happened.

Clearwater helped Cindric discover one of his finest talents—what cops called "the gift of bullshit." Before long, Cindric could bullshit his way into just about any place, and he could also spot a fellow bullshitter at a hundred yards.

He became Sonny Crockett, sort of. As a plainclothes detective and narc, he was soon playing roles that fit his rosy-cheeked, round-faced look. He pretended to be an ex-con who worked as a handyman at the Laurel racetrack, with a side hustle dealing meth and PCP. While undercover, he delivered more buy-bust operations than anybody else in his unit. DEA recruiters signed him up in 1996.

After a rookie stint in Newark, New Jersey, in 1999, he transferred to the DEA office in Washington, D.C., and was assigned to the inner-city drug task force, where he partnered up with the disciplined, unshakable Stouch. Pac-Man taught Ironman to forget about straight lines. Sometimes things go sideways and that's okay. Ironman taught Pac-Man intellectual rigor and finesse. As they went to other assignments, they stayed in touch.

In the summer of 2008, Milione recruited Stouch for the 960 Group's Africa team. Two days after he joined, the younger man found himself on a plane for Sierra Leone. He had no idea how to work in a foreign environment. "All I knew was the streets and how criminal minds function," he said. "It was enough." He looked for people who knew how the smuggling underground functioned and convinced them they had a better shot at staying alive if they worked with him.

The group ran a series of successful investigations in Guinea-Bissau, Sierra Leone, Ghana, and Liberia and disrupted a major Colombian pipeline that was spinning off cash to AQIM—Al-Qaeda in the Islamic Maghreb—one of the successor groups to Osama bin Laden's organization. AQIM was based in Sub-Saharan Africa.

In late 2011, the Africa team was rewarded for its triumphs with a bigger budget and more work. Milione was looking for another agent to join it. Stouch called Cindric. Milione interviewed him and liked what he saw—a street guy who could talk to crooks in a language they understood, who could flip them and send them back inside the criminal network as confidential informants. Milione sized up Cindric as a passionate, extremely bright guy, a little rough around the edges—someone who could sometimes get distracted, abruptly changing lanes and taking an off-ramp. But Stouch would be there to pull him back, keep the investigation organized and moving forward, and play devil's advocate.

The important thing was, Milione could see that Cindric and Stouch would stay out there in the cold until they got whoever they were after. Like all good criminal investigators, they were obsessed. That was true of all of Milione's agents. "The work is the vice," he said. "Not prostitutes, not gambling, not drinking. It's the work."

Cindric and Stouch saw the 960 Group as their opportunity to achieve the goal every agent dreamed about—to discover a new untouchable.

The definition of "untouchable" was, as Stouch put it, someone who is "constantly and overtly under the nose of global law enforcement but can't be touched. They have established so much power through wealth, political corruption, and permeating fear that their circle is virtually impossible to penetrate. Either everyone knows about them but can't get to them, or they may be invisible."

The way to tell if you had a bona fide untouchable was this: when you brought him in, other agents and cops would ask who the hell the perp was, and then, when they heard the story, raise a mug of draft in envy.

The talented Mr. LeRoux was the best candidate for untouchable they'd run across, even better than Viktor Bout, because he was on the way down when the 960 Group fixed on him. LeRoux was on the way up.

Cindric and Stouch hit the Internet and searched out everything they could find about LeRoux and anyone associated with him and his businesses. They started with La Plata Trading, the Manila-based front company that had paid for the Somalia project. La Plata Trading, it turned out, was the owner of record of the *Captain Ufuk,* the scow seized for gun-running on Bataan Island in August 2009.

Three people connected to the *Ufuk* had been killed, execution-style, after the seizure: Bruce Jones, the captain of the *Ufuk;* Noemi Edillor, purchasing manager for La Plata Trading; and Michael Lontoc, a well-known competitive sharpshooter and manager of Red, White and Blue Arms, the consignee of the arms seized from the *Ufuk*.

None of the stories in the press in the Philippines and East Asia mentioned LeRoux by name, but an associational analysis by the agents and their intelligence analyst, Carol Dillon, connected the dots and showed he was behind both Red, White and Blue Arms and La Plata. His subordinates were turning up dead. What was that about?

The agents contacted the DEA's Manila office. Agents there had heard of Paul LeRoux for several reasons. First, DEA Manila had received cables from the Minneapolis DEA office, asking about LeRoux and RX Limited. Second, the DEA agents in Manila had made inquiries about LeRoux to the Australian Federal Police officers posted to the Australian embassy in Manila. Because LeRoux was an Australian citizen by marriage and carried an Australian passport, that nation had a legal interest in him.

Third, and most intriguing, the Australian police had recently received some emails written by an anonymous tipster who wanted to blow the whistle on LeRoux. The email author signed himself or herself Persian Cat. He or she claimed to work for LeRoux in Manila and to be directly involved in handling LeRoux's financial affairs, including the financing of the *Captain Ufuk* and its cargo of arms. The person also claimed to have information about Southern Ace and the mysterious drugs and arms operation in Somalia that was the subject of the U.N. Security Council investigative report.

The Australian cops shared the emails with the Manila-based DEA agents, who forwarded summaries to Cindric and Stouch with a note cautioning that the content "remains unidentified and uncorroborated at this time. However, much of the information is plausible and consistent with other verified information."

Persian Cat said LeRoux had paid millions of pesos to police and officials in the Philippine Department of Justice to cover up his involvement in the *Ufuk* gun-running affair. Persian Cat claimed that LeRoux had personally ordered the murders of Jones, Edillor, and Lontoc. "The source believes they themselves will be a next target for assassination . . . ," the summary said. "The source notes that other people in the organization would like to turn on LeRoux but will not, as a result of the LeRoux apparent power." The whistle-blower clearly hoped to trigger an investigation that would lead to LeRoux's prosecution and imprisonment.

Persian Cat included a long list of bank account numbers, front companies, and properties in the Philippines, Hong Kong, Thailand, Djibouti, Singapore, Congo, Israel, Zimbabwe, and Somalia. There was a list of Filipino officials allegedly bribed by LeRoux.

Persian Cat's most sensational claim was that LeRoux was dealing with Iran in violation of international sanctions. Persian Cat also said that LeRoux had sent an emissary to Beijing to arrange arms purchases from NORINCO, the Chinese government's military weapons manufacturer.

The anonymous Persian Cat emails did not rise to the level of evidence that could be used in a courtroom. Prosecutors required live witnesses and plenty of corroborating documents. But they were a gold mine of leads. The emails, taken with the other material the agents were finding, encouraged them to believe that LeRoux was worth a hard look, and they contained some specifics they could check out.

Cindric went online again and pulled up a report by a Washington watchdog group, the Sunlight Foundation, summarizing a lobbying report filed by a Canadian consulting firm led by Ari Ben-Menashe, a notorious Israeli power broker whose name had cropped up during the Iran-Contra scandal of the Reagan administration.

The Sunlight Foundation reported that between 2007 and 2009, Paul Calder LeRoux had paid $12 million to Ben-Menashe to use his influence with Zimbabwe president Robert Mugabe to help LeRoux acquire a large tract of land seized from white farmers in Zimbabwe. (The agents later learned that the Israeli didn't deliver, so LeRoux, Smith, and Hunter discussed kidnapping Ben-Menashe from his residence in Canada and waterboarding him until he returned the money. The scheme proved logistically challenging and was dropped.)

Cindric and Stouch could see only the bare bones of the LeRoux/Ben-Menashe/Mugabe affair, but it reconfirmed that LeRoux was worth pursuing. Not many business people were willing to take a $12 million loss on anything, especially farmland in Zimbabwe. The purchase was a substantial capital investment for a lone-wolf entrepreneur. Add to that loss LeRoux's apparent loss of $3 million from the Southern Ace venture in Somalia, and LeRoux looked like a high roller who was taking crazy chances.

He was nothing like the familiar dope kings—the Escobars and El Chapos of the world. The Latin traffickers were hillbillies and party animals, but when it came to finances, they were conservative. They knew where every peso went, and they punished anybody who lost a single load or a few dollars. They wanted time-tested, trend-proof sure things. Take away the prostitutes and bling and they were predictable and boring.

LeRoux had to be a gambler—another name for an entrepreneur, really—and if that were the case, he must still be in business. Gamblers never quit.

The question was, what was he doing now and where was he doing it? Whatever he was doing, it wasn't likely to be boring.

Cindric went into his mantra. *What you believe, what you know, what you can prove.*

He believed that LeRoux was "a really good bad guy." The task was to move the needle to *know*, then *prove*.

"We need a source," Cindric said.

"Yep," Stouch replied.

Cindric called Atallah back.

"Hey, Rudy, we need a fucking source," Cindric said politely.

Atallah gave Cindric the name and contact information of a man who knew something about the African mercenary world—Joe Van der Walt, a former South African military intelligence officer who was director of Focus Africa, a Pretoria-based company that offered security services and risk management to corporations, mainly oil and mining companies in Africa and the Middle East. On the side, he had taken up the cause of stopping wildlife poaching. The same routes were used by smugglers of drugs and also guns, human body parts, drugs, gold, blood diamonds, and timber.

Cindric called Van der Walt. Yes, he had heard a few things about LeRoux. He would try to help. But, he warned, LeRoux was not to be trifled with. He had friends in high places in Pretoria.

"This guy's got a long reach," the South African said. "We'd better meet in Botswana."

Brown, Cindric, and Stouch flew to South Africa, picked up Warren Franklin, an agent in the DEA Pretoria office, and on January 19, 2012, drove over the border to Gaborone, the capital of Botswana. Not long after they checked into their hotel, Cindric's phone rang.

"Hey, Tommy, come on out front!" the caller boomed. "I'm the big ugly guy with the beard."

Van der Walt wasn't ugly, but he was enormous, with a barrel chest, ruddy face, and shock of red hair and beard. He and his partner, Nigel Morgan, a veteran of Britain's elite Irish Guards and, more recently, a specialist on corporate investment in Africa, led the agents to the hotel bar, where they talked into the night.

Van der Walt and Morgan had done some investigating. Based on notes and documents turned up by database searches and public sources, they believed that LeRoux was building a multinational criminal empire—a big one, but they didn't have proof, only some bits and pieces that needed connective tissue.

"He's a ghost, no real Internet footprint," Van der Walt said.

LeRoux was rumored to run a smuggling network across southern Africa. He had been spotted traveling in and out of South Africa, Namibia, Zimbabwe, Botswana, and Somalia, trading in a variety of drugs, arms, gold and diamonds and god-knows-whatever. They suspected him of laundering cash through the gold and diamond markets. He seemed to be behind at least a half-dozen paramilitary "security" companies that hired white mercenaries and sold protective services to prominent African figures, some legitimate, some in organized crime. Nobody bothered him, so they heard, because he had bought protection from high-level figures in the South African government and probably also Zimbabwe.

Physically, the South Africans said, they'd heard that LeRoux was a hulking great beast, a man mountain. Van Der Walt and his mates were, like many Afrikaners of Dutch and English descent, big guys, and very intimidating. If they thought LeRoux was more enormous and scarier, well, that was saying something.

When Cindric got back and told the story to Clearwater, his old sergeant said, nodding, "Fat Cobra." Fat Cobra was a villainous character in a Michael Douglas/Albert Brooks comedy they had taken in a few years back. LeRoux, whatever else he might be, was definitely fat, elusive, and venomous. The nickname fit, but Cindric and Stouch felt a little silly saying it out loud, so they modified it to a more prosaic shorthand—The Fat Man. As in, "hey, do you have a license plate for The Fat Man?" By any name, he was just what they were looking for—a fantastic creature nobody had corralled. He was out there somewhere, daring them to find him. Cindric and Stouch could manage cold, hunger, fatigue, and being scared shitless, but neither one of them could pass up a dare.

CHAPTER EIGHT

"WE'RE WAY BEYOND BIRTHDAYS"

LANDING AT DULLES AFTER THEIR TRIP TO SOUTHERN AFRICA, BROWN, CIN-
dric, and Stouch headed straight for Milione's office to brief him on
what they had learned. Halfway through their report, he interjected,
"That's kinda funny. You won't fucking believe this but . . ."

Not an hour earlier, Mark Nemier and Anthony Benedetto from
the SOD's Internet Crimes Section had been in Milione's office, seeking help for an investigation launched by DEA agents in the Minneapolis office against a shady Internet pharmacy called RX Limited.
Nemier and Benedetto thought that RX Limited might be the biggest
illegal online pill-peddling operation the DEA had ever encountered.
The Minneapolis agents had done a lot of digging and learned that
the figure behind it was a man named Paul LeRoux. They had come
to Milione seeking help to determine who this LeRoux guy was and
whether he could be charged with violating U.S. criminal laws. The
problem was that the pharmaceuticals sold by RX Limited were mostly
sleeping pills and tranquilizers. Sales without valid prescriptions were
illegal under the federal Food, Drug and Cosmetic Act, enforced by
the Food and Drug Administration. The FDA was almost toothless.
Unless the drugs involved were dangerous chemicals such as opioids
and were on the Controlled Substances Act list, they weren't even in
the DEA's jurisdiction.

Cindric and Stouch knew nothing about the case in Minneapolis. Brown knew a little, but he hadn't paid much attention to it. In
the SOD, there were hunters and gatherers. The 960 Group agents

were hunters, after big game. An Internet pill merchant didn't make their cut. But now, Milione put two and two together and realized that the suspected arms merchant and mercenary king who had piqued his agents' interest might be the same person the Minneapolis agents had identified as the owner of RX Limited.

Meanwhile, SOD boss Derek Maltz had gotten wind of the Minneapolis pill case because of the extraordinary amount of money involved. The agents in Minneapolis calculated that between June 2007 and August 2011, RX Limited and its subsidiaries had shipped nearly three million drug orders. The company had one of the biggest accounts on FedEx's books, the shipping bills running half a million dollars a month. Bank records from Hong Kong showed that RX Limited had deposited and withdrawn $276 million through a single bank in Hong Kong. The total in sales was probably much more.

But making money wasn't a crime. Neither the Minneapolis agents nor the SOD Internet Crimes unit had come up with solid evidence that RX Limited and its proprietor were engaged in a criminal enterprise worthy of a trial on the American taxpayers' dime.

Maltz thought evidence might turn up if the SOD agents worked it harder. When Maltz roared, people scrambled. In his fifties, the SOD chief had eyes like flares, a downtown New Yorker's seismic profanity, and a flamethrower rasp. He sprayed paragraphs, pounded his desk for emphasis, and bellowed, "Or am I fuckin' crazy?" No one said yes, though some wanted to. Every week Maltz made it a point to stick his head into the cubicle occupied by Nemier and Benedetto and bellow, "Hey, big boys, when are we going to step in and fucking DO IT? Hey, what are we doing? WHAT ARE WE DOING?" After yet another lacerating session with Maltz, Nemier and Benedetto showed up in Milione's office looking for help. By pure coincidence, they appeared on the same day Brown, Cindric, and Stouch returned from southern Africa.

Milione put his foot down. The 960 Group did not do pill cases, period. If the LeRoux in the Minneapolis case was the same LeRoux in Africa, they would certainly find out. But the 960 Group would not take over the Minneapolis case itself. Pill cases were complex, frustrating, and almost always a waste of time. An investigator could spend years in a paper chase accumulating documents, unraveling interlocking corporations and business fronts, and making charts, graphs, and Excel spreadsheets. Even then, prosecutors would rarely seek indictments for peddling pharmaceuticals because of the slim odds of winning convictions. "We will focus on him strictly as a target for selling drugs and arms," Milione said. By drugs, he meant hard drugs—heroin, cocaine, and meth.

Cindric and Stouch dug in. Quickly, they realized that the RX Limited pharmaceutical-slinging enterprise was the creation of the same man they were targeting. The discovery heightened the mystery of Paul LeRoux and was the first hint about the innovative way in which he was operating. What was groundbreaking was that there were only tangential links between the infrastructure of RX Limited and his other operations. They were completely stove-piped, except for LeRoux at the top. RX Limited was white-collar crime at worst. The activities Cindric and Stouch heard about in southern Africa were serious, top-tier transnational organized crime and violent crime. Usually, the criminals involved were two different species.

That's when intel analyst Carol Dillon discovered, by searching geek and hacker sites, yet another jarring fact about LeRoux. He was the cybersecurity specialist who had written the pioneering privacy program Encryption for the Masses—E4M.

"A fucking cryptographer!" Cindric beamed. "He's smart! Like my old man!"

"What the hell are you talking about?" Brown said.

"Fuck! My old man was a cryptographer. He was the smartest man I ever met. We're way beyond birthdays now!"

Brown and Stouch were confused. Birthdays?

The "birthdays" line was one of Cindric's mantras. He murmured it when nobody was listening. It came from one of his favorite films, *Clear and Present Danger*. It was spoken by a CIA computer geek who was helping hero Jack Ryan, played by Harrison Ford, hack into a corrupt official's computer. The point was, ordinary people made passwords out of their birthdays. The geek discovered that Ryan's nemesis was a brilliant villain who had devised passwords so complex they could be cracked only with a powerful computer that threw millions of combinations at the problem.

To Cindric, the birthdays line meant a puzzle that was extremely, delightfully challenging. When he found out that LeRoux was, among his many parts, a cryptographer, he thought about what someone had told him about his father: "Your dad used all quadrants of his brain. That doesn't happen very often." Cindric spent most of his life trying to be half as good at his job as his father had been. "I was chasing a ghost," he said.

Could LeRoux be another one of those rare human beings who could unleash his brain's larger capacities? But entirely on the dark side? Cindric dearly hoped this was true. An investigator was only as interesting as the people he investigated. An untouchable cybervillain with an unorthodox approach would be a fabulous creature, even rarer than Viktor Bout, who was highly intelligent and a big shot but very much in the predictable twentieth-century mold.

Milione picked up on the spark crackling around the room. Cindric could see it in his eyes, which were alive with interest.

"We need to infiltrate him with a person," Milione said. "Nobody has tried to infiltrate him in a clean, clear way."

Brown, Cindric, and Stouch murmured in agreement. Intelligence agencies used the term "assessment," which was often based on speculation, assumption, and RUMINT, the latter meaning third-hand accounts and rumor. At worst, an assessment was a WAG—wild-ass guess. Law enforcement officials didn't talk about assessments. The rules of criminal evidence didn't allow for speculation, assumption, and gossip. The rules demanded hard, direct proof. Agents and cops took the rules very seriously because they knew that if they didn't follow every one of them down to the last colon, comma, and footnote, they would lose their cases, get branded as losers, and, worst of all, get transferred to desk jobs where careers went to die.

In the courtroom, seeing was believing. The agents had to get to someone inside LeRoux's world. And, because the infiltrator's credibility would be attacked by defense lawyers, the agents had to make sure LeRoux's incriminating words and deeds were captured on video and audio.

The problem was, unlike cartel leaders they had investigated before, LeRoux seemed to be a solo act. Was he close to *anybody*? Cindric and Stouch sifted through the possible insiders who might be flipped—an ex-wife? A girlfriend? Persian Cat, whoever and wherever he or she was?

On the other side of the world, Warren Franklin, the DEA's man in South Africa, got one of those leads that agents dream about. After accompanying Brown, Cindric, and Stouch to Botswana, Franklin returned to the U.S. embassy in Pretoria and ran a routine name check on LeRoux. He asked the CIA station to run LeRoux's name, too. DEA agents routinely complained that dealing with the CIA was a one-way street, but in this case, a CIA officer generously shared the results. The name LeRoux got a hit in the agency's database. In October 2010, someone had sent a tip to the CIA's online threat-reporting link, offering to blow the whistle on Paul LeRoux. No one from the CIA had followed up. However, the CIA database retained the tipster's name and phone number. Franklin sent the details to Cindric and Stouch.

The agents grinned at each other. They had a name and phone number! Awesome! What were the odds?!

However, before they started high-fiving each other, they had to admit that this was probably a dry hole. The information was sixteen months old. It came from somebody who was on the run. If that person was smart, he or she would have changed his number and gotten a burner phone, or a handful of them. Even if the phone worked, how would a frightened person react to a cold call?

Usually, the agents found a middleman to make a friendly introduction and vouch for their sincerity and discretion. In this situation, they had nothing.

"How do we do this?" Stouch asked.

Should they try to circle around the tipster and learn more?

Should they make that epic flight to South Africa, again? He might not even be in Africa anymore.

Cindric thought a moment.

"Fuck it," he said, and started dialing.

A man with a deep voice and an accent answered.

"Hello, this is Tom Cindric with the U.S. government. Did you provide some information to the U.S. government a year or so ago?"

The man said that he did.

"We'd like to talk to you about Mr. LeRoux," Cindric said in his most polished voice. He explained that LeRoux sounded like a security threat. If the gentleman on the other end of the line would help make a criminal case against LeRoux, the DEA would protect his identity. He wouldn't have to worry about LeRoux coming after him because LeRoux would be out of business and locked up tight.

The man must have liked what he heard. He gave them his real name because he had put it on the CIA form. He said they could call him Jack, the *nom de guerre* LeRoux had given him. He agreed to meet the agents at Dubai International and fly with them to Larnaca, Cyprus, for a long talk. They chose Larnaca because it was a relatively quiet place, off the beaten track of the arms merchants. Jack didn't think LeRoux had business or personal interests there.

Cindric and Stouch headed for Dulles International to catch the next flight to Dubai. They kept their bags packed, because they spent more time in airports and in the air than at the office. That was a good thing, as far as they were concerned.

In Dubai, the agents walked to the gate for the flight to Larnaca. They had told Jack to meet them there. They spotted him immediately—six feet three inches tall, dark-haired, in his thirties. He looked as if he spent a lot of time in the gym. He had a chiseled face, broad shoulders, and narrow waist. He was quaking—shifting from foot to foot and glancing around as if he were on the lam. Because he was.

"He's sweating like a whore in church," Cindric muttered to Stouch.

Stouch squinted, which his partner took to mean agreement.

They greeted him and chatted for a few minutes. He was stammering out of fear and worrying about a guy named Hunter. They couldn't talk there. There were too many eyes and ears lurking about. Dubai International was the gateway to Baghdad, Kabul, Tehran, Sana'a, Benghazi, and just about any other hot zone. You couldn't spill a cup of coffee without splashing a soldier, journalist, lawyer, bagman, arms dealer, war profiteer, or spy of some sort. It was a hunting ground for intelligence services of many nations. The agents had to assume it was wired top to bottom.

Besides, Dubai International was a major international hub of the mercenary Facebook. Grab any stool in McGettigan's Irish Pub, the nearest thing the airport had to a dive bar, and you'd find yourself shoulder to shoulder with a bunch of mercs, also known as PMCs—private military contractors. Jack laughed at their attempts to blend in. He could spot them from the far end of Concourse C. They all wore the same non-uniform uniform, consisting of athletic-casual brands that gave discounts to U.S. military and government employees and contractors; Oakley sunglasses, Under Armour T-shirts, Casio watches, Timberland boots, desert-colored canvas pants, and brown or black North Face jackets. The most gung-ho sported tattoos with skulls, serpents, and inspirational sayings. All of LeRoux's American and European security men had probably stopped at the Irish pub at one time or another, because it was the only place to get a Guinness and a burger, watch football, and check their email in peace.

The three men boarded the flight to Larnaca. The agents rented a couple of rooms in the Hilton so they could debrief Jack and let him get comfortable with them, away from LeRoux's world.

"He's a genius," Jack began. His next words spilled out in a rush.

"Look, he doesn't do anything like anybody else. Nobody has ever figured him out. Nobody has any idea what is in his mind. He's had many partners, but he controls everything himself. Nobody else could make any decision without him. He's a narcissist. He's a sociopath. He's a nice guy one day. The next day he can wipe out your whole family with one call."

Over two days, several cases of water and many carafes of coffee, Jack told the agents his story and as much as he knew of LeRoux's story. He told them about the fishing business that turned into an arms business and the meth business. He described LeRoux's strange manners—friendly at first, then menacing.

"His craziness only grew with the more money he got," Jack said. "The more he got away with it, the more people that died, that made him feel that he was untouchable."

Untouchable! Jack didn't know how much the agents loved that word. Cindric and Stouch glanced at each other. They didn't want to look overjoyed. They needed things to stay cool, no sudden moves, sort of like inching up to a bird that had flown through the window and needed rescuing before his head slammed into a plate-glass window. They were the only way out for Jack, but he might not know that yet. The squints and twinkles that passed between them signaled that they were close to ecstatic. They knew they were incredibly lucky to have found a phone number that led to a guy who knew their target well and who might be willing to talk about him. That sort of thing just didn't happen in their world.

Jack knew he was taking a monumental risk. He was looking at two

Americans who wanted something from him that could cost his life or blow up the one he'd patched together with Anya. But maybe they could give him and Anya a new life.

Yes, he was scared, but he wasn't a coward. He proved that in Somalia. He proudly showed the agents a video of the battle with al-Shabaab, which he had made with his cell phone. He watched with satisfaction as their faces reacted to the explosions and screams emanating from the tiny speaker.

Dealing with LeRoux was a different kind of stress. He felt like one of those rats trapped in a maze. He had set off this chain of events when he gave his phone number to the CIA. Having grown up watching thrillers, he'd expected somebody from the CIA to get back to him and do something. He didn't know how to deal with silence. And suddenly, here were guys from another American agency that he'd never heard of. He didn't know anything about the DEA, but he was inclined to like these guys because they looked like what they were, cops. Clean-shaven, short hair, open faces, dressed like blue-collar workers. They weren't mysterious. They seemed sincerely interested in him.

He thought about Anya. He couldn't ask her to share his life so long as LeRoux and Hunter were roaming the world, looking for him. LeRoux held a grudge forever. Hunter was desperate to please LeRoux. They'd persevere. These two ordinary-looking Americans were his best shot at a somewhat normal future. If he could see that LeRoux and Hunter were locked up or dead, he and Anya could go where they pleased, without buying fake passports and sweeping their hotel rooms for hidden electronics for the rest of their lives.

Stouch watched Jack hesitate. What sensible person wouldn't? But Stouch had done this before, and he knew how to tilt the game. He leaned toward Jack, smiled his warmest freckled-farm-boy smile, and asked gently, "Wouldn't you feel better if he weren't in the picture? If he got locked up for good?"

Jack nodded vigorously.

"Too many people have died for little or no reason," he said. "It has to stop."

"We can do that," Cindric said, giving him his honest-cop baby blues. "But we're going to need your help."

"Okay, these guys mean business," Jack said to himself.

He stuck out his hand. Yes, they had a deal.

The deal, as they explained it, was for Jack to go back inside LeRoux's organization, this time as an undercover source. He had to work his way back into LeRoux's confidence, record their conversations, share all their communications with the agents, and let the agents write his emails and texts to LeRoux.

Jack was sure he could manage that. He thought that LeRoux had forgiven him when they last talked. He didn't expect LeRoux to be surprised and suspicious when he offered to come back. LeRoux's flaw was that he allowed his reality distortion field to work on his own head. He convinced himself that he was the Boss and no one who had ever met him would dare double-cross him.

The agents flew Jack to New York. On February 22, 2012, they escorted him into the U.S. attorney's office in Manhattan and filled out the paperwork that put him on the DEA payroll as a confidential informant.

They walked him across the street to City Hall Park, sat on a bench looking at the Brooklyn Bridge, and had Jack call LeRoux on a recorded line.

"Boss, it's not working out here in Dubai," Jack said. "If you have a job for me, I'm ready to start."

"Sounds good," LeRoux said.

He rang off.

They waited on the park bench. In less than ten minutes, LeRoux called back with an offer.

"Okay, I want you to go to Africa," he said.

LeRoux wanted Jack to bribe officials of various small African governments to give him bogus end-user certificates for small arms that LeRoux wanted to buy from Eastern Europe and China. Despite Jack's departure, he clung to his vision of building an Amazon-for-small-arms, and he was still searching for reliable suppliers. He had found that arms factory managers all wanted to see end-user certificates from official bodies. This was a CYA exercise. Nobody checked to see whether the certificates were genuine. So long as the paperwork had official stamps and seals, they were good to go.

The job would pay Jack three thousand dollars a month, a paltry sum. LeRoux promised to supplement Jack's base pay with expense money and bonuses for completed assignments.

"Take it," Stouch told Jack.

"Cheap Charley again," Jack thought. The agents would pay him an informant's fee, plus all expenses, and in the end, the prospect of freedom from fear of LeRoux. Priceless!

Cindric, Stouch, and Jack cooled their heels for seven full days. They whiled away the time setting up Jack's phone and laptop so they could control them and preserve all communications to and from Le-Roux.

On February 29, 2012, LeRoux sent an email to Jack with detailed instructions on how to get African bureaucrats for end-user certificates to provide cover stories for his purchases of small arms. He explained:

> For example let us say that you go to Eritrea (smaller countries work better for this, avoid big countries like ethiopia or heavily monitored countries that are involved in wars) then u get a contact in the police or security ministry, you find out what offices issues end user certificates, then u bribe them to produce a document that states that the police of Eritrea want to buy 100 x AK47 from Pakistan (we will supply the information on the products and the suppliers details) then they print it on their letter head and stamp it and sign it we pay as follows 25 000usd to the contact when he produces the document 25 000 usd when the document is accepted in pakistan as legit.

LeRoux emailed Jack a list of rules. Jack had heard them many times before, but LeRoux was pompous and liked to lecture. The rules: Never give anybody his real name. Never meet in his own hotel. Always use at least two phones, one to reach contacts, the second to call LeRoux. Always use the laptop that LeRoux had set up with encryption software. Never give anybody money up front. Concentrate on low-level bureaucrats—those with just enough power to sign end-user certificates.

"Do not fly in and expect to meet the president," LeRoux wrote. "It does not work. They are too high and will want too much money."

Jack promised to obey. He took off for Africa to start his new job, working for LeRoux and lying to LeRoux. The second part was harder. Jack wasn't a great liar, but he was learning.

Cindric and Stouch went back to Washington to talk endgame with Brown and Milione. They had to get LeRoux to go someplace where government officials would expel him when presented with a warrant from the United States government.

That ruled out the Philippines, where LeRoux had based his pharmaceutical operations since 2004, and Brazil, where he was in the process of relocating. LeRoux had recently taken up residence in a condo in Barra da Tijuca, an upscale beachfront neighborhood south of Rio. Now that his Plan B to build a new city in Somalia had fallen apart and he still hadn't connected with Mugabe in Zimbabwe, Rio was his Plan C—his sanctuary city if things got hot in the Philippines. Brazil's diplomatic relations with the United States were severely strained. Brazilian courts were unlikely to honor American extradition or expulsion requests, even for foreign nationals like LeRoux. Jim Sparks, an enterprising agent in the DEA São Paolo office, which covered Rio, had persuaded the Brazilian counternarcotics police to tap LeRoux's phone with a warrant based on the Minneapolis RX Limited case. The Brazilian cops were happy to pitch in. DEA agents like Sparks had been cultivating them for decades. Like other cops all over the world, the Brazilian cops and the DEA agents hated two things: dopers and politicians. The transcript of a wiretapped call showed LeRoux boasting that he had gotten a Brazilian mistress pregnant. Once she gave birth, he would qualify for Brazilian residency, and extradition would be off the table.

Where could the DEA agents lure LeRoux and be sure that he would be arrested? Western Europe was out of the question. London, Paris, Berlin, and Vienna were clean, scenic, and orderly, but their well-developed legal machinery could chew on extradition proceedings for years. Also, DEA agents could attract unwelcome attention from local politicians, American diplomats, and, not least, CIA officers who competed bitterly with the agents for sources and glory.

In places with legal systems in survival mode, DEA agents could make things happen. Local officials didn't have the luxury of time. If a criminal from some other country showed up, they just wanted him gone. Bad guys were willing to go to such places and wouldn't see the law coming.

Cindric and Stouch had Jack propose a meeting in Accra, Ghana. The DEA had an office in Accra and an agent, Joe Kellums, who had made good connections with the cops.

LeRoux said no.

How about Guinea? They could meet in Conakry, the broken-down capital city. They thought it sounded like the kind of dark, sexy place LeRoux would like. He would have no idea that Milione and Brown had developed a solid relationship with some of the cops there.

LeRoux wasn't interested.

What about Liberia?

LeRoux liked it. Loved it. It had just the right mix of political anarchy, modern communications, and good air and sea connections. He could use the Liberian ship registry, which was cheap and easy, to flag his growing fleet of yachts and the cargo ships he intended to buy for his arms business.

For the agents, this was excellent news. Milione was sure that Fombah Sirleaf, head of the Liberian National Security Agency, and stepson of President Ellen Johnson Sirleaf, would execute a clean arrest—no wavering, no screwups, no torture. LeRoux could not know that Milione and Brown counted Sirleaf as a personal friend, dating from 2010. At that time, Sirleaf's agents had picked up intelligence that Colombian cocaine trafficking rings were in Monrovia, trolling for powerful people they could bribe to let them use Liberia as a transshipment point between Colombia, Europe, and New York. "For a fledgling democracy, that kind of criminality would have tremendous impact on our national security," Sirleaf said. "We truly had to send a strong message that we weren't going to tolerate it."

Without resources to investigate and prosecute the traffickers on his own, Sirleaf contacted DEA agent Sam Gaye, who was posted in Lagos and covering West Africa. Gaye showed up with Milione and Brown. They had Sirleaf fitted with a DEA wire. Sirleaf invited the Colombians and their African middlemen to his home and, with the tape rolling, agreed to join their payroll. The traffickers laid out their plans to land six tons of cocaine, worth about $150 million on the street, in Monrovia, break it up, and ship it in smaller lots to New York and Europe.

Sirleaf and his men arrested a Colombian, two Ghanaians, three Sierra Leoneans, and their Russian pilot. President Johnson Sirleaf ordered them expelled to the custody of Milione and the 960 Group. "The Republic of Liberia is officially closed for business to the narcotics trade," she said. Milione and Brown flew them to New York, where they were prosecuted and convicted in federal court in Manhattan.

"In a place where bribes to government officials used to be as routine as the crow of the rooster every morning," *New York Times* correspondent Helene Cooper wrote, "the actions of Fombah Sirleaf still have Liberians shaking their heads in wonder."

Ever since, whenever Milione and Brown went to Africa chasing Colombians, they made it a point to stop by Monrovia. On some limpid nights, they could be found at Fombah Sirleaf's home, listening to his favorites, Mozart and Everclear, and sharing tidbits about all the intriguing new faces showing up in West Africa.

CHAPTER NINE

DAZZLE HIM

A STING IS A SEDUCTION. WHETHER IT'S AN ARMS DEAL OR A FLIRTATION, the tradecraft is pretty much the same. Be desirable, but play it coy. Let the target do the pushing. The more he wants it, the more he feels like a winner when he thinks he's getting it.

You know you're doing it right when he starts acting as if it's his idea.

The agents had to get LeRoux to think the Monrovia meeting was his brainstorm. He had to show up in the Liberian capital in person. That was going to be tricky, because LeRoux much preferred to use proxies for all major transactions. Jack told them how he had mocked Viktor Bout for doing a deal himself in Bangkok, face-to-face with people who turned out to be DEA informants.

What exactly would this weird, security-obsessed mogul find so irresistible that he would break his own rules and travel to Monrovia himself? How would the agents manipulate him into thinking he thought of it?

Milione didn't believe the answer was too complicated.

"He's a criminal," he said. "He wants to make money. It's power, it's access. He's looking for another country he can corrupt and be safe in and make money in. It's a money stream for him and a base of operations."

"I don't think so," Cindric said.

"Nope," Stouch said. "This guy isn't your average crook."

Sure, the agents said, he liked money, but he didn't love it best.

From all that Jack and others said, what he truly loved were his ventures. He loved finding angles that no one else had thought of.

And there was that volcanic rage boiling in him. What was novel, fascinating, and outrageous? What would make him infamous?

"Blood diamonds?" Cindric asked. The idea might play into the image he liked to cultivate as a cruel swashbuckler.

Stouch had a source who, he thought, could help. While investigating Colombians in Sierra Leone and Togo, he had befriended an Israeli gold and diamond merchant who had spent years in Sierra Leone and Panama, dealing in both commodities and laundering money in the Mideast and Europe. The Israeli sent Stouch some photos of uncut diamonds. Stouch had Jack show them to LeRoux.

No deal. LeRoux wasn't interested in blood diamonds. He had been there and done that—a few diamonds, a lot of gold. Now he was into arms, meth, and coke. He told Jack to focus on getting those end-user certificates for shipping arms.

"Holy shit, what are we going to do?" Cindric groaned.

"Meth?" Stouch said. "Chemicals?"

"Yeah, why not?" Brown shrugged. In the United States, trafficking large quantities of methamphetamine carried a mandatory minimum penalty of ten years and a maximum of life.

They pitched the scenario to LeRoux in a succession of emails they wrote for Jack to send LeRoux. The first message said that Jack's family had some rich friends who owned jewelry stores in major cities in northern Europe. Through them, Jack had met an Israeli businessman who brokered gold and diamonds and, as a sideline, laundered money in Liberia for some Colombian drug traffickers who were trying to set up a lab in a remote part of the country.

"These people want not to deal with the Mexicans anymore," the email said. "They think they can make money doing it themselves."

"He'll like that," Stouch said. "He knows the Mexicans will fuck them." LeRoux had dropped hints to Jack of a run-in with a Mexican smuggling family that controlled the Juárez/El Paso border crossing he wanted to use to have a proxy move a load of Tramadol pills into the United States. He grumbled to Jack that the Mexicans were low, dishonorable characters, in contrast to the Colombian traffickers, whom he revered as the gold standard in organized crime.

Through LeRoux's several attempts to get into the cocaine trade without a Colombian partner, his esteem for the Colombian traffickers of the *Miami Vice* age had risen to mythic proportions. To turn a profit in cocaine, he realized, a person had to master a range of skills and economic sectors, from agriculture to chemistry to shipping to banking. The Colombians had done it all, in the 1970s and '80s, before cell phones, GPS, Skype, and encrypted email. They had created a multibillion-dollar global industry out of a handful of seeds, a few go-fast boats, and Cessnas. They had balls like watermelons.

LeRoux must have figured out by this time, the agents theorized, that he couldn't beat them, so he'd better join them. Carving out his own cocaine pipeline was taking too long. Better to forge a strategic partnership with a Colombian cartel. In exchange for cocaine, he would offer the cartel the benefit of his connections in Africa and Asia, the biggest untapped markets for just about everything, legal and illegal. They would gain access to North Korean meth, plus his own brainpower. He was pretty sure the Colombians didn't have anyone like Paul Calder LeRoux.

"It'll appeal to him that the Colombians are trying to do their own entrepreneurial thing in Africa and ship it out from there" to the United States and Europe, Stouch said.

Cindric agreed, congratulating himself on finding such an ingenious partner. All that college psychology was coming in handy. To inflame LeRoux's desire for the deal, Cindric wrote a second email to go out under Jack's signature. It said that the fictional Colombians intended to ship partially refined cocaine to Liberia and finish transforming it to the fine white salt everyone recognized. Colombian cartel slang for the halfway-there stuff was *permanganato*. This was their term for coca paste, the raw extract from the coca plant, stabilized with potassium permanganate. The formal term, in Spanish, was *permanganato de potasio*.

Jack told LeRoux that the beauty of *permanganato* was that it was legal to ship. This wasn't strictly speaking true, but it was close. The stuff could be made to resemble ordinary toothpaste, and customs and border authorities didn't look for it. Cindric and Stouch were improvising off their perception that LeRoux was voraciously curious, driven to master all the minute tricks of the trade. If the Colombians had a gimmick to slip the surveillance net, he would want to adopt it for his own smuggling ventures.

More important, Stouch said, "He would think that it would give him access to Liberia and an opportunity to exploit and buy another third world country to grow his criminal network." If he thought some Colombians had bought the Liberian leadership, he would want to get in on that deal and piggyback on their control, using the relationship to make a profit for himself.

To underscore the fictional Colombians' special interest in Liberia, Cindric wrote another email for Jack to send LeRoux. This message said that in addition to refining cocaine in Liberia, the Colombians also wanted to produce an unnamed product. To do it, they were in the market to buy industrial quantities of pseudoephedrine, red phosphorus, iodine, and a few other items. They hadn't figured out where to buy these chemicals yet or how to get them to Liberia. They also wanted training for their "cooks," who were accustomed to making cocaine but were inexperienced in making other products.

When LeRoux got this email, he realized, from the list of chemicals, that the Colombians intended to manufacture meth. And he spotted an opening to cement a strategic partnership with a Colombian cartel. Cindric's message was devised to make LeRoux think that Jack had tapped into some Colombians who were novices at making meth.

It was designed to bait him into offering these fictional Colombians his superior expertise, plus all the ingredients for meth. The scenario would appeal to his vanity and his vision of an immensely lucrative underworld coalition, a superpower in which he would be at the helm, shoulder-to-shoulder with a regal Andean godfather.

To get there, he had to dazzle the Colombians. He had to assume that they were proud to the point of arrogance. They didn't know what they didn't know. He had to show them, with a *tour de force*, that he could bring important added value to the table, something no one else in the Asian underworld could do.

He told Jack to tell them that he had a far superior formula for meth. He listed the ingredients in *his* recipe and said he could deliver them to Monrovia.

"Best we give them a package which is chems + training," he wrote Jack.

The "package," he wrote, would include not only the chemicals themselves but also a "clean room," meaning a mobile laboratory where Colombian cooks—trained by LeRoux's people—would stir up sparkling batches of crystal meth. He attached a design.

The minute Cindric opened that email, he could see that LeRoux had taken the bait. They had captured his imagination. He was hot—*hot!*—to do the deal.

His response demonstrated a comprehensive knowledge of the fine points of meth manufacturing. Cindric showed it to DEA chemists, who concurred that the email proved that he was a meth maker of some sophistication and experience.

The dilemma remained—how could they be *absolutely* sure LeRoux would come to Monrovia?

It was Jack who nailed the landing. Spending time with two experienced criminal investigators like Cindric and Stouch had sharpened his gut and developed his intuition. Jack would never master all their tricks, but since he knew the stakes for an undercover operator were life

or death, he paid attention and caught on fast. He learned to interpret
LeRoux's body language, his grunts and stutters, to sense his uncer-
tainties and feel his obsessions.

Jack told the agents that the Boss was intensely focused on doing
the Colombian deal. The timing was critical for him because he was
in the middle of his move from Manila to Rio and was feeling a bit
vulnerable. His ambition to be bigger than Escobar and Bout hung in
the balance.

When he next spoke with LeRoux, Jack chose words he believed
would punch LeRoux's buttons.

"It would be disrespectful not to meet the guy," Jack told the Boss.
He said it quietly and without emphasis, but he made sure LeRoux
heard and digested the word "disrespectful." The lore about the Colombians, which LeRoux had absorbed, was that you never, ever *disrespect* a Colombian if you value your life. Imagine how *disrespected* the
Colombian representative would feel if, after going to all the trouble
to fly to Monrovia, LeRoux stood him up and sent a marginal instead!

LeRoux got it. He knew how peeved he felt when he had to talk
to marginals. Jack knew that he knew. His trick worked like a charm.
LeRoux promised he would definitely be in Monrovia.

Between LeRoux's email to Jack about the meth deal and Jack's
description of LeRoux's state of mind, Cindric was positive the sting
was going to work. He exhaled. He telephoned Stouch and Brown and
exulted, "We got 'em!"

One more hurdle had to be cleared. Jack had to meet with LeRoux
in person and discuss the Colombian deal on tape. U.S. attorney Preet
Bharara and his assistants in the Southern District of New York, who
prosecuted all 960 Group cases, wouldn't take the evidence to a grand
jury and seek an indictment until the agents could show that Jack and
LeRoux were conspiring face-to-face. They had to be able to prove that
LeRoux was personally acquainted with Jack and spent time with him.
On the stand, a good defense lawyer would raise questions about Jack's

veracity. Why should a jury believe that Jack really knew LeRoux? Jack could say anything. That didn't make it true. There were the emails, but they were digital documents, easily doctored. In the digital world, anybody could pretend to be anybody else. The agents had to convince a judge and jury that LeRoux was truly personally involved with Jack in major crimes. The agents had to have a massive pile of proof that LeRoux was, in the language of the court, guilty beyond a reasonable doubt.

Cindric and Stouch launched a subtle campaign to maneuver Le-Roux into summoning Jack to Rio for a personal meeting. They crafted an email designed to play to LeRoux's arrogant view that Jack was not an independent thinker, but a puppet, completely dependent on Le-Roux for orders. They had Jack inform LeRoux that he was flying to Panama to meet the Colombian cartel representatives. There, he hoped to cement the Monrovia meth/lab/cocaine deal. But he needed Le-Roux's guidance before the meeting so he'd be sure to say and do the right thing. Jack's email said:

> I think it would be better if I meet with you first, as there are a few things that we need to talk about and plan things out correctly, and I need your personal advice before I walk into a meeting with those guys.

On April 29, 2012, LeRoux responded by ordering Jack to meet at his apartment outside Rio on May 11.

Bingo! Cindric and Stouch were elated. LeRoux had totally fallen for it. They decided to push the edge. How far would he go? They had him on conspiring to deal in meth. Would he also conspire to sell arms?

Milione and Brown liked the idea. Small arms drifted around the planet the way factory pollution wound up in polar bears. Rival groups captured them and used or traded them. Many of the arms LeRoux had acquired for his Somali militia were probably already in the hands of African militant groups al-Shabaab, Boko Haram, and Al-Qaeda in the Islamic Maghreb. A few might have made their way to the big Middle Eastern terrorist groups—Al-Qaeda in the Arabian Peninsula, the Islamic State in Iraq and Syria, the al-Nusra Front, and Hezbollah.

They decided to up the ante. Would LeRoux sell SAMs—those diabolically effective shoulder-fired surface-to-air missiles? If he did, he was looking at twenty-five years in prison, mandatory, and possibly a life sentence.

Cindric and Stouch decided to have Jack tell LeRoux that he had a prospective buyer for arms, the Shan State Army, a rebel group that opposed the military regime in Myanmar. Shan tribesmen supported themselves and their insurgency by growing opium, refining it to heroin, and smuggling it to market through Thailand. The agents happened to know a Westerner who bought weapons for the Shan State Army. He gave them an authentic Shan State Army weapons wish list.

They figured this scheme would appeal to LeRoux because he had made noises about expanding his operations in Southeast Asia. He might jump at a chance to add the Shan State Army to his list of customers for arms.

Cindric and Stouch took Jack to Paris and had him write LeRoux that his new contact, a Shan State Army representative, was looking to buy small and medium-sized arms, including SAMs, antiaircraft missiles, specifically, Russian Strelas, models SA-7 and SA-14.

The email the agents wrote for Jack to send LeRoux said:

He has requested prices on the following items:

For area air defense: SA-7's or equivalent. They would like to purchase 50 kits (1 launch tube with 3 missiles—50 launch tubes 150 missiles). They would then like to purchase an additional 150 missiles.

For point air defense: SA-14's or equivalent. They would like to purchase 12 kits (1 launch tube with 3 missiles-12 launch tubes 36 missiles).

They also requested prices for:

M147- time delay firing device, M224- lightweight company mortar
system, M249 squad automatic weapon, M107 special application
scoped rifle, and M242 vehicle rapid fire weapon system.
They asked if you could package in weapon round containers or
missile round containers and delivered at sea either in Bay of Bengal
or South China Sea.
Advised they can get an euc [end user certificate], but would
prefer no paper trail.
I would like to be able to assure them we can supply weapons
to combat US and UN planes and helicopters involved in counter
narcotics efforts in the Shan State

Once they hit "send," they broke for lunch and wandered to a cafe
on Victor Hugo Circle. In minutes, the agents' phones went off one
after the other, with urgent texts from Milione.

"Call me now."

They called.

"What the fuck are you guys doing?" he said.

"We're sitting on the street in the Trocadero," Stouch said.

"Eating," Cindric said. "Food's pretty good here."

In so many coughs and grunts, Milione let them know that *somebody* had intercepted an email from Jack to LeRoux. *Somebody* had
asked him about it.

In more grunts and sniffs, they let him know that they had just sent
the Shan State Army shopping list to LeRoux.

"All right, I'll get this straightened out," Milione said. He was
laughing when he said it, so they finished their lunch and took a stroll.

Milione didn't tell them, then or ever, who *somebody* was, or anything else about the conversation. He didn't have to. If you're an experienced hiker, you don't have to meet a bear nose to nose to know

when one's been snuffling around the trail. The agents had been in the federal government long enough to assume that Milione's contact was somebody in the NSA or CIA, whose agency had intercepted the email with the Shan State Army weapons list. The mention of the SAMs might have triggered a red flag in some classified intercept system.

Several reasons: an ordinary hacker couldn't have broken into the encrypted channel Jack and the agents used to contact LeRoux. French, British, or Russian intelligence could have done it, but intelligence agents from these nations would not have contacted Milione in a matter of minutes, nor would they have told him what they had intercepted.

No, it had to be somebody from the United States—probably CIA. The agency had liaison officers inside the SOD. They knew what the 960 Group was, that the boss was Lou Milione, and how to get to him fast.

The cryptic coughs and grunts were Milione's way of warning the agents to go darker—that people in the CIA might be watching them and might figure out who LeRoux was.

"Dude, I think they were going to do direct action on him," Milione joked later. Direct action meant kill or capture, and "capture" meant kidnap, but neither he nor the agents seriously thought the CIA would kidnap a man out of the center of Paris or drop a drone on a luxury high-rise in Rio.

What they feared was that the CIA might try to poach LeRoux. It had happened plenty of times before. Somebody at the CIA could take it into his or her head to approach LeRoux, expose the DEA investigation, and make him an offer he couldn't refuse, to become an CIA "asset," meaning enrolled source.

"They might try to flip LeRoux and turn him to their own," Stouch said. "Why wouldn't they want him as a source? A guy operating in all these unstable countries? Embedded in the Philippines, with access to networks of terror, Iran and North Korea? If I were operating in that world, hell yeah, I'd try to flip that guy—grab him and put him on a plane. If he tells them he's on board, they don't have to play by the Constitution. But we don't play in that world. We go at somebody because he's committing crimes. We're pretty much black and white, and transparent."

Theoretically, CIA assets weren't immune to criminal investigation and prosecution, but in the real world, plenty of them cut deals with intelligence officers in order to beat the criminal justice process. Whenever somebody at the DEA, FBI, or the Justice Department wanted to charge a CIA asset with a crime, he had a fight on his hands. In some cases, disputes over whether to charge a CIA asset went all the way to the National Security Council. In many cases, the DEA and other law enforcement agencies just gave up.

These turf battles were happening with increasing frequency. Some senior CIA officials were rankled by the DEA's Operation Containment, an initiative launched after the attacks of September 11, 2001, that expanded deployments of narcotics agents to the Middle East, South Asia, and Africa. Mike Braun, DEA's chief of operations, devised Containment for all the right reasons, to help deprive terrorists of money derived from transnational organized crime, but in Washington, no good deed goes unpunished. CIA officials regarded DEA (and FBI) agents as clumsy interlopers who would surely mess with their carefully cultivated relationships with local officials. They complained bitterly when more DEA people turned up in Middle Eastern and Central and South Asian countries they regarded as their turf.

Having invested a lot of time and money in LeRoux, Cindric and Stouch were desperate not to lose him. They didn't know what Milione was going to do, but they trusted that he would quietly solve the problem. He generally did. Sure enough, they never picked up further hints of blowback from their Shan State Army wish list.

The day Cindric, Stouch, and Jack were to fly out of Paris, more evidence they needed to support conspiracy charges against LeRoux

arrived, in the form of a wiretap transcript. LeRoux had made a telephone call that was intercepted by the Brazilian police and forwarded
by Jim Sparks in Sao Paolo. In it. LeRoux was barking orders to an
RX Limited middle manager, Shai Reuven. LeRoux was trying to tell
Reuven to take care of a crucial detail in anticipation of his meeting
in Monrovia with the Colombian cartel representative. Determined to
wow the Colombian, he wanted to offer a master chemist to show the
Colombian's cook how to make primo meth.

LeRoux was trying to talk to Reuven in an impromptu code, but it
was too subtle by half. Reuven just wasn't getting it. The conversation
went like this:

LEROUX: We need to get us a cook.

REUVEN: Okay.

LEROUX: I like Mexican food and I want to get me a cook, you know
what I'm saying?

REUVEN: Yeah.

LEROUX: I have some guys out of Liberia. Liberia, okay?

REUVEN: Yeah.

LEROUX: Who are partnership with us, we need to send them the
cook, all right?

REUVEN: You mean a real cook, yeah?

LEROUX: No, no, no. *I am talking for meth, dude. Are you retarded?*

REUVEN: For what? For what?

LEROUX: For meth!

REUVEN: Okay, okay, I got you.

LEROUX: Come on now. JEEZUZ CHRIST!

The light evidently dawned on Reuven, who replied that he would
recruit a meth chemist from Florida.

LEROUX: (Exasperated) Bye-bye.

For Cindric and Stouch, the wiretap transcript hit jackpot. They could picture LeRoux getting madder and madder and redder and redder, until he finally blurted out that he was making and selling meth and planning to teach some Colombians how to do it. This was damning, irrefutable evidence, straight out of LeRoux's big mouth. It was *exactly* the evidence the prosecutors wanted—proof that LeRoux was ordering subordinates to put an illegal meth scheme in motion. His state of mind—what prosecutors call criminal intent—had to be crystal clear to a judge and jury. The wiretap, especially LeRoux's exclamation—"I am talking for meth, dude. Are you retarded?"—left no room for reasonable doubt about what he was thinking.

Cindric and Stouch strolled to the Eiffel Tower to watch the evening laser light show. It was springtime in Paris, a Van Gogh starry night. Perfect.

Cindric chose the moment to call his wife, Gena, and also Michael Lockard, an assistant U.S. attorney in Manhattan who had been assigned to handle the LeRoux case. He wanted to let them know he was on the job, slugging it out, working day and night. Gena had just come in from the stable where she worked and their daughters competed. Lockard was at his desk as always. Cindric decided he had better not rub it in about the Eiffel Tower and the stars.

Stouch didn't want to call his wife, Kelli, who rose early for her work in a medical practice. He had other ways of celebrating.

"I think we owe ourselves a crepe," he said.

He walked over to a kiosk and ordered a couple of thin pancakes drizzled with Nutella, a hazelnut and chocolate spread beloved by French children and so much classier and *je ne sais quoi* than the jar of Skippy that usually powered his twenty-mile runs.

Aw hell, Stouch decided, special occasion. A little sugar wouldn't kill him. He could put up with Paris.

Jack flew from Paris to Rio on Sunday, May 11, 2012, checked into his hotel, and donned two bugs, one that recorded audio, the other, an audio-video recorder. He was on his own for the first time. Cindric and Stouch couldn't accompany him to Rio because they couldn't get visas. Relations between the United States and Brazil were so sour that U.S. government employees faced long delays whenever they tried to visit Brazil on their official passports.

The agents flew on to Panama City, where Jack would join them after his session with LeRoux. Jack had told LeRoux that after they met in Rio, he would go straight to Panama to meet with the Colombian cartel people. Good tradecraft dictated that he go exactly where he said he was going to go. LeRoux would be scrutinizing Jack's expense accounts and airplane ticket receipts for any anomalies. He might even hire someone to shadow Jack, physically or virtually. Jack would follow the script—meet with LeRoux, as planned, then fly to Panama City, check into his hotel, hand off the body wires, and get some sleep.

Jack's cab pulled up outside LeRoux's condo in the Barra da Tijuca about 9 p.m. Sparks met him on a side street with a crew of cops from the Brazilian anti-narcotics unit. He told Jack that they'd hit a snag. The Brazilian cops had heard from the DEA agents in Minneapolis that LeRoux was extremely dangerous—a killer. They didn't want Jack to go into the building. If Jack went inside the condo and got shot by LeRoux, the Brazilians cops would be dealing with the corpse of an American operative. That would be impossible to explain to their superiors, much less the Brazilian press. Couldn't Jack talk LeRoux into coming out and meeting him in a public place? A restaurant, perhaps?

Jack didn't think LeRoux would pull a gun on him. They were going to talk business "like two best friends. I was his golden boy at that time."

He phoned Cindric and Stouch. "They want me to meet him somewhere else. Paul won't go for that."

Cindric and Stouch told Sparks that he had to convince the Brazilian cops they were overreacting. It was true that LeRoux had *ordered* killings. But he had paid hit men to carry them out. As Jack said, he was a klutz with weapons. Besides, he wasn't going to open fire in his own condo, in front of his own child.

Sparks told the Brazilians all that and explained that the recording devices Jack was wearing were tiny and well concealed. After some rapid-fire negotiations in Portuguese, Sparks convinced the cops to let Jack pass.

Jack headed up the elevator. A woman answered the door, holding a chubby, beady-eyed baby. "If that's not a little fucking LeRoux, I don't know what is," Cindric said when he saw the video.

The woman wasn't Cindy Cayanan, LeRoux's regular girlfriend. Cindy was model-thin, with high cheekbones and long, straight hair. This woman was short and chunky—maybe the Brazilian baby mama of LeRoux's anchor kid, or maybe yet another girlfriend. She averted her eyes and let the men get on with business.

Like LeRoux's places in Manila, the Rio apartment had a spectacular view and almost nothing in it. LeRoux motioned Jack out onto the balcony. More hospitable than their previous meetings, LeRoux offered Jack a stool and a Coke Zero and got down to business.

Jack launched into a spiel about the reasons for his visit. The Colombians wanted to make meth in Liberia, ship it to Portugal, store it there briefly, and then distribute it in smaller parcels to Europe and the United States.

LeRoux leaned in. Listening to the tape later, the agents could hear his intensity and excitement. LeRoux's command of detail was extraordinary. He had already thought out the minutiae of setting up a meth lab in Liberia, including which officials to bribe where. He knew where to buy supplies and how, when, and where to smuggle them. He knew chemistry and materials science.

"The deal's like this," LeRoux said. "Everything's cool, everything's good, the chemicals will be priced. I have the prices on the hydrophosphorus acid, I have the prices on the iodine crystal, the sulfuric acid—all that stuff's cheap. I'm waiting for confirmation on the pseudoephedrine. It's all straightforward to buy, there's no problem. As far as I'm aware, from China, we don't need a license for the hydro or the iodine or the sulfuric . . . we buy it in Hong Kong, no problem without a license. But the pseudo, yes, we will need a license, but if they have an EUC [end-user certificate] it's no issue."

Pseudoephedrine—pseudo—was the active ingredient in meth. Law enforcement agencies worldwide were always on the alert for shipments of this powerful chemical. LeRoux showed that he had researched how to get it by the barrel and the options. He knew that one course of action would cost more time. Another would cost more money. The Colombians would have to decide which was more valuable to them—time or money.

Chinese pseudo, he explained, was cheapest and he could order it by the ton, but Chinese chemical manufacturers required an end-user certificate and paperwork. It would take two months to ship.

Indian vendors, on the other hand, were faster. "We can ship any amount of pseudo they want from India right now. In fact, we have fifty keys ready to ship," LeRoux said. "It will make it much faster if we just ship it from India without a license. We could just ship it unofficial as pool chemicals from India or whatever.

"The difference is like this," LeRoux said. "On the one hand, the EUC will be cheaper because we don't have to pay any bribes [to the Chinese]. On the other hand, if we ship from India, we have to pay bribes through customs, [and] the price per kilo is around twice the Chinese price. So in China, instead of $1,500 it will become $2,500 or something like that. So, that's the difference. But we can send . . . whatever the fuck he wants. Anything! Either from India or from China."

As he listened to LeRoux, Jack glanced down to see the edge of the secret recording device coming out of its hiding place under his cuff. A spike of electricity ran up his spine. He slid his hand over the loose part, trying to keep his cool as he tucked it back in his cuff. If LeRoux grabbed his arm to inspect what was under his sleeve—catastrophe. The investigation would be blown, and Jack with it.

"Don't panic," Jack said to himself, starting to panic. "Lie. He'll believe. You're still his golden boy."

LeRoux's eyes followed his hand. He missed nothing. He looked at Jack quizzically but kept silent.

"Stupid diving gadget," Jack said, shrugging. "Always some problem."

LeRoux nodded and got back to business. Jack breathed. After swearing that he would never trust anyone, LeRoux was showing that he trusted Jack, at least long enough to make the connection he so desperately wanted with the Colombians. LeRoux started talking about the clean room, the meth industry term for a mobile lab. "Everything—the chemical, the fume room, the clean room—I suggest we containerize it and ship it to them," he said.

"Yeah, because it's Africa," Jack said. His heart had slowed to normal.

"Yeah, otherwise it will have been months trying to get all the parts and assemble it," LeRoux replied. ". . . Personally, you know, I know how these things work. It's better we just give them ready-to-go, otherwise you just fuck around, six months."

And, by the way, LeRoux said, "I'm ready to take the other product." He meant Colombian cocaine. He was eager to get his hands on a lot of cocaine, which he could sell for a whopping price in Australia, East Asia, and Southeast Asia. His previous attempts through people who were not Colombians had failed miserably. He was ready to buy from the factory.

"How soon can they get the other product to Europe?" LeRoux pressed. "I need it in those places I told you. Either UK or Spain." He wanted ten kilograms of cocaine to begin with and, if it was good, he would take up to fifty kilos.

He returned to the subject of the North Korean meth that he wanted to broker to the Colombians. "There's no top end on that, no top end," he said happily. "We can get, if they wanted, the highest-quality product. The highest-quality product! It's coming from the North Koreans, believe it nor not. They're manufacturing the shit! There's no control.

Up to six tons a month is available, I am told, [and] nobody is buying that quantity because that's the upper limit. The Chinese [Triads] are the biggest buyers. We buy from them. They deliver to us at sea."

North Korean meth was more expensive than Mexican or Colombian meth but, he said, it commanded a much higher price in Asia. He was getting it through Kelly Reyes Peralta, the bartender at Sid's Pub, and Reyes's connection, the Chinese Triad rep in Manila, Lim Ye Tiong Tan. LeRoux had recently agreed to buy forty-eight kilograms of pure North Korean for $60,000 a kilogram through Reyes and Lim. It was an exorbitant price. He could get acceptable meth for as little as $10,000 a kilogram wholesale in Thailand. But LeRoux knowingly overpaid for the sake of *guanxi*—connections—an all-important concept for anyone who wanted to do business in China. He was determined to cultivate contacts in the Chinese Triads so they would help him buy arms manufactured by state-run arms industries of the People's Republic of China. These factories turned out good-quality, cheap, popular guns, grenades, mortars, and mines.

LeRoux particularly wanted the Triad reps to help him get his hands on a PRC-made missile or a North Korean missile or guidance system assembly, so he could reverse-engineer it. He figured that access to either or both systems could do much to inform his precision-guided missile project for Iran.

He bragged that even at the excessive prices demanded by the Triads and the North Korean supplier, he could turn a profit. "You know, that shit, you can flip it for $150,000 a kilo depending on the market," LeRoux said. "The market is more than gold. The price in Australia is $150,000 a kilo. Japan is around $190,000 a kilo. So, if they need it in Asia, we can supply them as well, no problem . . . we have fifty units [of North Korean meth] just buried in the ground for a rainy day, you know what I'm saying? It's more valuable than fifty kilos of gold."

LeRoux said he had lined up a British chemist and an American chemist who would come to Liberia to give instructions to the Colom-

bian cocaine cook on how to make meth. (Evidently, Reuven, the aide
he had ordered to find a meth cook, had come through.)

LeRoux told Jack to find out how the Colombians smuggled contraband into the United States. He was curious because he was looking
for a better route for the opioids he wanted to ship from Mexico into
the United States.

"The oxys and the roxis are selling like crazy in the States," LeRoux
said. Oxy was street slang for oxycodone, a synthetic opioid painkiller
sometimes sold under the trade name OxyContin. "Roxi" or "roxy"
was street talk for Roxicodone, a related trademarked opioid pill.

LeRoux told Jack that he was shipping opioid pharmaceuticals via
Canada and Mexico, but his methods were costing too much. He complained that Texas law enforcement was aggressively checking trucks
and cars, not only at the border but also on at highway checkpoints
inside the United States.

"We have the stuff in Texas, okay, but it is still hard to get it,"
LeRoux complained. "It is like another fucking border. Believe me. I
mean, what you really want is the stuff in Florida, in New York, and
in California." LeRoux would do just about anything to avoid dealing
with the Mexican smuggling families who controlled the *plazas*, meaning, the various smuggling corridors.

He paused to indulge in a racist rant about Mexicans. "We lost a
million dollars on a deal with the Mexicans," he grumbled ". . . Low
level crooks who don't keep their word and start ripping off people and
fucks up the whole business. . . . I don't know if you've ever been to
Mexico, but it's a strange fucking place. . . . They don't work, dude.
Real lazy strange people."

By contrast, he declared, the Colombians were the most evolved
form of transnational organized crime.

"They seem like real business men and of their word," LeRoux said.

The Colombian networks had extensive wholesale and distribution
networks in New York and Miami. LeRoux hoped the Colombian car-

tel rep would advise him how to bypass Mexican smugglers on the south side of the Southwest border and the Texas cops on the north side and get his product up the East Coast.

"I like this Liberian deal very much, man," LeRoux said. He was practically drooling over the prospect of a deal with a Colombian group. "We will be a good partner for them. Anything they need. We know, we don't fuck people. And we won't rip them off. We have money. There's no problem."

By the way, he said, he was shifting to a new financial model. "Wires are easy, but we end up with a huge paper trail. It's dangerous," he said.

LeRoux told Jack that Hong Kong Organized Crime-Triad Bureau had recently seized $20 million of his gold bars. These, accumulated through various gold buying operations in Africa, had been held in a Hong Kong safe house in the name of Edgar Van Tonder, the South African who had also served as LeRoux's front man for Southern Ace. Most businessmen who lost $20 million would be drinking wine from the bottle, but LeRoux sounded merely irritated.

"Every day there's a fucking problem," he said, in a conversational, almost jocular tone. "Actually, the problem is too much wiring. Too much money moving around banks. We need to move to a better structure this year. Cash."

"Cash?" Jack said.

"Yeah . . . moving cash as cash. It's becoming too crazy—these fucking banks, too many regulations. Too many questions, seizing money. Fucking delaying things, a lot of bullshit goes on. Too much shit, my friend, but we have solutions. Don't worry."

LeRoux said he was going to ask the Colombians to give him cash in five-hundred-euro notes.

"It's surprising how much money weighs, dude," he explained. "A million dollars is a good couple of bags. You know, it's like two bags."

"Wow, that's a lot to ship, that's true," Jack said, wondering where the conversation was going.

"The euros, it's, what, a fifth of the amount for the five-hundred-euro note, something like that."

LeRoux's numbers were dead on. He was obviously experienced at packing large sums of cash into suitcases. He knew that $1 million in 500-euro notes would weigh just five pounds and could easily be concealed in a small valise. By contrast, $1 million in $100 bills weighed twenty-two pounds and needed a small duffel. Which is why high rolling crooks the world over favored the 500-euro note, which they nicknamed the Bin Laden.

He remarked that 500 euros were worth about $650 that day. Again, dead on—the bank rate for 500 euros was $647.10, slightly higher for ordinary transactions.

He walked Jack to the door.

"All right, thanks for the Coke and the lovely receivement," Jack said, trying to be sociable. "It's a nice place here. Beach volleyball?"

LeRoux brushed aside his attempt at small talk. "Well, just remember what I said. Recommend that you get the stuff from India to begin with."

By 10:10 p.m., Jack was back in his cab and on his way to his hotel in Rio.

He got up the next day and flew to Panama, where he met Cindric and Stouch and handed them the audio and video devices he had worn during the meeting.

In the hotel, Stouch took the video recorder to his room and downloaded it into his laptop.

"It's dark," Stouch said.

"Yes, but it makes the point," Cindric said. "You can see him there. It's fine. It's not crystal clear video that you like."

Cindric took the audio device to his own room, downloaded it, put on his headphones, and listened. It was sharp. And it was absolutely damning.

"It backs up everything we've read and said to each other," Cindric said jubilantly.

They called Brown at SOD and filled him in. "This is great, this is perfect," Brown said. "It shows that we have him! He's willing to do deals."

They needed one more piece of evidence—dope on the table. Talk was cheap. They had to get physical proof that LeRoux possessed a quantity of genuine crystal meth with intent to traffic it.

Jack contacted LeRoux and asked him to send him a sample of the North Korean meth, ostensibly to show the Colombians' cartel representative.

"No problem, I'll have Irish send it," LeRoux said. He was referring to Phil Shackels, who was from Northern Ireland. LeRoux had hired him and his partner, Scott Stammers, an English kickboxer and hustler, to be the arms-and-drugs division of his expanding business empire.

Jack gave LeRoux a Monrovia address for "Global Resources and Services." Jack explained that he had set it up as a front company for the cocaine and meth venture. In reality, Global Resources was a dummy corporation set up by Sam Gaye, who had retired from DEA and was now living in Monrovia, his birthplace, and working as a security consultant for the Liberian government. In the language of tradecraft, Global Resources was backstopped. If LeRoux became suspicious of Jack and had someone check Liberian incorporation records, they would show that business had been created exactly when and where Jack said he had done it.

In a week or so, Gaye phoned Cindric and Stouch to say that a parcel had arrived at the Global Resources mail drop. This was direct evidence of LeRoux's drug trafficking conspiracy and had to be handled according to established protocols.

Cindric and Stouch flew to Monrovia on May 31, 2012, to take custody of the parcel. Gaye drove them through the city to get to the mail drop. Nothing looked normal. As far as they could see in any direction, there was chaos—phone lines dangling to the street, scrap metal strewn about, and people living in shanties made of old packing crates. There was no electric grid. What little electric power there was came out of generators.

"Monrovia was beautiful at one time," Gaye said apologetically. The civil war that had raged between 1989 and 2003 had ravaged his city and much of the countryside.

They followed Gaye into the mail drop, pushing through a crowd of men idling on the curb. They were the only foreigners around. They gripped their backpacks tighter and hoping they could get in and out without a hassle.

They collected the parcel and drove to Gaye's house. Cindric slit the brown paper open.

"Fuck," Cindric said. "It's a photo album."

He opened cautiously. It was hollowed out. Little packets containing five or six grams of crystal meth were hidden underneath the paper that lined the cover and the pages. Very clever.

The agents had to get the meth to the United States to log as evidence, first with the DEA lab in suburban Virginia, then with the federal court in New York. To do that, they needed a direct flight from Africa to the States, not one that required a change of planes in Europe. The paperwork required by European border controls was onerous.

There was one flight from Accra to JFK International that suited their purposes. They put the meth in DEA evidence bags and flew from Monrovia to Accra. They walked up to Ghanaian border control, showed their credentials, and declared that they were carrying contraband drugs as official evidence. The airport authorities waved them through. No, they said, it wasn't necessary to search their bags.

After that, boarding the plane wasn't exactly comforting. What other bags had the Ghanaian authorities declined to search? Luckily, nobody got aboard with a bomb. The agents landed at JFK, reported the meth to U.S. Customs, and flew on to Washington to deposit it with the DEA lab in suburban Virginia.

The DEA chemists said that LeRoux was telling the truth about the quality of the meth. The crystals were 99.6 percent pure methamphetamine. It must have come from a state-sanctioned manufacturing facility. A grab-and-go mobile lab like the one LeRoux wanted to sell the Colombians couldn't make crystals like that.

There was something else interesting. The crystals in the packet contained a unique trace impurity, an organic chemical that served as a kind of signature. The DEA chemists had seen it just once before, in a batch of meth seized in South Korea and traced back to North Korea.

North Korea was stepping up its missile and nuclear weapons programs. The money had to come from somewhere. Meth was much in demand, especially in Asia. East and Southeast Asia and Oceania combined represented the world's largest market for meth and similar chemicals, according to the United Nations Office on Drugs and Crime.

"We gotta get the grand jury," Milione said. "We gotta take ground." "Take ground" meant nailing down a federal indictment against LeRoux. That required the prosecutors to present the evidence to the federal grand jury sitting in the Southern District.

Cindric phoned Lockard, laid out the agents' progress, and asked, "Grand jury next week?" This was shorthand for "Does the prosecutor think the agents now have enough evidence to support an indictment of Paul LeRoux?"

"Yeah, when you get back, we'll take care of it," Lockard said.

Lockard was as good as his word. He took the case to the grand jury promptly. He was a gentlemanly University of Virginia law school graduate who seemed to have memorized whole sections of the federal code and court opinions and who kept his cards close to his vest. Cindric and Stouch called him Atticus because he reminded them of the upright lawyer in Harper Lee's *To Kill a Mockingbird*. He was a man of unassailable rectitude and a perfectionist, qualities that were essential in the exacting New York City court system. A prosecutor who winged it wouldn't last an hour under a withering barrage from a high-priced Manhattan defense lawyer, nor could he or she withstand the scrutiny of a punctilious judge and a jury of fair-minded, skeptical citizens of New York.

Lockard and the other prosecutors in his unit served as a check and balance. To be innovative, agents couldn't hang back and stick to time-tested, conventional methods. The crooks read court records avidly, especially when they were behind bars and had nothing to do but study how the DEA had operated in the past. On the other hand, the agents couldn't swing wild or act like a cowboy, bending the rules. If they hit a legal land mine inadvertently, they could trigger a court case that might result in a negative legal opinion. They didn't want to risk a decision that could gut Section 960 and other narcotics statutes. They relied on Lockard and his colleagues to show them where exactly the line was, so they'd know when they were about to go over it.

Cindric and Stouch planted themselves at the Daniel Patrick Moynihan U.S. Courthouse on Pearl Street in downtown Manhattan. The agents weren't in the grand jury proceedings themselves, but they stood by, in case Lockard and his colleagues needed, say, a photo or a document. Oddly, for June, the days were brutally hot, climbing into the nineties and close to 100 percent humidity. The stone and glass buildings reflecting off the pavement turned the city to a steam bath, straining the dated building's air conditioning system.

On June 21, 2012, Lockard emerged from the grand jury room with a smile. The grand jury had just handed down a sealed indictment charging Paul Calder LeRoux with "conspiracy to distribute 100 kilograms of methamphetamine knowing and intending it to be imported to the United States."

After all the travel and agonizing over the case, Lockard said the grand jury had voted out the indictment quickly, with no reservations.

"You had them at Somalia," he said.

CHAPTER TEN

"I JUST DON'T WANT TO GET ON THE PLANE"

AMAZINGLY, THE DIPLOMATIC PROCESS WORKED THE WAY IT WAS SUPPOSED to. Officials at the U.S. embassy in Monrovia presented the indictment and federal arrest warrant to the Liberian Ministry of Justice. Since Le-Roux was not a Liberian citizen, formal extradition proceedings were not required. Instead, he could be expelled as an "undesirable alien" pursuant to the Liberia Aliens and Nationality Law.

Liberian Justice Ministry officials prepared an expulsion order and sent it on to the office of President Johnson Sirleaf. Since she was traveling at that moment, the order was signed by the acting president, Brownie J. Samukai, the minister of national defense, and dated September 21, 2012.

All Cindric and Stouch had to do was get LeRoux to Monrovia, and agents from the Liberian National Security Agency would put him on a DEA plane.

Jack messaged LeRoux that the meeting in Panama was a success. He said he had set up the meet with the Colombian cartel's man in Africa, a guy by the name of Diego. Diego would be played by a formerly high-ranking Colombian cocaine trafficker until he got arrested in the Midwest. He copped a plea, went to work for DEA, and became a U.S. citizen.

Cindric and Stouch cast Diego because he fit LeRoux's idealized image of a Colombian cartel leader. Diego was tall and elegant, with salt-and-pepper hair, an aquiline nose, high cheekbones, and a commanding aura. He joined Cindric, Stouch, and Jack in Monrovia to wait for LeRoux and play out their climactic scene.

Only, LeRoux wasn't in the air. Jack sent him an email drafted by Cindric and Stouch that everything was ready for the big Monrovia meet. LeRoux kept making excuses. There was only so hard Jack could push without arousing the Boss's suspicions.

So they waited. It was monsoon season in Monrovia. The rain wasn't the kind that cooled things off. They were staying at the RLJ Kendeja Resort and Villas, Monrovia's finest hotel. It was luxurious, for Monrovia, but since the wars, the beach was dirty and the pool was dirty. Stouch insisted on swimming in it anyway, to train for the next triathlon.

"You idiot, it's gonna be like that show, *Monsters Inside Me*," Cindric said. "God knows what you got growing inside you now."

Stouch ignored him. He ran as often as he could, jumping animal carcasses and piles of garbage. The rain was a problem. It was unrelenting. It kept them confined to their room much of the day. One day, as sheets of water pounded onto their dingy balcony, Jack popped in to say that LeRoux had just advised him of another delay in his travel schedule. Stouch lurched forward, stared at the window, and melted down.

"I can't fucking do this again," he groaned. He had a flashback from four years earlier, when he had collapsed in the backcountry of Togo and gone into shock. He had been interviewing Colombian traffickers imprisoned by Togolese cops extorting bribes. He was so thin and fit that he had no body fat to cushion the effects of dehydration and sickness brought on by tainted food. He had woken up in a local hospital and roused himself long enough to protest, "I don't want to die here."

Wim Brown, his partner at the time, found a French charity clinic that looked cleaner, and Stouch allowed a nurse to insert an IV into his arm. When he woke up, the place was deserted, because it was November 4, 2008, Election Day in the United States. The news had just broken that a son of Africa would be the next American president. All the clinic employees were outside, chanting "*Obama, Obama*." Stouch yanked the needle out of his vein and took off for the sad old hotel where he and Brown were staying. He crawled onto his bug-covered cot, drank a couple of bottles of water, ate a protein bar and a banana, and made a solemn promise to whoever was listening that if he got out of Togo alive, he wouldn't be back. Now, here he was in soggy, stinking Monrovia.

"I'm sick and tired of this shit," he said. "I've done this before. I CAN'T DO THIS."

"It'll work out," Cindric said, and tried to believe it himself. The air smelled of diesel from generators that ran day and night because there was no central power. The walls were specked with bullet holes. He imagined the place during the civil war, with the sickly-sweet smell of blood and rotting flesh in the air.

They sat for a while in silent despair.

"Fuck it," Stouch said finally. Time to shake it off. They went down to the bar, ordered beer and shots, sang *Get Down on It* along with Kool & the Gang and other eighties, late-disco-era dance favorites, and chatted with the bartender and waitresses. They closed the place down.

They got up the next day, wrote some more emails for Jack to send to LeRoux, and waited. And waited.

Finally, on September 25, 2012, a week after they arrived and four days after the expulsion order was signed, LeRoux texted Jack that he and Cayanan were heading for the Rio airport, on the way to Monrovia.

Milione and Maltz flew in from New York on a rented Bombardier Global Express executive jet that, assuming all went well, would deliver LeRoux to custody in New York. More agents from the 960 Group and from posts in the region filtered in to help.

The agents set up a command center in a room in the Kendeja. Milione, Brown, Cindric, Stouch, and the newly arrived agents went over the arrest plan and sketched it out on a white dry-erase board. As

Milione urged, they kept the plan simple because it would be easier to remember and there would be fewer chances of screwups. It went like this:

Jack, accompanied by some of Fombah Sirleaf's men from the Liberian National Security Agency, would meet LeRoux and Cayanan at the airport and whisk them through, bypassing the usual border control line. This little flourish was meant to signal LeRoux that Diego had bribed the cops, Liberian border control, and everybody else who mattered.

Outside the terminal, the "corrupt cops" would hand off LeRoux, Cayanan, and Jack to a chauffeur—in reality, another National Security Agency agent—who would deliver the honored guests to their hotel, the Palm Spring Resort, a gated, secured affair, apricot-painted concrete, with a view of the Atlantic, a pool, and a casino. It was about seven miles from the Kendeja. The paint, inside and out, was dingy, but rooms were comfortable, by Liberian standards. The agents picked it for its location, well away from town and from the sights and sounds of police and DEA activity.

LeRoux and Cayanan would have second-floor suite with a balcony. The room was L-shaped, with a king-sized bed, a minibar, a flat-screen TV, and Wi-Fi. Jack had a standard room below them on the ground floor, with a view of the parking lot. The room next to LeRoux's suite would be occupied by DEA agents.

DEA agent Matt Keller from the 960 Group would handle the overnight shift in the surveillance room, listening to the feed from a bugging device planted in the room. It was like a baby monitor. Keller needed it to make sure LeRoux didn't slip out of the hotel during the night. The agents assumed that LeRoux would sleep off the long flight from Rio. The next morning, LeRoux would meet with Jack, and then Jack would escort LeRoux to Diego's hotel and introduce them. In their meeting, LeRoux and Diego would put the finishing touches on the North Korean meth/cocaine deal. At that point, the NSA men would move in, arrest LeRoux, process him, and expel him to DEA custody. Happy ending.

Only, stuff happened.

Before LeRoux landed, Keller, Joe Kellums, an agent posted to the DEA Accra office, and the Liberian agents went into LeRoux's suite to plant the bug, which was hidden inside a clock the team had brought from Washington.

PFFFTTTT! FUUCCCK! As soon as the clock's plug touched the wall socket, the thing blew up. The voltage from the hotel generator was greater than American voltage, and it fluctuated unpredictably.

Kellums looked at the clock melted around the bug and turned to the Liberian agents. "You guys have anything?"

The Liberians went back to their office and returned with a gizmo made in China. It was a big ugly clunker, about the size of an old-fashioned walkie-talkie. Kellums turned it over in his hand, then stuck it in a vase under some flowers and set it up in LeRoux's room.

LeRoux shambled off the plane, wearing a blue polo shirt the size of a pup tent, khaki shorts, and flip-flops. He and Cayanan went straight to their room.

An hour or so later, Keller called Cindric and Stouch from the surveillance room. He held his cell phone up to the audio feed from the bug. The fat man was in heat. Even over the cell connection, Cindric and Stouch could hear Cayanan screaming.

"FUCK ME, LEROUX! FUCK ME, LEROUX!"

Then came a cascade of thumps, bumps, growls, yips, and creaks. It sounded as if somebody were shooting a bondage movie during an earthquake. How did a 110-pound woman handle loud, rough sex with a man the size of a baby grand? Cindric started laughing. Keller did not.

"Thanks, guys. I gotta listen to this shit all night," the younger man snarled. "You OWE me."

Cindric and Stouch slept better than they had in weeks.

Keller didn't sleep at all. He wasn't supposed to. The bugging device didn't record anything, only broadcast sounds to the surveillance room so Keller could tell if LeRoux slipped out the door. Finally, LeRoux's humping and grinding gave way to very loud snoring. He sounded like a rhino with indigestion.

Deep in the O-dark hours, Keller heard LeRoux speaking. After moving from Manila to Rio, then flying to Monrovia, his body clock must be totally confused. Keller felt a glimmer of sympathy for LeRoux. If the guy knew it was his last night of liberty, surely he'd be out clubbing. Of course, from what Keller had heard, he didn't like to talk to people. Still, he might have liked a cocktail. Keller would have liked a cocktail. He popped a bottle of water instead.

The next morning, while LeRoux and Cayanan were at breakfast, Kellums joined Keller in the surveillance room. They saw LeRoux's room door open and the maids preparing to make it up. They were changing out flowers in vases in rooms along the hall. If they lifted LeRoux's vase, they were bound to find the bug.

Kellums dashed into the corridor, did a pirouette around the maids, and, channeling Nathan Lane's drag queen in *The Birdcage,* began gushing about the wonderful lotions, marvelous soap, and gorgeous flowers. He twirled into LeRoux's room, declared that he absolutely had to have those glorious blooms in his own room, snatched up the bugged vase, and stuck the flowers on his head like an Easter bonnet. They were plastic, but he acted as if they were fresh from a palace garden.

Kellums had been a sniper with the U.S. Army Rangers in Iraq and had served with the DEA contingent in Jalalabad, a heroin smuggling center in Southeast Afghanistan. In the war zone, he grew out his black beard and hair and looked like a Cajun moonshiner. Nobody would take him for a dancer.

"What was *that*?" Keller asked.

"I pulled out my crazy," he said. "We all have it. We just don't go there."

After breakfast, LeRoux dropped Cayanan at their room and met Jack at 10 a.m. in the hotel cafe for a prebrief before their meeting with Diego. The breakfast room was supposed to look Chinese. Its red-orange walls and gilded fixtures glowed oppressively in the wet heat.

LeRoux, who had changed into another gigantic royal blue polo shirt, didn't seem bothered. He had good news to share. Jack had rarely seen him so pumped. He had been trying to make a deal with the Iranian Defense Industries Organization to supply small arms for his Amazon-style arms business. He had just gotten word from the two emissaries he sent to Tehran that the deal was a go.

All he had to do was come up with an African military officer and an end-user certificate with a lot of official-looking rubber stamps. These would provide cover for the arms sales, in case anyone questioned the Iranians about the buyer. This was the breakthrough LeRoux had been after since 2008.

"Everything we want, even bigger shit, is available in Iran," LeRoux rejoiced. "And there's no questions asked! They will deliver to us in any Muslim country anywhere in the world—Indonesia, for example. But we need to fetch up with a general or some fucking lieutenant from an African country, and they front the deal. It doesn't have to be a Muslim country. Just fetch up with a fucking general or a lieutenant with some official paperwork."

"What about here?" Jack asked, meaning, what about a Liberian military officer.

"Yeah, that's fine," LeRoux said. "If we can fetch up here with a general, all these items we want are available. I mean, the stuff they have for sale is unbelievable. They will deliver the goods anywhere in the world, no problem. The prices are higher but the bullshit is less."

LeRoux was practically giggling as he gave Jack instructions.

"Work on getting me a guy I can show to the Iranians," he exulted, "because I'm telling you, my friend, everything you want . . . even shit the Russians won't sell us, we can get there, even seven-meter-long rockets the size of this room! They sent me a catalogue! It's unbelievable, you can fucking buy whatever you want!!"

LeRoux said there was one item the Iranians wouldn't sell—SAMs, which he needed to fulfill the Shan State Army order. If a passenger airliner were knocked out of the sky and the killer missile were traced back to Iran, the blowback from the international community would be terrible. Officials in Tehran evidently didn't want to fade the heat.

China wouldn't sell SAMs, either. LeRoux had tried through Lim, the Chinese Triad rep, to buy small arms from Poly Technologies, the behemoth manufacturing company owned by the People's Republic of China. The company made, among many other things, large quantities of good-quality, inexpensive infantry weapons for the People's Liberation Army. On the side, it sold small arms to nearly all comers. (In 2014, the U.S. government would blacklist Poly Technologies for illicit arms sales under the Iran, North Korea, and Syria Nonproliferation Act.) But it wouldn't sell LeRoux SAMs for the same reason as the Iranians cited—blowback.

Unfazed, LeRoux said he thought he could get SAMs from Russian or Serb mafia gun-runners. His face was alight with anticipation. He badly wanted to pick up the Shan State Army as a client. The group occupied contested real estate in the Shan Mountains north of Myanmar, Thailand, and Laos. Shan buyers would always have money to spend because they had a renewable resource. Their one cash crop was opium, China White, the champagne of heroin.

Opium flourished in the Shan hills in the heart of the Golden Triangle. Shan tribesmen and Nationalist Chinese had been cultivating agribusiness levels of opium since 1949. A big bump in production occurred during the Vietnam War and again at the turn of the new millennium. Now, however, the Golden Triangle couldn't compete with Afghanistan in terms of quantity. But aficionados still considered the quality of Myanmar heroin unrivaled and would pay top dollar for it, so it was making a comeback. The numbers and possibilities excited LeRoux.

LeRoux turned to the arrangement he wanted to make with Diego. He had found a source in Mumbai for pharmacy-grade meth chemicals—pseudoephedrine and ephedrine. He said he could buy a ton of the meth precursors for $1 million or so and sell it to the Colombians for $50 million.

"It's like gold dust," LeRoux told Jack. "Like gold dust! Let's take the first delivery. Something like one metric ton to begin. A thousand kilos. First order."

The only tricky part would be avoiding naval patrols around India and Africa. He had studied government surveillance of maritime shipping lanes and thought he knew how to navigate around areas that were being watched.

"Not the Malacca Straits!" he said. "That area is very heavily monitored. Anywhere in the South China Sea, like Thailand, Vietnam, but not in in the actual Chinese waters itself. In international waters."

LeRoux had plans for the cocaine he expected to get from Diego's organization.

"I need as much [cocaine] as he can supply," he said. "I have at least a demand for 200 units a month to 1,000 units a month." He calculated that he could sell the coke to the Chinese Triad for $20 million to $50 million a ton.

If he moved as many tons of chemicals, meth, and cocaine as he anticipated, he would quickly enter the rarified circle of drug billionaires. Only El Chapo and maybe three or four other kingpins had attained billionaire status, an achievement that enhanced not only their professional reputations but also their untouchability.

LeRoux and Jack pushed back their chairs to head for the meeting with Diego at his hotel, the Golden Gate. On their way out the door into the downpour, LeRoux turned to Jack, handed him a couple of U.S. hundred-dollar bills, and told him to find a cheap laundry in town.

"These fuckers charge crazy money," he grumbled. "It's like, two bucks for a shirt here."

"It's Africa," Jack sighed with feigned sympathy.

"Cheap bastard," Jack said to himself. "Fatty's making millions and he won't pay a lady who makes a dollar a week to wash and iron a shirt?"

At the Golden Gate, Jack introduced Diego. The Colombian, dressed immaculately in a crisply ironed collared shirt and neatly creased slacks, rose and solemnly offered a manicured hand, like a Spanish grandee. He flashed his professional smile, which he had perfected over years of playing the part. It was the body language of a man who was slightly interested, slightly chilly, and wanted to signal, "I know everything, so don't mess with me."

LeRoux lowered himself into an overstuffed leather sofa, sat up as straight as his belly would allow, and put on his London manners. He apologized profusely for a delay in shipping the mobile meth lab. "If you have any problem assembling it," LeRoux said, "I'll send guys in— like that." He snapped his fingers.

Diego said he was curious. Why was LeRoux using the Philippines as a base?

"It's the best shithole we can find in Asia, which gives us the ability to ship anywhere," LeRoux replied airily. "We can ship to Hong Kong, Japan, Australia and the prices are very good. For the product that you're manufacturing [cocaine], in Australia it's around $150,000 a kilo. If we move the other one you want [meth] to Japan, it's around $100,000 a kilo. It's the best position in Asia, and it's also a poor place, not as bad as here, but we can still solve problems."

Diego said he was impressed with the quality of the meth in the sample LeRoux had supplied. "It is awesome," he said.

LeRoux nodded proudly. "That stuff comes from the North Korean government. They can make it. They don't care there. They have a building *this* size to make it," he bragged, sweeping his hand to suggest a hotel-size lab. "We can get around six hundred kilos a month."

LeRoux explained that he was getting the meth through one of the Chinese Triads, which smuggled it out of North Korea and brokered it to the outside world. He thought he could talk the Triad rep into lowering the price, if he would sell his organization 200 kilos of Colombian cocaine a month, which it would distribute in Asia.

"If we give them good quality coke, I don't see how we need to pay more than $20,000 or $25,000 maximum for the meth," LeRoux said.

Diego nodded and, to flatter his subject, said that he had heard that despite his success and wealth, LeRoux chose to live modestly. LeRoux, who never did get irony, responded happily that he drove an ordinary car, not a "fancy" one. By ordinary, he meant his Range Rover, which cost $90,000 or $100,000 in the United States and at least double that in the Philippines. He launched into a long rant about how he had killed his lieutenant, Dave Smith, for spending ostentatiously and driving a Lamborghini and Mercedes around Manila.

"You know what really pissed me off?" LeRoux said. "His yacht was bigger than my yacht."

He jumped subjects again, to Iran. He was buying guns from Iran, but he needed some end-user certificates. Could Diego help him?

Diego, baffled at this twist in the conversation, changed the subject back to the meth transaction. His instructions from the DEA agents were to seal a deal for meth. He was not supposed to allow LeRoux to wander off into uncharted territory.

Diego said his organization would take delivery on one hundred kilos of North Korean meth to start with. It would be distributed in New York through the Colombians' outlets there.

LeRoux nodded. Done, he said.

Diego stood and offered his hand. LeRoux, rising, took it, motioned to Jack and headed back to his hotel suite.

Diego went to the DEA control room in the Kendeja to hand off his recording devices. As the agents hooked them up to a computer to download them, he collapsed into a chair and popped open a bottle of water.

"Holy shit, this guy is talking about all kinds of crazy shit," he gasped. "He was talking about making people *disappear*. Talking about *Iran*!"

That was LeRoux, Stouch said—grasshopper mind, but he wasn't a fantasist. He was eager to please the Colombians. He thought they enjoyed killing as much as he did. Or maybe, Stouch thought, LeRoux was a bit nervous in the presence of a real Colombian and wanted to let Diego know that he, too, killed mercilessly.

Stouch called Brown to fill him in.

"What are we waiting for?" Brown said. "What more are we going to get?"

"What do you think?" Stouch asked Cindric.

"If you think it's good, I think it's good," Cindric said.

Cindric went outside, met the two Liberian National Security Agency agents assigned to carry out the arrest, and escorted them into the command center. They were both about six feet two inches tall and 250 pounds, lighter than LeRoux, but all muscle. They looked as if they spent a lot of time in the weight room.

"We will take care of this," the senior officer said.

"The arrest will be very anticlimactic," Stouch whispered to Cindric. "Just hang out in the back and let them do their thing."

They took a convoy of SUVs over to LeRoux's hotel. The rain had slowed to a drizzle. The air was heavy as a wet, woolen overcoat. Cindric and Stouch followed the Liberian agents to the second floor and stood a short distance behind them as they knocked on the door to LeRoux's suite. Brown trailed some steps behind.

"Room service," one of the cops said in a low, rumbling voice. He sounded nothing like a waiter, but the gambit never failed. Cayanan dropped her iPad on the bed and answered the door.

LeRoux had changed into an orange polo shirt. He was sitting at the desk, his face fixed on his laptop screen.

"Mr. LeRoux! Put your hands up!" the senior officer shouted. "You're under arrest."

LeRoux jumped to his feet, leaving his laptop open and unlocked.

"What did I do? What did I do?" he shrilled. He had changed into his orange polo shirt and looked like the Great Pumpkin.

"Sir! Put your hands up!" the Liberian repeated, his tone sharpening.

LeRoux kept his hands down. Cayanan stood frozen to the spot.

"Don't move," Cindric called to her.

LeRoux lurched toward his computer. Cindric got to it first and snatched it so he couldn't launch a command to wipe the machine's data.

LeRoux slumped toward the floor, all passive resistance. The Liberian agents couldn't get his arms together to cuff them. Stouch jammed his thumb under LeRoux's jawbone, searching for the pressure point that caused blinding pain and submission, but no lasting damage. The big man didn't budge. His pain threshold must have been off the charts.

"Fuck it," Cindric said, starting toward LeRoux. The rain and the heat had gotten to him. Was he flashing back to his bar-fighting days? Brown saw Cindric's face reddening and his fist clenching. He knew that look. Cindric was about to knock the fat bastard's head off.

"Don't do it, Tom!" Brown shouted.

"Sir! Quit resisting or I will shoot you," the senior Liberian commanded.

Stouch was hanging on to LeRoux's neck and shoulder, still looking for a pressure point that worked. He was starting to wonder if the man felt pain. LeRoux was trying to shake him off like a horsefly.

"If you resist, I'm going to shoot," the Liberian said.

"Eric, move!" Cindric yelled. The Liberian was seriously fed up.

Stouch jumped back from LeRoux. He heard one of the other DEA men, he wasn't sure which, shout to the Liberian, "Put that fucking gun away."

The Liberian ignored him and shouted his warning again.

After what seemed like an hour, but was probably a minute, LeRoux loosened his arms and allowed himself to be cuffed.

Stouch sidled over to Cindric. "Really, it's normally a lot more anti-climactic than that."

"Fuck you," Cindric replied. He turned back to face LeRoux.

"Mr. LeRoux, I'm Tom Cindric, a special agent with the U.S. Drug Enforcement Administration," he said. "We have a judicial expulsion order for your arrest."

"You have been indicted for conspiring to import and distribute one hundred kilograms of methamphetamine into the United States," Brown said.

LeRoux ignored them and turned to the Liberians.

"My brothers, we can work this out, we're all Africans. Except for him," he said, gesturing at Cindric. "Don't take me to your police department. What can I give you? What do you need?"

"There is nothing you can give me, sir," the senior Liberian said. He nodded to his partner, and they hustled LeRoux into an armored police SUV. Cindric jumped in behind them.

Jack, in his first-floor hotel room, was peering out of his window at the parking lot as the Liberian agents frog-walked LeRoux to their SUV. LeRoux was calm. Jack thought LeRoux must be collecting his thoughts, figuring that he could pay his way out, once they got to the police headquarters.

Jack heard knocks on his door. It was Stouch. His face was flushed with adrenaline. "Pack your bags and let's go!" he snapped.

Jack obeyed. He trotted out to the parking lot and got into a police car, which delivered him to the Kendeja Hotel. The agents there took him to a room and made sure he locked himself in.

Stouch, meanwhile, collected LeRoux's seized computers and phones, which he would give to the DEA techs to download and analyze. He sped off in a second Liberian National Security Agency SUV with Cayanan, who had been detained but would be released to return to Manila.

Stouch's ride pulled into the National Security Agency headquarters—a dilapidated, three-story concrete affair with no elevator—about the time Milione and Brown arrived in their rental car.

As the three climbed the steps to the booking room, they could hear LeRoux shouting, offering bribes all around. He was demanding a Liberian lawyer. He wanted to see a Liberian judge. The Liberian cops were shaking their heads and doing their paperwork.

Through all this, Cindric dialed Jack and held his cell phone aloft. "Listen to this, you deserve it!"

This was the first time Jack had ever heard fear in LeRoux's voice. The cops weren't going to hurt him physically, but they had taken away his control. They didn't want his money. If there was anything LeRoux needed, it was control. Now that he had lost it, he was close to hysterical.

When Cindric hung up, Jack threw his phone on the bed and did a face plant into the pillow. He'd forgotten what sleep was like.

Inside the building, the Liberian agents were winding up their paperwork. LeRoux, his voice hoarse with shouting, turned to Milione, who had been quiet up until now. LeRoux correctly divined from the agents' deferential body language that Milione was the senior DEA man present. Cindric was the biggest, Stouch the fittest, and Brown the most clean-cut, but Milione was definitely in charge.

"I apologize in advance, but I really don't want to get on the plane," LeRoux said.

"I know you don't want to get on the plane," Milione replied. His voice was even and firm.

LeRoux, shackled now, went dead weight again. Underneath all those layers of lard, he was incredibly strong, with shoulders like a Russian power lifter and short hard legs.

It took four Liberian agents, plus Cindric, Stouch, Brown, and Milione, to hoist LeRoux and haul and drag him down three flights of steps to the parking lot in the steaming rain.

LeRoux collapsed in the parking lot, screaming that he was being kidnapped. The eight men dragged LeRoux to the door of the twelve-seat passenger van the DEA agents had rented for the occasion and shoved and pulled until LeRoux's butt was on a seat. The Liberian agents climbed in next to LeRoux. The DEA agents surrounded them, and Carol Dillon, the analyst, hopped in behind, taking notes to document the expulsion for the U.S. court record. They slammed the van door shut and locked it.

Milione turned around to stare at LeRoux, nose to nose, like a football coach chewing out an unruly junior varsity player.

"Paul, just stop it," he snapped. "You can't act like this. It's undignified."

LeRoux snickered. All that stress and adrenaline came out as a man-baby giggle.

"I did apologize in advance," he said. "I told you I wasn't going to get on the plane."

"Are you going to behave yourself?" Milione said sternly.

LeRoux snickered again. "Yeah, I will."

"Are you sure?"

"Yes, yes, yes."

He sniffled to suppress a laugh.

Cindric and Stouch saw Milione's face harden. "You better not resist in this plane," he said. His voice was still low, but his tone was one that the agents never wanted to hear directed at them.

"We are not going to have a problem on that plane," Milione said. "You're going to end up on the worst end of this. We're not going to get hurt in this. You are."

The agents knew that Milione would never abuse a prisoner or allow anyone else to do so. He said it was against the U.S. Constitution and just wrong. But, if he had to subdue someone to protect the lives of others, they were sure he wouldn't hesitate to inflict real damage. Cindric said, "If you get in a fight with Lou, you better pack a lunch because it's an all-day job."

That was quite a statement coming from ex-bouncer Cindric, who practiced an aggressive kickboxing style called Muay Thai.

The packed van trundled toward the airport. The rain was coming down again. The humidity in the van was close to 100 percent.

And then they heard a pop and felt the vehicle sag. They all knew the sound. Flat tire. What's next? An earthquake? A flood?

The Liberian agents jumped out, jacked up the van, and changed the tire. They were good at it. Flats were commonplace on Liberian roads.

They got to the airport around 10 p.m. A short time later, they were strapping LeRoux into his seat. Once the airplane door was screwed shut, a new LeRoux personality suddenly appeared, one they had never seen before.

LeRoux took in the situation inside the plane, eyes twinkling like a computer rebooting. Cindric and Stouch watched LeRoux's process, briefly mesmerized. They saw him reach his "aha" moment.

Jack! He's working with them! LeRoux must have thought. *Which means that the DEA has everything I said and wrote to Jack. I'm fucked. Okay, time to unfuck this.*

His orange shirt, drenched in sweat and rain, stuck to his belly. His hands and feet were manacled. He reeked. They all did.

And yet this hot mess of a man in desperate need of a bath suddenly transformed into CEO Paul—magisterial, as if calling a board meeting to order. He was starting to assert command by sheer force of person-ality and ego. If he had been arrested by younger people or people who weren't prepared for him, Cindric thought, LeRoux could have done it. He could have taken control of the room.

He squared his shoulders and smiled benevolently. "Well played, gentlemen," he said.

He paused for dramatic effect. "But if you're looking at me, you're obviously looking for bigger things."

"Not really," Stouch said. "You're the prize."

"No, no, no."

"What then?" Cindric said.

"Nation-states, gentlemen. Nation-states."

Cindric shot Brown a look that said, *Fuck, where is this going?*

"What?" Stouch said.

"Iran. North Korea."

CHAPTER ELEVEN

QUEEN FOR A DAY

IT WAS ON.

"What have you got?" Cindric said.

"What are you going to give me?" LeRoux replied.

Cindric shook his head. "We can't make any promises."

"I need some assurances."

"To be clear, this is not our first rodeo," Milione said. "This team and others on the team who aren't here brought down Viktor Bout. He was given every opportunity, and he decided to go to trial."

This went on for two hours until fatigue and hunger set in. LeRoux asked for a Diet Coke and a sandwich, any kind.

The agents fetched themselves sandwiches and soft drinks. After his blood sugar bumped up to normal, Stouch turned back to LeRoux. "If you don't want to talk, that's fine," he said. "Look, here's how this works. I can't make you any promises. Tommy can't make you any promises. That's our boss"—he pointed to Brown. "He can't make you any promises."

"That's *his* boss"—he pointed to Milione. "He can't make you any promises."

"You see that guy there?" He pointed to Derek Maltz, whose black eyes were boring into LeRoux's skull like carpenter bees. "He's the boss of the whole group, and he can't make you any promises. So you either talk to us now, or we'll wait till we get to New York and we're with the prosecutors."

God, I hope he doesn't talk because we're both fucking exhausted, Cindric said to himself.

"Okay," LeRoux said. "I understand." Stouch read him his rights. He signed a statement waiving them.

He didn't shut up for thirteen hours.

"Viktor Bout was a very foolish man," LeRoux began.

He knew plenty about Bout. Specifically, that Bout was doing hard time for agreeing to sell 700 to 800 shoulder-fired, antiaircraft Russian Igla surface-to-air missiles—SAMs—to men who he thought were Colombian FARC guerrillas. Bout had advised the fake FARC guerrillas on tape that the terrorist group could use the missiles to take down American helicopters and kill American troops. The prosecutors used his words to argue for the maximum sentence under the law, life in prison. They didn't get their way because federal judge Shira A. Scheindlin harbored deep skepticism about the sting and Bout's culpability. "You may not like the business he is in—but he is a businessman," she said during the proceedings. Even so, the judge acknowledged that she had had no choice but to send Bout up for the mandatory minimum of twenty-five years in federal prison. Bout was forty-five at the time.

LeRoux couldn't count on getting a judge so lenient. He wasn't willing to risk doing twenty-five years, much less life. He knew that his agreement to sell SAMs was on tape and in emails between him and Jack. He was sunk, unless he avoided going to trial on the SAMs charge. To do that, he would have to offer up evidence leading to more important criminals. He knew the mantra the agents and prosecutors lived by—*flip and go higher*. What leverage did he have?

LeRoux described multiple projects on multiple timelines. He sounded like a chess master playing a dozen opponents simultaneously. He had been darting among the chessboards, using people as his chess pieces. One board was about Somalia. Jack knew all about that, because he was LeRoux's pawn in that game.

Jack had picked up bits and pieces of what LeRoux had been doing in Iran, North Korea, China, Brazil, the Philippines, and Africa, but he didn't have the whole picture because LeRoux compartmentalized his business activities. Once LeRoux started talking, it was clear that he had created his own universe of games and pawns, a bewildering tangle to anybody except himself. The agents could see in his eyes that his mind was racing faster than he could form the words to articulate his vision. They struggled to slow him down to human speed.

"Okay, let's whiteboard this," Cindric said. "Who would you put up at the top of the whiteboard?"

"On the right, Kim Jong Un," LeRoux said. He meant the Dear Leader of North Korea, with the strange hair and the nukes.

"On the left, Ayatollah Khamenei." Khamenei was the Supreme Leader of Iran, presiding over a regime racing to develop the capability to build nuclear weapon and arming Hezbollah and other proxies to the teeth.

LeRoux launched into a stunning admission of a conspiracy the agents had not suspected existed. He said he had been helping Iran develop the capacity to build advanced navigation systems for its rockets and missiles—the weapons systems that most directly threatened Israel, Iran's regional rivals in the Arab world and U.S. and allied forces in the region.

As LeRoux unspooled his tale, it started with a relatively low-key overture to Iran in late 2008, shortly after he founded Red, White and Blue Arms. LeRoux needed a steady supply of small arms—"heavy weapons, rockets, machine guns and explosives," as he later put it— for his new venture. He intended to start with local sales and scale up quickly to regional, then global sales, much as he had done with his pharmaceutical business. He knew that Iran was unlikely to bend to Western pressure to refuse the sale. According to LeRoux's plea agreement he sent Nestor Del Rosario, a Filipino middle manager at RX Limited, and his assistant Rogelio "Ogie" Palma, to Tehran, with instructions to sound out the Iranian Defense Industries Organization, the state-owned military-industrial conglomerate. He thought that Del Rosario and Palma, who were slight, brown-skinned figures, wouldn't seem threatening to Iranian officials, nor arouse suspicions. The Iranians were more likely to suspect a Brit, Australian, or white southern African like himself of being a spy for the CIA or MI5.

Upon their return, Rosario and Palma gave an optimistic assessment. They had met with the head of the DIO, and he had indicated interest. But they hadn't closed a deal. It took them two more trips to Tehran to get a verbal commitment to make the purchase and a catalogue of Iranian small arms. After their third trip, in mid-2009, they returned with a long shopping list of specialized electronics components, high-performance materials, and technologies the Iranians wanted to buy through LeRoux.

At the time, Tehran was struggling to enlarge and modernize its forces and weapons systems, which were outdated and depleted after the Iran-Iraq War. Iran's progress was hobbled by draconian trade sanctions levied by the U.S. and international community aimed at forcing the radical regime to shut down its nuclear enrichment program and stop arming its militant proxies. Iranian DIO officials were always on the lookout for unscrupulous businessmen who would act as straw purchasers. Was LeRoux a good candidate? The Iranian shopping list appeared to be a test.

"The Iranians have been at this since 1980, and they're very, very good at playing people who think they're playing Iran," said Anthony Cordesman, an expert on Iran's military capabilities with the Center for Strategic and International Studies, a highly regarded Washington think tank. "They're always willing to see if somebody can come up with this stuff. There's no risk to them."

There were a few random items on the shopping list that could be used in nuclear devices. The request for an explosives formula using only unmonitored materials seemed destined for the Iranian Revolutionary Guard Corps—Quds Force and its proxies, among them Lebanon's Hezbollah, the Palestinian groups Hamas and Islamic Jihad, Iraqi Shia militias, and the Houthis in Yemen. But most of the list consisted of missile parts and the technology to make them. The Iranians wanted, for reverse engineering, a Phoenix missile, an air-to-air tactical missile used until 2004 by U.S. Navy and Marines Corps fighter jets such as the F-14 Tomcat. They wanted a cruise missile design, also for reverse engineering. They were seeking fiber optic gyroscopes available only in the United States and Western Europe and enhanced guidance systems for missile navigation; and vibrations platforms and supersonic wind tunnels for missile testing.

LeRoux understood why. Someone like him, interested in military weaponry, could find terabytes of white papers about Iran's military machine, plus the U.S. intelligence community's conclusion, repeated throughout the 2000s, that despite sanctions, Tehran had managed to assemble the largest and most diverse stockpile of ballistic missiles in the Middle East.

Missiles were Tehran's top priority because they were cheaper to build and operate than fighter planes. Small rockets and missiles could be easily shared with mobile teams of Hezbollah and Hamas fighters.

Iranian missiles lacked range and accuracy. Most of the Iran-made projectiles aimed at Israel landed harmlessly in the desert. "The limited lethality and accuracy of most of Iran's rockets and shorter-range ballistic missiles mean that most Iranian missiles cannot hit a point target and would not produce significant damage if fired into an area target," Cordesman wrote in a white paper published in October 2014 by CSIS. "They lack advanced precision guidance systems or terminal homing capabilities that could make them more political weapons and sources of intimidation than effective war fighting systems."

When LeRoux's emissaries came calling, Iran's DIO was trying to develop missiles capable of precision strikes and with longer ranges, even to intercontinental missiles that could strike the United States.

The DIO was working on a land-attack cruise missile system, a formidable threat to all its neighbors, and was seeking improved accuracy for its close-range ballistic missile systems. Its personnel were searching through multiple clandestine channels for advanced missile navigation technology. Smart missiles would be a game changer for Iran's perpetual conflict with Israel and for Iran's ally Bashar al-Assad of Syria, who was struggling to win a civil war that had killed at least half a million people and driven millions of people from their homes.

LeRoux said his emissaries were told that if LeRoux came up with a guidance system for Iran's short- and medium-range rockets and missiles, he would be paid $100 million in gold.

LeRoux was all in, calculating that he could make himself indispensable to the Iranians. It wasn't just the money, though $100 million was an attractive figure. He embraced "projects," as he called new ventures, with a passion he never expressed for his children, wives, lovers, or kin. For him, the Iranian opportunity was like walking into a room full of fresh chessboards. He saw it as an opportunity to scale up to a larger arena—from weapons to weapons systems and eventually weapons of mass destruction.

He immersed himself in the world of clandestine missile design. He wasn't a rocket scientist yet, but he saw no reason he couldn't become one. He hadn't met a problem he didn't think would yield to him. He wasn't shy about letting the Iranians know it.

He sent word to Tehran that the shopping list was unrealistic. Some of the items could be bought only in the United States, which had stringent export controls, over and above international sanctions, for militarily useful items. U.S. enforcement agencies were aggressive. Even if the DIO got a sample or two, Iran's engineers and manufacturers didn't have the expertise to copy them. U.S. and NATO-level weapons systems were hard to build, hard to keep up, and ruinously expensive.

He offered an alternative: missile technology simpler than what the Iranians wanted but better than what they had. Modern missile guidance systems achieved precision by a combination of GPS, inertial navigation, and radar technologies. Iran could not legally obtain GPS receiver technology and also certain inertial navigation aids because of an international anti-proliferation accord called the International Traffic in Arms Regulations (ITAR), adopted by the industrialized nations (Canada, France, Germany, Italy, Japan, the United Kingdom, and the United States). The ITAR rules at the time required the chips in commercial GPS receivers to be degraded so that they stopped working when they reached 60,000 feet altitude and 1,000 knots velocity—in other words, in a missile—or when they were in an unmanned airborne device carrying a 500-kilogram payload.

LeRoux said he told the Iranians he believed he could create a GPS-based navigation system "ideally suited for deployment in low-cost mass-produced tactical or ballistic missiles." He said he could reprogram the chips in cheap commercial GPS receivers and turn off the anti-proliferation restrictions so that the Iranians could mass-produce small, smart rockets and missiles.

If he succeeded, the consequences would be dire. In 2017, the U.S. Air Force's National Air and Space Intelligence Center (NASIC) reported, "If the Iranians and North Koreans use satellite navigation systems (such as GPS) onboard their CRBMs [close range ballistic missiles], then the miss distance of these CRBMs could be reduced to tens of meters. High accuracy of CRBMs would be a force multiplier for both the Iranian and North Korean artillery forces by giving them precision strike capability against high priority targets."

In other words, the U.S. Air Force believed that an Iranian ballistic missile with good GPS guidance could strike targets within a circle as small as thirty-three feet across. Its controllers could pinpoint a specific building, even a specific room in that building. They could aim at a particular car or truck conveying a particular military commander, spy, or scientist.

Listening to LeRoux, Cindric and Stouch grasped immediately the implications of his missile navigation research, which he recited in a matter-of-fact voice, as if he were talking about designing next-generation hay balers. If Iran achieved its goal, its arsenal would advance from a tactical to a strategic threat to Israel and the Middle Eastern nations. Anyone who wielded so-called smart rockets could program them to strike specific buildings and critical infrastructure targets such as water purification plants, command-and-control hubs, communications links, airfields, military installations, and more. Batteries of smart rockets could overwhelm Israel's Iron Dome missile defense system, cripple other defenses and government functions, and inflict incalculable civilian casualties. Israel would strike back furiously at Iran, and the conflict would escalate, embroiling the Persian Gulf nations in a hot war in the Middle East, this one involving at least two nuclear powers—Israel, certainly, and, possibly, Iran.

They could only imagine the cost in human suffering.

To carry out the project, LeRoux assembled a technical team and set it up with a lab in a warehouse in the province of Cavite. An electronics engineer and a computer programmer were already on his payroll, developing a cell phone intercept device he called the "X station." It was supposed to alert when the Philippines authorities were skulking around his offices and research facilities. He was already paying hefty bribes and didn't want the cops or military to pile on to shake him down for more than he was already paying. "Every little while the Filipinos try to fleece me for money," he complained to Jack in Rio. "I mean they try to fuck my ass." He certainly didn't want the Iran missile project, which was far more extensive and potentially lucrative, to be interrupted.

He reassigned the technical specialists to missiles and, during 2010, brought in twenty to twenty-five more engineers, computer programmers, and scientists, mostly from Eastern Europe. These people were his research and development team. Essentially, he became an outside contractor reporting to Iran's DIO, just as Boeing, Lockheed, Motorola, and other American corporations collaborate with the Pentagon.

He broke up the project into thirty or forty components. Besides the guidance system project, he agreed to have his team design a cruise missile, something like the U.S. Navy's Tomahawk cruise missile. The Iranians wanted their Tomahawk-clone cruise missile to have a range of 1,000 miles, plus stealth capability to evade radar. LeRoux boldly told the Iranians that the stealth missile would take several advanced components and a couple of years, but it could be done.

He did not divulge the scope and true aims of the surreptitious Iran project to the engineers who staffed it. He told them various lies, for instance, that they were working on a "spectral analysis" project or that they were building a new kind of drone to be used to search for mineral deposits in the remote reaches of the Mindanao islands.

The Iranian DIO officials seemed to believe that LeRoux was on the right track, because they asked him to move his R&D team to Tehran. LeRoux refused, saying that his Eastern Europeans didn't look Iranian and would be instantly spotted by Western spy services. Also, he said he didn't want his people to travel to Iran with disks that might be seized.

As usual, he had his own agenda. According to Jack, he was going to double-dip. He figured that if he could make $100 million from the Iranians, he could make the same amount from other buyers. He intended to piggyback on his smart missile research to create inexpensive knockoffs—the missile equivalents of Saturday night specials. Jack believed, based on some hints LeRoux dropped, that LeRoux intended to sell cheap precision-guided rockets and missiles to African and Asian warlords, dictators, and guerrilla armies. Who wouldn't want a smart missile? Possessing just a few of them would serve for bragging rights and blackmail.

He didn't tell the Iranians any of that. He wanted to preserve the option of using Iran as his bolt hole. He was getting worried that the

Philippines officials he had bribed wouldn't stay bought. In late 2009, after the *Captain Ufuk* was seized for gun-running in Bataan, LeRoux learned that agents of the Australian Federal Police were investigating him. Australia had strict gun control laws and put a high priority on arms trafficking in the region. LeRoux prepared to retaliate against the Australian cops if they caused him trouble. He bribed an official in the Philippines Department of Foreign Affairs 50,000 pesos, about $1,200, to slip him a dossier on the SOP Australian Federal Police agent posted to the Australian embassy in Manila. The dossier contained the Australian cop's home address and the names of his wife and two daughters. LeRoux said he thought about having Dave Smith stalk the man but decided against the idea because he might be discovered.

LeRoux did his own cyberstalking by gaining access to an Internet chat group where wives of American and other diplomats posted to Manila discussed their families and social plans. He didn't say what he planned to do with this information, but his casual tone implied that he saw nothing wrong with trolling the spouses and children of law enforcement officials and diplomats.

He got more leaked documents from his Filipino sources and realized that the DEA agents in Minneapolis were onto him. He knew he might need to ask Iran for asylum. Iranian citizenship would make him the ultimate untouchable.

To please his Iranian client, he set up an FTP server—a sort of private cloud—where his team would post plans and diagrams as they developed. Iranian scientists and engineers at the DIO could hop on the server and download whatever they liked.

He programmed the server so it wouldn't create a cybertrail. It didn't log when the Iranian scientists entered the system and downloaded documents. This was another security measure: if his server were ever compromised or seized, no one could determine what missile technology the Iranians had obtained through LeRoux.

In 2010, LeRoux delivered his first commissioned products to the

Iranians, two explosives formulas, both based on chemicals derived from unmonitored household chemicals.

The first formula used scrap silver jewelry and some chemical salts. The second was based on coffee sweetener that contained erythritol tetranitrate, ETN. It was related to pentaerythritol tetranitrate, PETN, a component of military plastic explosives.

The coffee sweetener formula was especially insidious. Police and border control agents in most countries were trained to recognize common ingredients in IEDs—ammonium nitrate fertilizer, for instance, pool chlorine, and brake fluid. They weren't told to look for a stash of coffee sweetener.

Yet this coffee sweetener bomb might pack a wallop. LeRoux calculated that it could reach a detonation velocity of 7,000 feet per second, compared to 8,000 feet per second for C4, the standard military explosive.

The product fulfilled the DIO request for a recipe that could be transmitted to terrorist cells a long way from Iran. A terror cell's bomb maker could buy the ingredients at a local grocery and whip together a serviceable IED, with no need for smuggling, bribing, ducking, and covering.

The DIO officials paid up as agreed—$5 million in gold bars, delivered in late 2010 to Dave Smith aboard LeRoux's yacht, the *Mou Man Tai,* in international waters off the coast of Indonesia. LeRoux never saw the gold bars. He said Smith stole them, which is why he had to terminate Smith. It was just business.

For LeRoux, the coffee sweetener explosives project was a one-off. It generated cash flow for salaries for his team while the more expansive and lucrative missile navigation project was under way. It was a practical short-term means to a long-term triumph, or so he hoped.

He acquired certain American-made electronic components and technologies on the DIO shopping list, in violation of U.S. and international sanctions. LeRoux told his Kentucky-based purchasing agent,

Jonathan Wall, to buy some items that could have either military or civilian uses and that were regulated for export as so-called "dual use" goods enforced by the U.S. Department of Commerce. Because sanctions banned the sales of dual-use items to Iran, LeRoux had Wall acquire them and ship them out of the United States. Wall's purchases included jet engines for testing; X-Plane flight simulator software; GPS chips; a HEATCON carbon fiber oven, presumably for nose cone construction; potassium perchlorate, nitric acid, and liquid mercury; a fume hood; vacuum pumping equipment; and electronic capacitors.

LeRoux told the DEA agents that he had no idea why the Iranians wanted those things. Nearly all could be used in weapons systems, in some cases, a nuclear weapons program, (though Iran had long denied that it was making nuclear weapons). For instance, the liquid mercury ordered by the Iranians could be destined for innocuous items such as thermometers. But it was also essential to a process for making lithium-6, an isotope that played a key role in producing tritium, an unstable form of hydrogen gas that could enhance a nuclear device's blast and cut its weight for missile flight.

Similarly, a vacuum pump had many applications, some innocent, but one was not: pumping the air out of a centrifuge used to enrich uranium for the core of a nuclear device.

Capacitors are electronic one-off switches. A simple capacitor makes the flash of light in a copying machine. Sophisticated high-speed electronic capacitors are used as, among other things, as nuclear triggers, to slam bits of fissile material together to assemble a critical mass at the core of a nuclear implosion bomb.

Cindric and Stouch pressed LeRoux to explain what exactly he did with these items and several others that might have applications in weapons of mass destruction. LeRoux claimed that he hadn't consciously helped the Iranians develop nuclear weapons—as far as he knew. What his clients did with goods he purchased for them was beyond his control. In law, the concept is called willful ignorance or willful blindness. For an arms merchant, it was just good business. Ask "why" and he might lose the sale.

Even as he was moving into major weapons systems, LeRoux took on a few more small jobs to get something he needed, or just to stretch. The more chessboards, the better. On a separate track, he was developing components for small, portable weapons of terror for a completely unrelated client, the New People's Army, an armed communist separatist group that occupied part of Batangas Province, about sixty miles south of Manila. The U.S. government had designated the NPA a Foreign Terrorist Organization.

Somewhere along the way, LeRoux had bought a boatyard in Batangas Province to service his own yachts and those of others moored in the area. It was his only legitimate business, though bent to a nefarious end, to maintain his smuggling fleet. In 2010, LeRoux got worried that the boatyard would come under attack by NPA guerrillas. He decided to get an insurance policy. He approached a man he knew only by a *nom de guerre*, the Accountant, and offered to pay the guerrillas for protection.

The Accountant asked for money and lethal goods—explosives, blasting caps, igniters, and cell phone detonators. LeRoux gave him some C4 military explosives from his inventory at Red, White and Blue Arms. He had no ready-made detonators, so he decided to make some himself. This wasn't a high-tech job, but—why not? Wasn't the customer always right? And besides, LeRoux was curious to see if he could do it, hands-on, on top of his desk. He found some instructions someplace, probably on the web, crafted two or three detonators from cell phones, and handed them over to the Accountant.

The detonators apparently worked, to LeRoux's delight. He said he got a call from the Accountant that a bridge in Batangas had been blown up. But the news wasn't all good. The Accountant added that this was a message that LeRoux wasn't paying enough for protection. He had to send the NPA 50,000 pesos a month, about $1,200, which he did, for about a year. Later, the Accountant told him that a Philex Mining company office had been blown up, more proof, LeRoux thought, that his detonators worked.

If LeRoux had wanted to affect political change through violence, he could have been the dark world's new Q, the gadget guy of the James Bond franchise. He could have crafted an array of clever electronics for the terror underground. He could have enlisted customers in twenty or thirty countries.

LeRoux didn't want to go into the business of retail violence, inflicting casualties one or two bombs at a time. This wasn't because he had grown a conscience, far from it, but because it was dull and repetitive, not innovative. People had been bombing bridges since the invention of black powder. Cell phone detonators were as old as cell phones themselves.

His purpose was to do something white-hot brilliant, like nothing before it, and very, very big. He wanted to be king of dystopia, beyond anyone's imagination. When he was onto a new project, he got a rush of energy that came out as a brainstorm, and the brainstorms took him in new directions that were exhilarating. He had to generate awe. Not fear, not admiration. Awe. That's what a god did, and he was getting closer.

While working on the missiles and detonators, he had a brainstorm, one of the best yet. Owning a boatyard on a remote, guerrilla-infested stretch of coastline wasn't a liability. It was an asset that would solve a problem he had been pondering.

His engineers were asking for certain rocket fuel chemicals for testing. These included potassium perchlorate, to be used as an oxidizer and an igniter for solid rocket engines; ammonium perchlorate, another oxidizer; HTPB, a binder; and powdered aluminum, an explosion intensifier. These items were available in Hong Kong but could not be imported into the Philippines. Border control authorities would be watching for them and might seize them.

One day, Reyes Peralta, the ice-dealing bartender at Sid's Pub, and Lim from the Chinese Triad happened to mention that the North Koreans had a surplus diesel-powered submarine for sale.

Just the ticket! LeRoux thought. If he had a submarine, he could evade the import restrictions. He could buy the chemicals in India or China, load them onto his sub, and drive it right up to his dock.

LeRoux negotiated for the sub. The talks broke down over the asking price of $5 million. LeRoux declared he would build his own sub. He promptly organized five of his engineers into a new "naval team" and told them to design and construct 10-meter and a 30-meter submarines. He started construction on a submarine dock at the Batangas boatyard.

Just before LeRoux was arrested, he learned that the design for the ten-meter submarine was done. It would have a range of two hundred miles, enough to smuggle the chemicals he needed from a larger vessel waiting in international waters. LeRoux estimated it would take just a month to build the sub.

"How do you know if it's going to work?" Cindric interjected. "Are you going to test it?"

"Me? Noooo." LeRoux laughed.

He had planned to order a couple of his Filipino employees to climb into it and submerge.

And if they stayed submerged?

"Ah, they're marginals," he grinned—throwaway people.

LeRoux said the Iran missile project was making progress, though it had some way to go. He said he had set up a wind tunnel and test facility in Batangas. In late 2011 or early 2012, his team set off a small test rocket, to study the effect of G-forces on the gyroscopes in a part of the missile navigation system under development.

A week later, the team spotted a small airplane flying over the site, checked out the tail number, and got some confirmation that the plane might belong to the government. LeRoux jumped to the conclusion that he was under surveillance, had been put onto a kill list—he wasn't sure whose—and was being stalked. He used his cell phone intercept platform to scan the airwaves for signals that would indicate that police or military units using mobile phones were approaching his clandestine lab.

Many people would have run for cover. Hardly a week passed without news of a U.S. drone strike that killed some alleged terrorist somewhere. But for all LeRoux's frenetic pace and impulsive ways, when he was deeply invested in a project, he didn't run.

He burrowed underground. He dug a bunker near the Batangas test facility. The engineering team used a U.S. Federal Aviation Administration simulator to run algorithms that approximated missile tests.

The simulations weren't very satisfying. LeRoux started planning a better, aboveground launch testing facility in a remote area of South Africa. He thought he would be safe there from spy drones and overflights. He set up a South African company called Maple Africa Tech and erected a website to make it look legitimate.

For a while, he thought of moving the research facility to an island he had bought, but before he could pack up the gear, it was overrun by militants from Abu Sayyaf, a small but vicious Muslim separatist group in the southern part of the Philippines.

"You have an *island*?" Cindric and Stouch exclaimed, almost in unison.

He smirked. Just the reaction he was after.

"Every villain needs his own island."

He laughed, but he was also dead serious. He *owned* an *island*, no joke. He had bought it to advance his career as a villain. A *supervillain!* He hadn't forgotten those Russian oligarchs on the Côte D'Azur, idling on their superyachts. Okay, they had big-ass boats, and they had their girls and guards and steel-gated villas. But they didn't have their own *islands*. The island was a message to the Russian oligarchs, the Colombian cartel leaders, the Chinese Triad leaders, and anybody else he envied. *Check out my island, bitches!*

The killings looked like another kind of message, to people who had bullied him when he was a fat nerdy kid. *You picked on me? Now go fuck yourself. I got you, and not only that, I got you even worse because I can snuff you out.*

"I think he has the opposite of White Knight syndrome," Cindric said. "He's not the guy who comes in on the white horse with the sword to save the world. He is going to come in on the black horse and he's going to conquer the world."

LeRoux was the Black Knight, and he was damn proud of it.

Hours into the flight, LeRoux's interview had filled dozens of pages of Carol Dillon's notebook. The agents were struggling to grasp the details of the missile guidance project. At one point, LeRoux got frustrated and turned to Brown, who was sitting quietly behind Cindric and Stouch and who looked as if he might have a technical bent. "Can you get a couple of guys who understand what I'm talking about?"

There was a twist to LeRoux's confession about Iran and missiles. Milione picked up on it first. Like they say, takes one to know one. As a master of the sting, Milione could spot another world-class seducer. LeRoux had guessed, correctly, that the agents would be transfixed by the yarn he was spinning out.

LeRoux *appeared* to be cooperating, and he was, up to a point, but he was also creating a massive distraction, like the flash-bang grenades SWAT teams used to cause bad guys' heads to swivel so the snipers could shoot them. It would take months for the agents to corroborate LeRoux's claims about his transactions with Iran, if it could be done at all, and to what end? Experts would have to be consulted. If he had violated U.S. export control and munitions laws and international sanctions, he could be prosecuted, but enforcing those statutes was the responsibility of an alphabet soup of agencies—FBI, ICE (Immigration and Customs Enforcement), and multiple branches of the departments of Treasury, State, Defense, Commerce, and Justice. An investigation of LeRoux's dealings with Iran would inevitably become a committee effort.

Milione hated multiagency collaborations. The technical term was "cluster fuck." If everybody had a voice in a decision, a decision never got made.

Milione wanted Cindric and Stouch to settle down and get back to a crime the DEA agents could prove on their own—a solid dope case. They had to elicit LeRoux's confession to trafficking in meth. They had to support the charge in the indictment—"conspiracy to distribute 100 kilograms of methamphetamine knowing and intending it to be imported to the United States." Everybody in the plane knew 100 percent of the facts in the meth case. A meth trafficking charge was simple, clean, and damning. If LeRoux lied about a single fact, they would know—and he would know they knew, and so on. If this was, as Milione suspected, a battle of wills, they needed to win it by preventing LeRoux from fabricating and delaying.

He had to admit trafficking in meth while they were in the air. Once on the ground, LeRoux could change his mind, invoke the Fifth Amendment, lawyer up, and shut up. They didn't need his confession to convict him on the meth charge, because they had more than enough evidence—the sample, the recordings—that he was trafficking. But if they got him into a plea agreement straightaway, they could keep debriefing him and pursue spin-off investigations, chasing his many intriguing leads into the arms and meth trades in Iran and North Korea. They could turn their energies to finding his co-conspirators. There were, apparently, quite a few, in unexpected corners of the world.

Milione conveyed all that in a terse conversation when the agents took a break and Cindric flopped down next to him.

"You're going to get a statement from him?" Milione said. It was not a question. "He's going to admit his guilt, right?"

"Yeah," Cindric said.

"Good. Good. Good," Milione said.

He spoke softly, but everybody knew that if he had to ask—tell, really—an agent twice, the guy or gal was off the team.

Cindric slipped into his seat and told Stouch, "We're getting back to meth."

Stouch nodded, relieved. He had worked cases involving weapons technology smuggling to Iran before. He knew they were gnarly and didn't always produce a guilty verdict. Milione was right. They had a slam-dunk meth case. Meth was poison. Juries totally got that.

Every time LeRoux tried to change the subject, Cindric and Stouch changed it back to meth. Meth, meth, meth. Finally, LeRoux confirmed what the undercover tapes showed, that he had tried to sell North Korean meth to Diego, knowing that the meth would be smuggled to New York. The confession was in the can.

Milione and Brown exchanged a look—*that's a wrap*. They nodded to Cindric and Stouch. Good work all around.

The agents weren't done, though. They wanted to squeeze LeRoux for more information about his most serious crimes before they landed. As the hours wore on, Milione, watching as Cindric and Stouch continued the interview, noticed that LeRoux had a tell. Whenever the agents raised names of people LeRoux was reported to have ordered killed, LeRoux said nothing, but he started coughing.

"Cottonmouth," Milione called it. He had seen it before. It was a signal of discomfort. It meant that LeRoux was lying or evading. Milione edged a little closer to LeRoux and said, solicitously, "You seem a little thirsty. Your mouth seems a little dry. Do you want some water?"

LeRoux nodded and accepted a bottle of water. He gave Milione a look that said, *You know. I know you know. You know I know you know . . .*

The DEA plane landed at the White Plains, New York, airport early on the morning of Thursday, September 27, 2012. Cindric, Stouch, and Brown drove LeRoux to federal court in Manhattan and presented him for his first appearance. He was fingerprinted, photographed, and booked. He met the defense lawyers the court had appointed to represent him until he could hire a legal team of his own.

Then they took him to the Brooklyn Bridge Marriott and rented a suite with tables and chairs. They allowed him to take a shower. They handed him his overnight bag, brought from the Monrovia hotel. He changed into fresh clothes, a blessing for everyone.

It was time for LeRoux to play queen for a day. That was courthouse slang for the negotiating process that led up to a plea bargain.

Nobody prosecuted in the U.S. District Court for the Southern District of New York got immunity in the traditional sense. Nobody, not even if he claimed he could deliver the devil himself.

Southern District prosecutors had moved to a process known as a "plea agreement." It gave judges and prosecutors leverage to persuade someone who participated in a crime to testify against others involved in the same conspiracy.

In the plea agreement, a criminal defendant agreed to admit guilt to certain crimes and to talk about his knowledge of other crimes, presumably more serious than those he committed. The prosecutors might agree to limit the charges to certain crimes and to recommend a sentence lower than the maximum.

However, the prosecutors honored the plea agreement only if they were convinced that the defendant had testified honestly and completely. If they found out that the defendant held back information or lied, they could void the plea agreement. Nor could they control what a federal judge would do at the time of sentencing. The judge could ignore their sentencing recommendations.

The plea agreement route was highly risky for the defendant. He had to tell all and was guaranteed nothing. Someone caught redhanded was looking at hard time. It was in his interest to make a plea agreement anyway, because the alternative was worse. That was LeRoux's situation.

The prosecutors didn't have to make a deal with LeRoux or anybody, ever. They did it when a criminal defendant had something important to say and his testimony was vital. If he offered testimony

and evidence they couldn't get any other way, they would consider—
consider—a deal.

How would they know what he could offer? He would make what
was formally called a "proffer," short for "offer of proof." This was in-
formally known as a "queen for a day" disclosure. With his defense lawyers present, the defendant spelled out what he knew about the crimes
under investigation, and other crimes the government didn't know
about. After days or weeks of debriefings, depending on the complexity
of the case, the prosecutors and defense lawyers agreed on a written
summary of the expected testimony, laid out in a "proffer letter."

The federal courthouse in Manhattan was a gossipy place, and
so were the usual lockups used for defendants-turned-witnesses. The
agents didn't know what they wanted to use LeRoux to do yet, but
whatever it turned out to be, they needed to preserve the element of
surprise.

LeRoux's court-appointed lawyers, Jonathan Marvinny and Sa-
brina Shroff, arrived at the suite and discussed the opportunities and
pitfalls of the plea-bargain process. They were joined by prosecutors
Michael Lockard and his boss Michael Farbiarz, co-chief of the Terrorism and International Narcotics Unit at the U.S. Attorney's Office for
the Southern District of New York.

LeRoux had been told that the prosecutors, not the agents, would
decide whether he could have a plea agreement. When they walked in,
he went into full CEO mode, gracious, not disdainful. A client, not an
employee. He put out his hand and said, "Hello, Attorney Lockard.
Paul LeRoux. How are you?"

"Hello, Mr. LeRoux," Lockard responded, just as formally. "I understand we're going to talk about some things today."

Lockard laid out the queen-for-a-day process. "This is your opportunity to tell your story without fear of it being used against you,"
Lockard said. "The only way it can be used against you is if you take
the stand and you lie."

However, he said, the prosecutors and investigators could use his disclosures during the proffer sessions as leads to open new avenues of investigation. If these investigations brought in new evidence against him—something that didn't come up in the initial proffer—he could be indicted on the new evidence.

All the more reason for LeRoux to tell the whole truth. That was not as simple for LeRoux as it sounded. He was a businessman who made his living negotiating deals. In business, negotiators never showed all their cards. Besides, he had no built-in moral compass. How would he even know when he was—or wasn't—what these American lawyers called *truthful*?

Still, he wanted to get on with it. "He was driving that train," Cindric said. He wanted to make a deal, fulfill the terms and the deal, and move on. He signed a statement saying that he understood what the prosecutors were saying. One of his attorneys initialed it, as did Lockard and Cindric. The statements and signatures would be collected every day, day after day after day until the prosecutors heard all the evidence he had to offer and decided whether they wanted to make a bargain with him.

LeRoux narrated the history of his early years, his young adulthood as a programmer and his turn to entrepreneurial ventures—founding RX Limited, escalating into arms and hard drugs, coming up with his idea for creating a global arms transshipment platform in Somalia. He explained how seemingly unconnected deals fit together like Legos. If he wanted to buy small arms made in China and meth from North Korea, he had to give the middlemen—the Chinese Triads in this case—something they wanted, which was cocaine. That meant he had to cut a deal with a Colombian cocaine manufacturer. If he wanted to sell arms to the Shan State Army, he needed to come up with Stinger missiles, which meant he had to get to know key people in the Serb mafia and find out what they wanted and couldn't get from other sources.

LeRoux bought and sold influence as easily as pills and guns. Surprisingly, for a man who rarely spent time with strangers, he had gotten to be adroit at using relationships and money to lubricate societal gears, or throw sand in them. As he later put it, "I pay bribes everywhere. . . . I paid bribes to facilitate criminal conduct wherever I worked in the world."

Sometimes he made payoffs just because he could. For instance, in 2007 or 2008, one of LeRoux's Israeli employees told him that an Israeli tech entrepreneur had massive legal problems and could use his help. Kobi Alexander, CEO of Comverse Technology, a billion-dollar enterprise headquartered on Long Island, had recently fled to Windhoek, Namibia, a few steps ahead of an indictment in the Eastern District of New York, which was in Brooklyn, and SEC complaint charging him with a $140 million stock manipulation. The U.S. Justice Department was putting pressure on the Namibian government to extradite Alexander to face the federal charges in Brooklyn. Since Alexander was a megarich business celebrity in Israel and son of the head of Israel's national oil company, LeRoux thought that Alexander's goodwill might be useful someday. Perhaps, now that he carried himself as the Dark Prince of the Cyber Realm, he considered it the thing to do for a fellow royal. He flew to South Africa with $750,000 in cash in a bag and gave the money to a fixer named Chris Miller, who drove to Namibia. What happened then? LeRoux didn't have firsthand knowledge. He said Miller assured him that the money had been funneled to someone in the office of the president of Namibia. From there, it was supposed to go to the judge hearing the Alexander extradition case. Miller died of heart disease soon after his journey. LeRoux never found out exactly what happened inside the Namibian bureaucracy. He was pleased to hear that the judge was replaced and that the extradition proceedings dragged on for years. Alexander and his family stayed on in Windhoek, living comfortably and donating generously to local charities until 2016, when he was able to negotiate a settlement with the U.S. government to pay $53 million in fines and forfeiture and to serve thirty months in prison. In March 2018, after serving about thirteen months, Alexander was transferred to the custody of Israel and quickly released for "good behavior." If he was grateful to LeRoux, he didn't show it. LeRoux said he was never reimbursed his $750,000.

As he told the story, LeRoux didn't seem particularly bitter. Corruption was just another routine business exercise, so, win some, lose some.

Just before his arrest, LeRoux had devoted most of his energy to his clandestine missile technology lab that was researching ways to reprogram cheap commercial GPS chips to improve Iran's missile navigation systems. The agents and prosecutors asked LeRoux to write a memo spelling out what exactly he sought to sell the Iranian Defense Industries Organization. The memo, which was highly technical, suggested that he had already given significant useful information to the DIO to put together a missile guidance system that was "NOT ITAR restricted," meaning, not hobbled by U.S. regulations meant to prevent rogue regimes such as Iran from harnessing GPS technology to navigate projectiles with precision.

The agents gave LeRoux his personal laptop so that he could demonstrate what he had done for Iran. He proudly showed off videos of small prototype missiles created by his engineering team.

He also demonstrated videos of a drone his engineers had made. He said it could be outfitted to deliver explosives.

What was striking about his demeanor was his lack of remorse. It didn't matter to him that his handiwork might eventually play a part in flattening the soaring skyscrapers of Tel Aviv and destroying the priceless world heritage that was Jerusalem. That awful prospect actually seemed to amuse him. He wasn't even motivated by practical considerations. In the worst-case scenario, unrelenting Iranian missile attacks on Israel could kill his business associates and employees and destroy his server array there. Yet he expressed no concern about these possible misfortunes to his company or his people. He loved the Iranian missile guidance project, and nothing and no one else. His only regret seemed to be that the project was still a work in progress and had not achieved its terrible ultimate goals. He took solace that the Iranians might still achieve precision-guided rockets and missiles by implementing the technology he and his team had shared with them. If they succeeded and acknowledged his contribution, he implied that he would be very happy indeed. He might even win a place in infamy, if the Iranians gave him proper credit. That was a long shot, though.

LeRoux talked to the lawyers and agents through the night and into Friday, September 28, 2012. He tried hard to seem upbeat and reasonable.

"He's very self-assured," Stouch said. "He can turn it on and turn it off. He can be very charming, depending on who's in the room."

LeRoux worked especially hard to win a smile from Lockard, who would decide whether he got the plea agreement he wanted. He was disappointed. Lockard gave him his standard poker face. Everybody got Lockard's civil nod that gave nothing away.

Lockard, Cindric observed, was "passionate about what he's doing, but if you want to see his pulse go up or down, forget it."

By the afternoon of Friday, September 28, LeRoux and the agents had been awake for close to sixty hours. LeRoux was still full of energy, but the agents had to pack it in or they'd start drooling. They adjourned the session, bid the lawyers good-bye, and checked LeRoux in at the Metropolitan Detention Center, a federal holding facility for pretrial detainees in Brooklyn.

They took the train to Washington, saw their families, did their laundry, hit the sack, and were back in Brooklyn Sunday night.

The next week's drill went like this. Every day, Cindric and Stouch drove LeRoux from the Brooklyn lockup to the Marriott for his meetings with the prosecutors and defense lawyers. Brown usually joined them, and sometimes other agents from the 960 Group stopped by. Cindric and Stouch decided to do the interviews at the Marriott rather than the courthouse because the hotel afforded more privacy. They didn't know whether LeRoux might have underworld connections in New York who might spot him walking in and out of the courthouse interview rooms.

The walk through the Marriott lobby and trip in the elevator was the trickiest part. The agents threw a jacket around LeRoux to hide his gray (not orange, gray) prisoner garb, but they forgot to consider what might be going on in his head until an elderly woman stepped into the elevator next to him. They gave each other a look and sideways nod that said—*watch out that he doesn't grab this poor lady and make a scene.* If he did, they'd have to knock the crap out of him in front of her, not to mention the hotel staff and everybody in the lobby. They could make him let her go, but it wouldn't be pretty.

Their fears were groundless, as it turned out. LeRoux was on his very best behavior. Not because he had repented but because he was creating a character, a genial, courteous Paul. This was an act for their benefit and for the benefit of Lockard and eventually, the judge who would sentence him. Fine. Polite Paul made life easier for everybody.

DEA technical specialists set up LeRoux's email and text channels so the agents could monitor the messages and respond as LeRoux. LeRoux supplied them with his passwords and encryption keys so they could read all his incoming and outgoing messages.

They maintained the fiction that LeRoux was carrying on business as usual from Brazil. No one on the dark side could know that he had gone missing and might be in custody and talking. During their sessions, they gave him his laptop and let him answer routine inquiries promptly. The DEA techs recorded his keystrokes so he couldn't pull any tricks. The agents arranged to pay his staff out of his bank accounts in Hong Kong, so everybody stayed happy and productive and nobody started looking for him.

He often exchanged messages with Cayanan. She believed that he had faked his kidnapping in Monrovia to freestyle through brothels someplace.

"How's Cindy the dragon lady?" Cindric would ask, though he knew, because he had cloned LeRoux's email.

"Aw, she's killing me this week," LeRoux would groan. But he seemed to enjoy her scolding. They had a spiky relationship. She wrote that she might go to law school. She'd be a fine lawyer, the agents agreed.

Great debriefings don't just happen. They depend on keeping the person content, relaxed, and talking. Stress makes people shut down. Cindric and Stouch spent hours thinking about how to develop rapport with this strange, perverse character. They knew that on an IQ test, he would leave them in the dust. It was incredible that the stars aligned so that they had found him and reeled him in. He had been in the wrong place at the wrong time, like a guy sitting in a Starbucks when a drunk driver plowed through the window. Now that they had him, they had to figure him out, because he was obviously spending every waking minute figuring them out. They had to stay a step ahead of his connivances. They had to become the friends he relied on to meet his every need. They had to think upside down and backward—and fake love for him, knowing that love wasn't a word in his lexicon.

"His confidant, brother, mother—whatever he wants you to be— you become," Cindric said. "We said, 'We care about you. We know it's a business decision for you.'"

They got him Diet Cokes and Big Macs. When he started to sag, nothing cheered him up like a big, sloppy burger with a glob of Special Sauce.

As they wrapped up the first weeks debrief, Cindric and Stouch concluded that things had gone smoothly—for LeRoux. He played the queen-for-a-day game adroitly. He seemed to think he was well on his way to securing his liberty. And he might be, except for one thing.

He didn't want to talk about the murders.

Paul Calder LeRoux in one frame of a video shot by undercover source "Jack" through a camera lens hidden on his body. *DEA source*

Dennis Gögel, German ex-sniper and one of LeRoux's paid killers, sent to Monrovia to kill two men in what was a DEA sting. *DEA source*

Slawomir Soborski, ex–Polish special operations soldier turned LeRoux mercenary, caught in a DEA trap in Estonia. *DEA source*

Joseph Manuel Hunter, LeRoux's chief enforcer, working out of Phuket, Thailand. *DEA source*

DEA agents Milione and "Taj" undercover on the street in Monrovia. Staged surveillance photo. *DEA source*

"Georges," the French pilot under contract to the DEA as undercover facilitator for the Monrovia sting. *DEA source*

Lou Milione with Donald Sutherland and Will Smith during filming of the 1993 film *Six Degrees of Separation*. *Lou Milione personal collection*

Lou Milione as "Agent Joey Casich" in staged surveillance to lure the LeRoux hit team to Monrovia. *DEA source*

Staged surveillance photo of "Taj" as Sammy the Libyan, in target package supplied to LeRoux hit team lured to Monrovia. *DEA source*

DEA agent Eric Stouch at Hunter's safe house in Phuket, Thailand.
DEA source

Top row left: LeRoux yacht *Texas Star II* moored in Fort Lauderdale. *DEA source* *Top row right:* One of LeRoux's yachts moored off the Thai coast. *DEA source*

Bottom row left: LeRoux's Westwind executive jet. *Bottom row right:* LeRoux's Antonov AN12 cargo plane parked at the Galkayo, Somalia,

Penthouse in the Salcedo Park Twin Towers similar to
where LeRoux lived and worked when in Manila.

Manila's Salcedo Park Twin Towers, site of LeRoux's
twin penthouses. *Jacqueline Hernandez*

Above left: 204 kilograms of cocaine found in the wreck (*below*) of the LeRoux yacht *JeReVe. Right:* Twenty kilograms of high-purity North Korean crystal meth smuggled to Phuket, Thailand, by LeRoux henchmen. *DEA source*

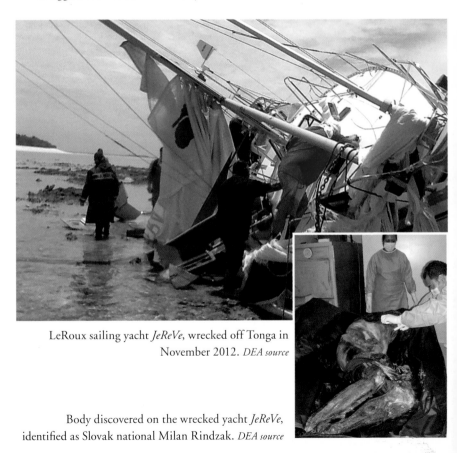

LeRoux sailing yacht *JeReVe*, wrecked off Tonga in November 2012. *DEA source*

Body discovered on the wrecked yacht *JeReVe*, identified as Slovak national Milan Rindzak. *DEA source*

"Jack," major DEA informant undercover within the LeRoux organization in Somalia. *DEA source* *Below*: LeRoux's plan for a forward base in arms trading and coca and opium poppy cultivation.

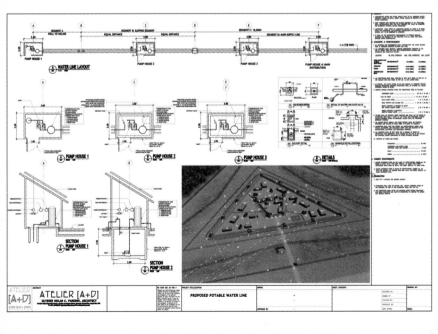

Above left: Paul LeRoux in a booking photo taken when he testified against confederates in federal court in Minneapolis.

Above right: Paul LeRoux in an undated airport surveillance photo. *DEA source*

Bottom left: Paul LeRoux's fake Zimbabwean passport in the name of "Bernard John Bowlins," one of his many aliases. *DEA source*

Bottom right: Cindy Cayanan, LeRoux's accountant and mother of two o

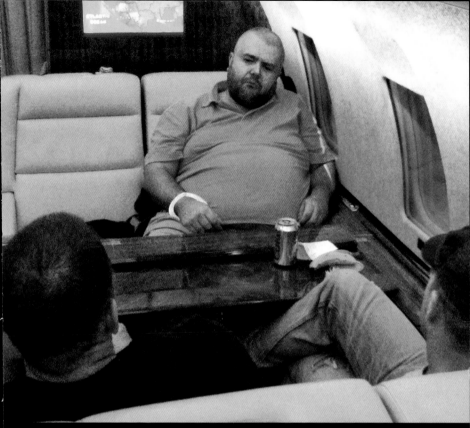

LeRoux under arrest with Cindric (*left*) and Stouch (*right*) en route to New York. *Derek Maltz personal collection*

Derek Maltz, DEA Special Operations Division chief, on the plane with LeRoux. *Derek Maltz personal collection*

Above left: Monzer al-Kassar, Syrian arms dealer active from Black September during *Achille Lauro* to Columbia's FARC, lands in New York, June 13, 2008, with 960 Group agent John Archer, left. *Louis Lanzano/ Associated Press* *Above right:* Legendary Russian arms merchant Bout caught in 960 Group trap, extradited to New York on November 16, 2010, flanked by DEA 960 Group agents Robert Zachariasiewicz (*left*), Wim Brown (*right*), and 960 Group leader Lou Milione, behind, in glasses. *DEA source* *Below left:* Joseph "Rambo" Hunter being led to federal court in New York by DEA agents Tom Cindric (*left*) and Eric Stouch (*right*). *Christopher Sadowski* *Below right:* LeRoux, after expulsion from Liberia, debarks from DEA plane in Westchester County, New York, between Cindric (*front*) and Stouch (*behind*). *Derek Maltz personal collection*

CHAPTER TWELVE

ALL THE PIECES ON THE CHESSBOARD

LEROUX WAS WILLING TO ADMIT USING HIS SECURITY TEAM TO HARASS and threaten people. But when it came to acknowledging that people had been killed on his orders, he dismissed the stories as "exaggerations."

He would say something like, "I just told so-and-so to deal with that problem."

Or, "I don't know anything about that. That was Dave Smith." Smith, of course, was conveniently deceased.

Or, "That was Hunter."

His tells appeared whenever the topic of murder came up. He got cottonmouth. His answers shortened to a few syllables. He tightened up, slumped, and fidgeted.

As the days wore on, the agents stopped all pretense of friendliness and bore down on him. They could not and would not use the techniques of military and CIA interrogators to force confessions—stress positions, sleep deprivation, loud music, or threats of physical harm. It was an article of faith among law enforcement—DEA, FBI, local police, and the rest—that brutal measures didn't get at the truth. People under extreme stress would say anything to get their interrogators off their backs.

They deployed other techniques. Stouch liked to use logic. He showed LeRoux how his answers made no sense. He wore LeRoux down like his old running shoes.

"What do you mean Monday? You just said Sunday. Which is it?" Or, "You said you were alone. Now you're saying you were with Smith." Or, "Okay, Marius shot first? Or the other guy? Make up your mind. You seem confused. Let's start again."

Cindric used emotion. When LeRoux denied something, Cindric roared, "Come on, Paul, you're full of shit. You've gotta give it up."

To which Stouch would respond, slightly more reasonably, "Come on, Paul, we're trying to help you here."

Brown didn't join in. Sometimes he uttered pleasantries to lighten the mood. Cindric and Stouch didn't want the mood lightened.

"You know, guys, he all but admitted it," Brown said at one point.

"Come on, Wim, gimme a fucking break," Cindric snorted.

Brown understood very well what they were up to. He disagreed. He thought the agents were being too rough on LeRoux. He didn't see the point of browbeating the man about crimes beyond the reach of American law. Whatever the truth was, he didn't think it all had to be on the table the first week.

Cindric and Stouch thought it did, because LeRoux was a manipulator. Engaging in a contest of wills with the agents was like oxygen to him. Whenever Brown suggested that the guys slow it down, Cindric snarled, "Fuck that! He knows he did these murders. He's gotta be honest. Fuck him until he gives it up. We know he ordered them. You can just tell. He's a fucking liar. He's not telling us everything. FUCK HIM."

"We need to establish our position, our control," Stouch said. "He's a smart guy, probably a lot smarter than us. But at this game, I think we're ahead of him. We can read him. We know it and we want him to know. You talk to enough bad guys and guys who have killed, and you just know."

It was going to be tricky for the prosecutors to make a plea agreement with a confessed murderer, but there was no way around it. DEA agents had a saying. *A deal with the devil is better than no deal at all.*

"Mike, I just hope you're prepared," Stouch told Lockard. "He killed them."

"Really? You think so?"

"Oh no, he did it. It's just whether he's going to admit to it now."

On the night of Friday, October 5, 2012, after the lawyers and Brown left, Cindric and Stouch escorted LeRoux back to the Brooklyn lockup. On the way, both agents got up in LeRoux's grill, so close he could tell their eyes were bloodshot, and they came at him from both sides, bad cop/bad cop, in stereo.

"Look, Paul, we're going to get to a point. . . . If you get a cooperation agreement, people are going to come in and talk about you," Stouch said. "And, if we find out you did things we don't know about, you're fucked."

"Paul, you're not telling us everything," Cindric said. "You're not telling us about the murders."

"We don't believe you," Stouch said. "You gotta have a come-to-Jesus moment with yourself because all that time we spent together is hanging out there now, because we're going to find out. You've survived by manipulating, but we see through you. You've got to make a decision."

"This is how this works," Cindric said. "You're going to take the weekend, and I want you to think about it. If you're not honest with us and we find out about these murders and you're in a cooperation agreement, you're FUCKED. No matter what good work you did, you're FUCKED because you're going to violate your cooperation agreement. I understand HOW hard it is. It's not easy to admit you did this, but if we're going to get to where we need to get to, you gotta do this."

LeRoux stared wordlessly as they handed him off to the guard who would take him back to his cell. The agents headed for Penn Station and took the train to Washington.

Come Monday morning, LeRoux sat down at the table and said, "Guys, I talked to my attorney."

They were looking at CEO Paul—controlled, in command, not at all defensive, but pragmatic. He had weighed the odds.

"I've had some time to think," he said, "and I'm ready to talk about a few things."

LeRoux launched the story of each homicidal episode, speaking briskly and remorselessly, as if ticking off his latest mergers and acquisitions.

He admitted to paying for the hit on Bruce Jones, the captain of his gun-running ship, the *Captain Ufuk*. He said Dave Smith had given the contract to John Nash, a sinister British character who skulked around Subic Bay and Angeles City. LeRoux said he also paid Nash to kill Jones's lawyer Joe Frank Zuñiga, officially missing since June 2012. Nash had showed LeRoux a cell phone photo of a plastic-wrapped corpse that he said was Zuñiga, or what was left of him. LeRoux said that Nash told him the body had been "disposed of." (In May 2014, the Philippine National Bureau of Investigation arrested Nash. NBI director Virgilio Mendez was quoted in the *Philippine Daily Inquirer* as saying that Nash had rammed an NBI vehicle while trying to escape and was considered an "alien who poses national security risk"; Mendez added that Nash was under investigation for links to an "international gunrunning syndicate operating in the Philippines" and that he had been found to be using the identity of a deceased person, from a California death certificate. NBI officials contacted by the author declined to say how the Nash investigation was resolved, citing their agency's "confidentiality rule.")

LeRoux described the deaths of Dave Smith and those in his circle in glowing detail. He spent a lot of time obsessing about Smith.

"If that son of a bitch came back as a poodle," LeRoux crowed, "I'd get out of the car right now and kick him square in the ass."

There was nothing funny about a murder, but at the thought of Smith, the gaunt, meth-head executioner, as a poodle, Cindric started laughing so hard he had to clutch his stomach—for a moment. As LeRoux continued to talk, laughter turned to horror. LeRoux was all vengeance and retribution. He had no love or loyalty to give, yet he had expected complete devotion.

The agents could see that LeRoux had thoroughly enjoyed killing Smith. The event had whetted his appetite for terminating more of his problem workers.

LeRoux said that in early 2011, when Hunter returned to Manila after spending Christmas with his family in Kentucky, LeRoux told him that Dave Smith had been executed for stealing, that he, Hunter, was the new chief enforcer, and that he was to organize "kill teams."

According to LeRoux's statements, incorporated in his plea agreement filed with the federal court, Hunter's first kill team was "Christophe"— Chris for short—DeMeyere, a Belgian veteran of the French Foreign Legion who had worked with LeRoux and Dave Smith since 2005, from the earliest days of the RX Limited, and an enormous dark-skinned New Zealander who called himself Mack Daddy or sometimes Daddy Mack. (The author's efforts to locate DeMeyere and Mack Daddy for comment have been unsuccessful.)

LeRoux gave Hunter names of people he wanted dead.

Nestor Del Rosario, LeRoux's lead emissary to Iran, was on the list. Sometime in 2011, according to his plea agreement, LeRoux came to believe Del Rosario had embezzled between $2 million and $4 million. LeRoux confronted him and told him that if he had stolen, he was a dead man. Del Rosario took that as his cue to disappear. The agents did some checking of their own and concluded that Del Rosario was probably Persian Cat, the tipster who had approached the Australian police and through them, the DEA.

Next on the list was Noemi Edillor, the thirty-one-year-old purchasing manager at Red, White and Blue Arms.

LeRoux said he sent a gofer named Tony to the Red, White and Blue Arms arsenal to find a Smith & Wesson .22 pistol with a silencer and deliver it to Hunter.

Edillor sometimes acted as a real estate agent, so Hunter alleged in his plea agreement that he told Demeyere and Mack Daddy to contact her about buying a property. On June 23, 2011, he alleged, they met her at the gate to her subdivision and shot her dead. The Manila newspaper reported that were no witnesses and no arrests. Hunter thought his kill team handled the job with finesse. "They shot her at the door," he boasted in a conversation captured by a Thai police/DEA bug. "Left her there, but it was raining that day so no, there was no people out and they did it perfect, no problems."

As commandos and professional killers knew, killing someone in the rain was good tradecraft, because the storm muffled the sounds of cars, footsteps, screams, the clicks of silencers and gunshots.

But the job wasn't perfect, as LeRoux wasted no time pointing out. "I wasn't happy," he grumbled later. "it was only by luck that there had been no witnesses. . . . Essentially, the kill team . . . had just got lucky because on that day it was raining." He told Hunter he was not going to pay DeMeyere and Mack Daddy their bonuses until he saw proof that Edillor was actually dead.

Hunter was furious. What did LeRoux know about killing? The only person he ever personally shot, as far as Hunter knew, was already a corpse. Hunter sent LeRoux a blistering email with a link to an online news report about the Edillor murder. It quoted her husband as saying that he personally found her bloodied body on the street near the gate.

"There is your fucking proof," Hunter wrote in an email discovered by the DEA agents after Hunter's arrest. "Have my guys money tomorrow. They're running around doing your crazy shit and you insult them. Have everyone's money tomorrow . . . both their pay and bonus money. No more bullshit."

Hunter's uncharacteristically sharp rebuke must have startled LeRoux, because he paid up, shut up, and raised Hunter's salary from $12,000 to $15,000 a month. And then he added more names to the kill list.

Two of the names were Dave Smith's widow and their son. LeRoux was still stewing about Dave Smith's treachery. Just knowing that Smith died horribly wasn't enough. LeRoux wanted his family wiped out, too. In one of his few displays of compassion, Hunter told DeMeyere not to do it.

The next names on the kill list were of LeRoux employees and contractors. DeMeyere and Mack Daddy refused. They were done with LeRoux. DeMeyere said he was going home to Belgium, Mack Daddy back to New Zealand.

LeRoux didn't want to talk about what happened next. Over many hours of prodding and prompting, he admitted that Hunter put together a new kill team and started going down the list. He knew that Hunter's second kill team killed Catherine Lee, a real estate agent who had helped LeRoux find properties to buy and who, LeRoux believed, had skimmed during the deals. LeRoux claimed he couldn't remember the names of the hit men who carried out the Lee murder.

The agents checked the Manila newspapers. Sure enough, the body of Catherine Lee had been found on a trash heap in the Manila sweat shop district, early on the morning of February 13, 2012. There were a few promising bits of evidence. Manila was a high-crime city, but this was no robbery. A gold ring was on the dead woman's hand, a silver bracelet on her wrist, and a Nokia C3 cell phone in her purse.

There was something else, which the agents learned from a local police report. She had been shot at close range under one eye, then under the other. There was no way her manner of death could be taken as an accident or a case of mistaken identity. Two shots carefully placed under two eyes at close range meant she knew and trusted her killer. The killer got very, very close and then struck without warning. It amounted to a statement that said, to any LeRoux associates who were thinking about cheating him, "This is what you get if you mess with LeRoux. You'll wind up as a corpse with no eyes, on a pile of garbage."

Once he started talking about killing, LeRoux couldn't hide his pleasure in his grisly memories. His face became animated and his eyes lit up. He was clearly proud of what he had done, and he wasn't sorry.

"There were going to be more killings," Stouch told Cindric. "He was just getting started. No question, there were going to be more. He's like, 'I'm smarter than everybody. I can do this and get away with it. I kinda *like* it.'"

The debriefings continued at the Marriott for another week, then moved to an interview room in the federal courthouse on Pearl Street. U.S. marshals escorted him into the federal courthouse cuffed. They put him into a holding cell and uncuffed him. From there, one of the agents immediately cuffed him and walked him sixty feet to the interview room, a small, windowless room with a conference table and chairs from the 1960s or '70s; dingy, white walls; and light, brownish-greenish carpet ripped in the corners.

Once they were sure he was cooperating, Cindric and Stouch let LeRoux become CEO Paul. They always seated him at the head of the conference table and let him speak expansively. They asked his opinion and treated him like a consultant. These were psychological tricks, and he probably knew that on some level, but, as a mental survival mechanism, he allowed himself to forget for a few hours a day that somebody else was pulling the strings and he was returning to a cell at the end of each day.

One day, Keller from the 960 Group happened to walk into the witness room while all this was going on. Keller had not forgotten the night before the arrest, monitoring the bug in LeRoux's hotel suite as LeRoux and Cayanan flung each other around. That was something Keller couldn't unhear.

LeRoux glanced sideways and said haughtily, as if he were a CEO, rudely interrupted by some minion, "I don't know if you know this, but me and the guys are working on a project."

Keller shot Cindric a WTF look.

"Aww go with it," Cindric whispered. "If he wants to think he's in charge, fine."

Keller complied, but he was glad to get out of there.

LeRoux warmed to agents, most of all Cindric, who could make him laugh. Cindric and Stouch didn't think he had ever had a relationship with another adult man, but he was such a shape-shifter, it was hard to say which Paul was genuine. Sometimes they caught a glimpse of Orphan Paul, lonely genius abandoned by his parents. Occasionally they heard that with his lawyers, he had broken down and cried that his parents—they didn't know whether he meant the adoptive parents or the biological ones—had betrayed him.

They resisted the urge to pity him. This was a form of street theater and he was a pro.

As Cindric and Stouch listened to LeRoux unpack his many schemes, they imagined all the ways they might use his position in the underworld to go deeper, darker, faster.

"Paul can get you to think that anything is possible," Cindric said. "The world is your oyster. He really believes that, too."

Even in the lockup, LeRoux still believed in magic, and he could still cast a spell over others.

Just for fun, Cindric and Stouch went with it. They kicked around ideas for using LeRoux as their agent of penetration into the chains of command in Iran and North Korea. North Koreans had been making meth for years to earn hard currency, but nobody had gotten deep into the inner workings of the Pyongyang pipeline. Nobody had proved that the regime itself used meth to finance its military activities, especially its nuclear program. All the circumstantial evidence suggested that this was possible, even likely, but as Cindric's mantra went, "There's what you believe, what you know, and what you can prove."

LeRoux told the agents he was willing to go to North Korea, or, failing that, to arrange a meeting in a third country, and to wear a wire to collect proof. Who authorized meth manufacturing? Who supervised it? Who collected the money? What bank accounts and front companies were being used? And much more.

Cindric and Stouch also thought sending LeRoux to Iran. He said he had a standing invitation to visit the DIO there. They decided to have him pursue the connection. On October 23, 2012, they sent a letter on Red, White and Blue Arms stationery over his signature, addressed to the Marketing Department, Defense Industry Organization, Tehran. The letter asked for the price of 250 units of 5.56 cartridges, standard NATO rounds. He requested a DIO catalogue.

The tiny prospective order was a probe, and it worked. On January 29, 2013, a fax landed in LeRoux's Manila office, which the DEA agents were monitoring. It was an invitation and an itinerary inviting LeRoux or his representatives to visit Iran. "Please inform us your view point that which field you like to cooperate with our organization," it said. It was signed by Morteza Farasatpour, the DIO's deputy managing director for commerce. (In 2017, Farasatpour would be blacklisted by the U.S. Treasury Department for aiding Syria's chemical weapons program.)

The agents wanted to know much more about the Iranian war machine. They thought that LeRoux could open a new window into the DIO, its missile development, its activities in Syria and Lebanon, and the Islamic Revolutionary Guards Corps, whose Quds Force provided training, supplies, and money to militants and terrorists in many countries. For instance, the agents wanted to know what happened to the coffee sweetener explosives formula LeRoux invented for the DIO. And they hoped to find out how Iranian engineers had made use of the missile navigation technology LeRoux's R&D team had shared through the FTP server.

Their plans foundered on one reality—to use LeRoux's talents, they'd have to put him out in the wild—set him free with a wire and a couple of cell phones.

Cindric put the idea to Brown. "We want to get him out," he said. "Paul is a game changer as an informant. He's got balls the size of grapefruits."

Brown grinned. He belly-laughed. He slapped his knee. That was the best one he'd heard in months.

The agents, he said, were bewitched and beguiled. What DEA agent didn't want to be Indiana Jones—plunging into forbidden lands, taking extreme risks, grabbing glittering prizes? Brown sure as hell did, and he knew that Cindric and Stouch did, too. So did everybody else in the 960 Group. If they didn't want that life, they wouldn't be in the group in the first place.

"Look, I'm with you guys, but it's not going to happen," Brown said. Still teary with laughter, he walked the agents around to Milione's office in the corner of the second floor.

"Tom and Eric have a proposal for you."

"We want LeRoux out," Cindric said.

"Are you fucking kidding me?" Milione said. It wasn't a question. He caught Brown's eye. Now they were both bent over laughing. Cindric and Stouch were aggressive, for sure, and immensely entertaining.

"Well, this is what we see, Lou," Stouch said, putting on his serious face. "You can't get to the devil using priests and nuns. If you want to get the next big bad guy, who do you go to? A Paul LeRoux."

Milione regained his composure. "It's not gonna happen, guys, but do you understand why?"

He went over the risks, which were monumental. They knew, they knew. But they pushed anyway. As they saw things, an agent's job was to push the edge, and a supervisor's job was to say, not so fast. Everybody in the room was earning his pay.

Milione sent them back to their beige cubicles with a kindly smile that they interpreted to mean that he also felt the pull of LeRoux's spell and he'd do the same thing if he were an agent.

But he was the ASAC, assistant special agent in charge, and his answer was clearly *Not only no, but hell no.*

Once away from LeRoux's reality distortion field, Cindric and

Stouch had to admit that Milione was right. They would never sleep; never have a moment's peace, if LeRoux were in the wild.

There was another reason they couldn't stage long-running penetrations of Iran and North Korea. Close to Christmas 2012, LeRoux had given them a Holy Shit revelation. He started talking about Rambo.

Rambo?

"Yeah, he calls himself Rambo," LeRoux said. "He's one of my security guys. Joseph Hunter. An American. He took over after Dave Smith."

LeRoux described Hunter as a retired American soldier who had executed a couple of people on LeRoux's orders and was hiring more former military men for more contract murders.

Jack had mentioned that he was terrified of Hunter because he was LeRoux's killing machine and had briefly stalked Jack on orders from LeRoux. But the agents had not realized the breadth and depth of Hunter's involvement in assassinations until LeRoux spelled it out.

Once that happened, Cindric and Stouch reset their priorities. Here was someone using the soldierly skills his nation had taught him, at the expense of the American taxpayers, to expand the reach of a transnational organized crime network and to kill people.

They had to find and stop Hunter. LeRoux said that Hunter still held at least six or eight unfulfilled murder contracts, and nobody knew how many freelance gigs he was taking on. But they hated to give up on the other threads of the LeRoux empire, especially LeRoux's North Korean meth operation.

They handed LeRoux off to one of the U.S. marshals, who would take him back to the lockup in Brooklyn. They took the subway back to Brooklyn and found a dim bar near their hotel.

"Shit, what are we going to do with all this?" Stouch said.

Cindric thought. And thought. Then he had an epiphany. He set down his beer.

"Let's put all the pieces on the same chessboard."

"I like it," Stouch said. "How?"

"I don't know but we'll figure it out."

They ping-ponged ideas for a scenario they could orchestrate. It was a lot like writing a play, only the stakes were higher.

"We'll make Hunter put together a security team," Stouch said.

"I fucking like that," Cindric said.

"We can get resumes."

"We'll ask for people who speak English and can move around in Europe. We can draw the security team out and use that to our benefit."

"That's good."

"They could do the meetings with the North Korean meth guys."

"The security team could be protecting our Colombians and the North Koreans."

"Okay, here's how it works," Cindric said. "Hunter becomes security for a Colombian organization."

"They're getting NoKo meth from Lim and Kelly," Stouch said. Lim was Lim Ye Tiong Tan, the Chinese Triad rep in Manila; Kelly was Kelly Reyes Peralta, the bartender and meth distributor at LeRoux's bar, Sid's Pub. "Stammers and Shackels—they just won't fucking go away," Cindric said. "We're going to have to do them on general principle."

Stammers and Shackels were living in Thailand at the time, moving cocaine from there to Australia. Like LeRoux, they had a brainstorm a minute. The problem was, many of their ideas were bad.

Before LeRoux was arrested, they set up a meth lab in Shackels's apartment in Manila. They hadn't mastered the chemistry, so no meth was produced. Then they made a deal with a Cambodian general to set up a meth lab inside his country. The plan foundered when they discovered they didn't have the right chemicals to make the meth solution crystallize properly.

LeRoux had a couple of false starts of his own, when he tried to move into cocaine, which in East Asia and Japan was an exotic and desirable commodity that commanded much higher prices than meth, which was commonplace. Between 2010 and 2012, he bought twenty to thirty kilograms of cocaine from a former Philippine National Bureau of Investigation official. The source said that the Philippine Drug Enforcement Agency had recovered the drugs from a larger shipment of cocaine lost at sea and washed up in the Cimarron Islands. The cocaine turned out to be too salt-damaged to sell, and some of it was fake.

Then he arranged through an Israeli gangster to buy fifty kilograms of cocaine from the Ecuadorean branch of a multinational trafficking organization headed by Daniel "El Loco" Barrera, a ruthless Colombian trafficker who aspired to succeed Pablo Escobar and was known as "the last of the great kingpins." Whatever hopes LeRoux harbored of cementing a long-term business relationship with Barrera foundered in mid-September 2012, when he was arrested in Venezuela and deported to Colombia. He would be extradited to the United States to face charges of trafficking in tons of cocaine and laundering tens of millions of dollars; he would be convicted and sentenced to 35 years in prison. LeRoux sent a yacht to Ecuador to collect the load of cocaine consigned by Barrera. After the cocaine was on board, the yacht set sail, but its mast broke in a storm. It had to return to port in Ecuador to make repairs. The cocaine was probably seized—LeRoux didn't know for sure.

In early 2012, Stammers and Shackels put together a deal with some Serb mafia characters to buy 150 kilograms of Peruvian cocaine, intending to smuggle it to the Philippines and sell it to Lim for his Chinese Triad group.

LeRoux dispatched his yacht the *JeReVe* to Peru to pick up the cocaine. His plan was to have it transferred on the high seas to a larger vessel that could manage the perilous voyage across the Pacific to the Philippines. But just as the scheme was coming together, LeRoux got arrested and was not in a position to provide a suitable smuggling craft.

Stammers, Shackels, and the Serbs, unaware that LeRoux had been locked up and had switched sides, decided to make do with the *JeReVe*. The yacht, crewed by central Europeans, set sail from Peru, heading west toward the other side of the Pacific Rim. The yacht encountered treacherous waters in the South Seas and wrecked. In November 2012, authorities in Tonga found it on a reef at Luatafito Atoll in northern Tonga. Captain Ivan Vaclavik was missing, and there was a desiccated corpse in the hold, along with 204 kilos of cocaine—LeRoux's 150 kilograms plus another 54 kilos the Serb mafia guys had gotten on their own. According to Australian and regional news reports, the Australian police identified the dead man through a passport found on the wrecked yacht and DNA samples as Milan Rindzak, a Slovak, the yacht's first mate.

Stammers and Shackels were not discouraged. They filled up Le-Roux's inbox with proposals for elaborate trafficking schemes involving both drugs and guns. Cindric and Stouch read all their ideas. Some were cockeyed, but some would work. They had to be taken down, along with Hunter and the mercenaries.

"We can use them for transportation," Stouch said.

"Yeah, maybe they can be the ones who move it to the U.S."

They diagrammed the play on bar napkins. The next day, when they went to the courthouse, they laid it out for the prosecutors. Lockard and his colleague Rachel Kovner looked at them with eyes that Cindric thought said, *You are fucking crazy.*

"Okay, well, after all this is over," Cindric told Stouch, "we're going to be remembered like Babe Ruth pointing at the wall."

Over the next few weeks, they refined and elaborated the scenario, seeking advice from Milione and Brown whenever they hit a pothole. The play would go like this:

Diego and his partner Geraldo, also a Colombian-American and an informant, would hire Hunter and his mercenary team to kill a DEA agent and his informant. Hunter would be told that the pair was interfering with drug deals cooked up by LeRoux and his Colombian cartel partners. Killing an American official, anywhere in the world, to interfere with the performance of his official duties was a federal felony punishable by death or up to life in prison. The law extended to foreign nationals who helped American officials—informants, translators, guides, and the like.

LeRoux said that Hunter and his mercenaries hung out in Phuket, the Thai beach resort. They were using a safe house he had recently bought there.

Thailand was an excellent place for the DEA to arrange a take-down. The DEA had cultivated the Thai counternarcotics police unit since the Vietnam War. Many Thai cops had been exchange students at the DEA Academy in Quantico, Virginia. DEA agents regularly partnered with the Thai cops and gave them equipment. The Thai cops could help them wire the safe house and other meeting places with video and sound.

The agents decided they would have LeRoux invite the meth ring to Phuket to pick up product and collect payment. The Thai cops could arrest them after Hunter and his mercenaries were in custody.

For safety's sake, they would need to split up the mercenaries. That's where Liberia came in. They could tell Hunter to send a hit team to Monrovia to carry out the contract assassination. They could rely on Fombah Sirleaf to make the arrests.

To make the play realistic, Cindric and Stouch would need to phony up a target package that LeRoux would pass to Hunter. They'd need photos of the fictional DEA agent and informant.

They invented a narrative, that the informant would be a Libyan boat captain. He would be Westernized, like many worldly young Mediterranean guys. His name would be Zaman—Sammy to his American friends.

"Taj," both agents said in unison. "He'll do it."

Taj arrived at the 960 Group in March 2012. He was deep into an investigation that he hoped would result in the indictment and arrest of two of the biggest heroin kingpins in Afghanistan, quite possibly the world. Making cases against them would take him a while.

"Sure," he said. He would be one of Rambo's targets. He had plenty of time to pose for a few snapshots.

Who would play the other target, the fictional DEA agent they named Casich?

"I'll do it," Milione said.

"Really?" Stouch said.

"Yeah."

"All right." Nobody was going to tell the boss to stay back at his desk.

"I wasn't trying to be a hero," Milione said afterward. "I knew we couldn't pick an image from the Internet. I wanted to keep it in-house. I thought it was cleaner and easier. We didn't want to use a random identity." The gunmen might try to match a stock photo to a real person.

Besides, he said, he was the only guy in on the team who had the time to play the role of Casich because it involved flying to Monrovia and posing for snapshots with Taj.

That part wasn't exactly true. As the ASAC, Milione had more to do than anybody else in the 960 Group. He was in charge of four groups of aggressive DEA agents. The fact was, if something went wrong, he didn't want anybody else to be on the firing line. He was very confident he could take care of himself. Also, he was proud of the work Fombah Sirleaf was doing to professionalize the Liberian National Security Agency and he wanted to get to Monrovia to urge him on.

Cindric and Stouch briefed LeRoux on the idea. He loved it. Other crime barons would balk at dismantling their hard-won empires, but to LeRoux, building and demolition were the same. Life was like chess. There were plenty of boards and chess pieces. He could get other hit men. He could get other traffickers. Money? He'd have to give up a pile of it, but he had accounts the agents would never find, and he could raise more money when he was released, and maybe even while he was in prison. The Internet was the gift that kept on giving. He lived for two things—a new project and power over others. This plan offered him both.

Day after day, sitting in a bare interview room in the courthouse, LeRoux took his place at the head of the table, playing chairman of the board. He held his head high, squared his prison-gray-clad shoulders, and presided courteously, a master of the universe on his best behavior.

Every session began the same way. The agents handed him his computer and watched as he tapped emails to Hunter and other employees they had targeted for arrest. He made sure that his people in Manila, Phuket, Jerusalem, and Rio were paid, supplies ordered, and equipment kept in good working order. In all, he authorized expenditures of more than $1 million, principally for salaries. He handed off his yachts to the DEA agents, to use in other stings. (In April 2013, Milione and his men would board one of them and lure a former navy chief of Guinea-Bissau, former rear admiral Jose Americo Bubo Na Tchuto, into international waters so that they could arrest him for facilitating the transshipment of Colombian cocaine through West Africa to the United States. He pleaded guilty and cooperated with the agents to identify other African officials selling access to Colombian traffickers.)

It was easy to see why LeRoux's weight had ballooned when he moved to Europe and became a computer programmer. Faced with a keyboard and monitor, he entered a trancelike state geeks call zombie mode. He could spend all day banging on his laptop without moving.

Lunch came from a kiosk inside the courthouse. LeRoux was a man of simple and inflexible tastes. For breakfast every day, he had a plain bagel with plain cream cheese and a Diet Coke.

Lunch was always a chicken quesadilla, hold the chicken, plus fries and a Diet Coke.

"Why don't you like chicken?" Cindric asked.

"Ah. It's okay, Tom. But I like the other stuff better."

He liked salsa, lettuce, pico de gallo, and cheese. He could have had those *and* chicken. He didn't have to choose. He didn't bother to explain.

He drank Diet Coke or Coke Zero. Rarely, a coffee. Very rarely, a Sprite.

The lunch lady knew his order by heart. The minute she saw Cindric or Stouch, she shouted, "Chicken quesadilla no chicken Diet Coke!" and she started slapping pico de gallo into a tortilla.

New York pizza was, as everyone in the galaxy knew, the best in the world, so one day, Cindric and Stouch tried to reward LeRoux with a slice of the real thing. He barely touched it.

"I like Domino's better," he grumbled.

On another day, Cindric walked to a Shake Shack for a fancy burger dripping with trimmings.

"Eh," LeRoux frowned, "I'd rather have a Big Mac."

Why?

"I like the Special Sauce."

They probed to find out if LeRoux was making friends inside the lockup. "When you're in jail, do you talk to the other guys?" Stouch wondered.

LeRoux said he did. He looked forward to meeting the white-collar defendants. He liked to play chess, and many of them knew the game. Especially the black-hat hackers. Of course, he could beat them.

Most of the guys, though, were street criminals. They bored him. LeRoux expressed a low opinion of nearly all of the other prisoners, the American educational system, and most of all, the Kardashians. The prison TV was constantly tuned to the Kardashians' reality show. He could not figure out why. Why weren't the inmates trying to learn something to better themselves?

When they talked, it was about sex. He got a kick out of impressing them.

"I've got the most baby mammas of anybody in the jail," he beamed. "I've got seven."

Seven women. And how many children?

Maybe eleven? They counted them off. There were the four by Lillian, two by Cindy. Then, five more that he knew of by various other women. He said he could be off by a couple.

"What the fuck are you doing?" Cindric said. "One woman is enough for any man."

"Ah, I'm not married to Cindy, but she's kinda like my wife."

"What about all the other women?"

"Ah, I don't know if all the kids are mine."

One day, he received an email from a woman in the Philippines. A photo of an infant was attached. The agents intercepted the email as usual and showed it to him.

"Paul, you're proud father to another baby," Stouch said.

LeRoux shook his head. "I gotta start getting these kids DNA-tested," he said. "They're getting uglier and uglier."

Cindric, who had a wife and two daughters he adored, must have looked aghast, because LeRoux said quickly, "Tom, you don't realize it's not normal until you're not there. In Asia, it's normal."

"It's *not* normal for girls to wear numbers like cattle," Cindric said. "It's *not* normal to buy human beings."

"In Asia, it's normal." LeRoux shrugged.

The agents left these sessions with splitting headaches, yearning for a beer and a shower. Keeping a step ahead of LeRoux and stroking his gigantic ego for six or eight hours a day was exhausting. It was like trying to train a wolf. He might look like a German shepherd, all furry and playful, but get distracted or stare at him too hard and you could lose a hand.

Still, there was something about LeRoux that inspired the agents to new fantasies of badass.

"How about this?" Cindric said. When they enticed Hunter's mercenaries to Monrovia, they wouldn't have the cops pick them off when they walked off the plane. That was the usual MO, since the targets to be arrested would be traveling unarmed.

Instead, the mercenaries would go to their hotel. The agents would plant Georges, the French pilot, inside Hunter's team, posing as Le-Roux's man on the ground in Africa. Georges would escort them to a shooting range and hand out the banned Heckler & Koch MP7 sub-machine guns they coveted. Sirleaf's men, in plain clothes, would be there to take videos of the men blasting away at human-shaped targets. If the jury had any doubts about the mercenaries' destructive potential, the horrifying images would resolve them.

"I like it," Stouch said.

"No, we can't do that," Milione said firmly.

"Why not?" Cindric protested. "We can control them."

"NO! We're not putting weapons in their hands."

"You guys have lost your fucking marbles," Brown said.

"You're going to put FUCKING WEAPONS in their HANDS?" Maltz, the SOD chief, roared. "I like it! But HAVE YOU GUYS LOST YOUR MINDS?"

Okay, Cindric said gloomily, no guns.

Plan B was vanilla: lure the four mercenaries to Monrovia, get the Liberian cops to arrest them coming off the plane. Have the Thai police arrest Hunter and the meth ring in Phuket.

Milione okayed the vanilla plan. Fewer moving parts, less chance of a screwup.

As winter gave way to spring, Cindric and Stouch could no longer sit with LeRoux every day, as he tapped out orders to Hunter in Phuket, the RX Limited crew in Manila and Jerusalem, and Stammers and Shackels wherever they were. Other agents from the 960 Group divided up the watch. Two of the younger agents—Matt Keller and Taj—often pulled LeRoux-minding duty.

Keller was immune to LeRoux's force field. "He's a scary man,"

Keller said. "He's at minimum a sociopath and probably a psychopath." Keller was an abstract thinker who excelled at the thirty-thousand-foot view. He saw no need to cultivate this fat weirdo.

Taj, on the other hand, relished his days with LeRoux. They were hard work-outs. As an undercover specialist, he was always dirt-level—eyeball to eyeball with someone who would enjoy killing him. His life depended on his ability to read his adversary's mind. He had to customize every character he invented to be the person his target desperately wanted to please.

LeRoux was the finest example of the deviant brain Taj had ever come across. As LeRoux wrote emails to his employees, Taj imagined the undercover scenarios he would run if LeRoux were his target. How would he crack him? How would he get into his head? Taj wanted to climb inside LeRoux's mind and stay there for a while, like a kid playing with the best model train set or newest computer game on the market.

"I'd love to spend two weeks with him so he could openly talk to me," Taj said. "Imagine how much we can learn from him. Imagine talking to him, understanding his fundamental thought process, and how he thinks about people."

Taj was an instinctive actor who could bend himself into whatever form somebody else needed to see—dealer, shooter, muscle guy, schemer, student, immigrant, diplomat, and so on. He realized early on that his ability to play roles convincingly was the only thing keeping him alive. All that stood between him and death were his mind and instincts. On the street, there was no such thing as probable cause. No second chances. Drug dealers were unscrupulous. What was to prevent a bad guy from shooting him and robbing him of his $100,000?

"Nothing," said his partner and training agent, Gina Giachetti. "Nothing but you."

The lesson Taj learned was this. When you were undercover, you were on your own. Your backup team was there to cover top management's butts. It would be six or eight seconds away, behind cars, trucks, and passersby. If a guy on the other side of the deal decided to take you out, he could, in two seconds. Survival was all about how fast you could think on your feet and whether you could eliminate issues and keep things calm. If things started going bad, you'd better be quick pulling your gun. Every time he went out on an undercover gig, Taj stuck his baby Glock 27 in the waistband of his jeans. It wasn't much for distance, but at close range, it might stop somebody.

He became adept at slipping into the skins of a mangy assortment of dirtbags—Crips and Bloods; Norteños, who were Chicanos from Northern California and spent most of their time menacing *Sureños;* Chicanos from Los Angeles; and Indian Sikh truckers who smuggled cocaine and meth to Canada in their eighteen-wheelers and smuggled ecstasy and BC bud, the expensive, potent strain of marijuana produced in southern British Columbia. When he screwed up, he covered by going all *chingón.* The word meant many things, but two meanings were big fucker and super badass. When his targets doubted him, he yelled at them that they were probably narcs and he was done with them. They inevitably apologized. Fooling them wasn't about languages or cultural authenticity. All he needed was a little superficial knowledge and brass balls.

Taj used his hours with LeRoux to practice on someone so different from anyone he had ever met. He heard that the prisoner didn't like to talk to other humans and took that as a challenge.

"I'm going to be spending today and possibly the following day with you," he told LeRoux at their first session. "If you want to chat and take a break, I'm here."

"Great, good meeting you," LeRoux said brusquely. "My computer, please."

Taj handed him his laptop. LeRoux sat down and started communicating with his men in the Philippines and Thailand.

During the morning, Taj asked if he wanted a drink.

"Yes, I'll take a Sprite." Curt, again.

Taj fetched the Sprite.

"What do you want for lunch?"

"Chicken quesadilla, no chicken."

Taj knew that. He fetched it. LeRoux ate without speaking.

But after lunch, LeRoux began to warm to the younger man. He took a couple of breaks to tell Taj stories about the Philippines, Cindy, how the Abu Sayyaf terrorists stole his island, and some of his dealings with the Chinese Triad and the North Koreans.

"How do you feel being in prison?" Taj asked.

"Well, you know, I'm here now," LeRoux said. "They got me on meth charges, but I don't see myself being here that long."

"Tell me about these guys you're communicating with," Taj said, referring to Hunter and the mercenaries.

"They're a bunch of junkies," LeRoux sneered. "They're pathetic, they're money-hungry. They'll do anything I tell them to do if I offer them money. We're just trying to put this together. We can make this happen."

LeRoux could sense the kind of person his visitor would like to see, and he could become that person for a little while. For Taj, LeRoux acted humble and courteous, which were qualities Taj admired.

LeRoux told Taj he identified as an Australian. How could LeRoux have possibly known that, outside of the DEA, Taj's best friends in Afghanistan were Australian soldiers? Taj had deployed for several years with the Australian special operations troops because their area of responsibility was northern Helmand Province, which the DEA agents considered the home base of the Afghan heroin cartel, the Medellín of Afghanistan. Taj hadn't told LeRoux anything about his past. LeRoux had that knack that a lot of criminals possessed, for guessing a man's thoughts by throwing out words until he saw his quarry's eyes flicker.

When Taj looked at the undercover videos of LeRoux before his arrest, he saw a different man—a guy snapping orders and laughing as he dealt in instruments of mass murder. One role-player to another, Taj thought LeRoux was damn good.

When normally under cover, Taj probed for something his target took pride in. He would act enthusiastic about whatever it was. The person would feel good and talk more.

LeRoux was obviously proud of his intellect. So Taj flattered him for his brains. During a break, Taj said, "I hope things work out for you. I'd rather have a person like you out there in the world working for me than being in prison."

LeRoux beamed with pleasure.

"You know what? I can do a lot of great things," LeRoux said.

"I think we'd make a great team," Taj replied. "You're a smart guy. We need to work with people like you."

"Oh, thank you."

"No, I'm being serious. People like you are a great asset."

Taj had succeeded in penetrating his world.

But, at the same time, LeRoux had gotten into Taj's head. Taj mentioned that he was after a guy in the Taliban. Did LeRoux know anybody in the Taliban?

LeRoux said he did. He was so persuasive that, for a moment, Taj wondered if he could use LeRoux to help with his unfinished Taliban heroin case. Maybe, if they released LeRoux to the wild, he could con the kingpin to a tropical paradise where Taj and his mates would be waiting. . . .

No! Taj had to wrench himself back to reality, just as Cindric and Stouch had done.

This was the old spider-and-fly routine. LeRoux looked harmless, sitting there in his gray prison jumpsuit, tapping on the keys of his laptop. But he was sending out invisible threads that aimed to convince somebody, maybe Taj, to set him loose.

On February 4, 2013, LeRoux got the first part of what he was after—a plea deal. Lockard and Kovner wrote a formal sixteen-page memo to their superiors recommending that the Southern District enter into a cooperation agreement with him. U.S. Attorney Bharara approved the agreement.

LeRoux would plead guilty to seven felony counts—conspiracy to import methamphetamine into the United States; violating Iran sanctions; money laundering; wire fraud; hacking; aiding and abetting a felon by paying a bribe in Africa to assist Kobi Alexander, a tech company executive accused of stock options manipulation in Brooklyn; and a violation derived from the Minneapolis investigation of RX Limited. These charges exposed him to a minimum of ten years in prison and a maximum of life; he hoped the judge would give him twelve years or so. LeRoux went into federal court on February 19, 2014, and entered his plea.

The plea agreement said that LeRoux would not be prosecuted for conspiracy to murder seven people in the Philippines. The prosecutors concluded that the U.S. government had no jurisdiction over those murders. Murder was treated a local crime, with rare exceptions. A U.S. law enacted in 1996 to fight terrorism made it a federal felony, punishable by up to life in prison, to conspire to kill or kidnap anyone living overseas. To convict someone under this law, government prosecutors had to prove that the conspirators committed at least one act on American soil. The prosecutors had no evidence that LeRoux had traveled to the United States in years, so he could not be shown to have taken any action while on American territory to advance murder plots. The plea agreement contained an immunity clause that was no real concession to LeRoux, but the prosecutors could use it, if they chose, to fend off extradition requests from the Philippines government.

They also agreed not to charge LeRoux with conspiring to sell surface-to-air missiles to terrorists. As a practical matter, they would have had a hard time making that charge stick because LeRoux didn't physically acquire the weapons nor deliver them to the fictional Shan State Army representative.

Even so, making a plea agreement with a man like LeRoux was not an easy decision for a U.S. attorney, especially Bharara, who prided himself on his reputation as Manhattan's most ferocious gangbuster. When the deal became public, and it would, it would be hard to explain why he okayed a deal with a man who admitted that he was responsible for a string of murders. But Bharara and his assistants did it anyway because LeRoux was about to deliver something they considered of greater value: a team of contract killers, assembled by a forty-eight-year-old Kentuckian named Joseph Manuel Hunter.

Or, as Hunter liked to be called, Rambo.

CHAPTER THIRTEEN

HUNTING RAMBO

WHO WAS JOSEPH HUNTER?

The agents knew a few facts about him, but was he the cold-blooded, robotic killer LeRoux and Jack described?

Or was LeRoux exaggerating to get himself off the hook? LeRoux knew that the worse the agents perceived Hunter to be, the more valuable they would consider LeRoux's help to bring Hunter in.

On paper, Hunter's U.S. Army record was unblemished. An entry in his personnel record, dated March 18, 1991, said:

Staff Sergeant Joseph M. Hunter selected as the Distinguished Graduate for the . . . Class 3-91. This high honor was won in very stiff competition with all the students in an academic/ leadership environment. His sustained superior performance, his determination to excel, coupled with his intense desire to accomplish all missions was an example for the remainder of the class. This individual is now ready for positions of higher responsibility.

But a person could change over two decades. The way to find out what Hunter had become was to observe him closely when he was making decisions to commit violent acts. "We get to see them when they think nobody's watching," Milione said. "But we're watching. There's a certain purity to seeing them for what they really are."

To do that, the agents needed to put someone wearing a wire across the table from him. Cindric and Stouch decided to play on the cover story that LeRoux had relocated to Rio in order to forge an alliance with a Colombian transnational organized crime group.

The head Colombian would be played by Diego, the suave former trafficker who had been on the DEA payroll for years. He was a perfect fit for the part, having already immersed himself in LeRoux's operations and associates as he prepared for his previous role, as the fictional Colombian cartel rep who lured LeRoux to Monrovia. Diego's chubby buddy Geraldo, also a reformed Colombian trafficker, naturalized American citizen, and longtime DEA informant, would pose as Diego's lieutenant.

Cindric and Stouch concocted an email for LeRoux to send Hunter from "Brazil"—actually the federal building in Manhattan—that he should get to Bangkok to meet his new Colombian partners. The email said:

The meeting in thailand is for the colombians to meet and discuss what they need for their personal protection while travelling and what will be expected of the people hired. These guys are business people. i am working with them on several projects out of south America and in Africa. they asked if I had someone who could help them with the personal protection when they travel and for security assessments on jobs.

The black jobs will be discussed and planned. The security guys will need to be capable guys who are willing to do black ops jobs, but initially it will be personal protection and security assessments. They need to be able to travel without issues

The tools for jobs will be arranged on our end. In some countries it may not be good to have certain tools so there are no detention issues. Tools for black ops jobs will be provided by me and my partners.

Let me know if you can meet the partners in thailand and speak with them regarding these things. They are going there on other

business and plan to be there around the end of January. I will send
you the cash necessary for travel and expenses. Let me know if any
of the guys you plan to use will travel with you to meet the partners
so I can send money for their travel and expenses also. the future
housing and transportation arrangements can be organized through
contacts in that country when needed. Organize your visa so there
are no issues.

Hunter didn't question the story. He knew that LeRoux was doing business with a Colombian group. He also knew that "black jobs"
meant contract murder.

Hunter agreed to meet Diego and Geraldo on January 26, 2013, at
the Landmark Hotel in Bangkok, a sleek, impersonal tower with more
marble than a necropolis.

Hunter arrived looking nervous. He had long believed that LeRoux
might have him killed for some imagined slight. He feared he might
be looking at his executioners. The two Colombians encouraged this
impression. Diego shot him a look that could slice open an envelope.
Geraldo was stout and merry, but in that menacing way that signaled
that he'd laugh while blowing somebody's brains out.

Settling into three leather chairs in the bar, Diego and Geraldo
nodded politely as Hunter stated that he didn't party. He didn't care
about fine food. He didn't chase women. He didn't want a drink. They
ordered soft drinks and water and got down to business.

Diego and Geraldo said that they had been partners with LeRoux
in drugs and gold mines for several years. They were moving a lot of
cash and looking for security to protect their people. They were good
in South America, where the right-wing death squads served as their
guards and enforcers, but they needed a security team for Asia and
Africa. The work involved drugs, weapons, money, and killing. They
would pay bonuses for contract killings.

Was Hunter interested in "bonus jobs"?

He said he was.

The audio and video recorders hidden in the Colombians' clothing captured Hunter's affirmative answer and his monologue on his favorite subject, himself:

Served 21 years in the Army. You probably heard of 1st Ranger Battalion. Long range surveillance 32nd Airborne. I retired as a commander of a special reaction team. We focused mainly on entries. I fought in Grenada in 1983, Panama in 1989 and then I went to Iraq three times as a civilian contractor. I worked for two companies. Triple Canopy and DynCorp. And my military training, Ranger School, I've been through various amount of training. Highly specialized, most of it was dealing with entry. I used to be a Heckler & Koch instructor, specialized in the MP5, what they call a master MP5 instructor, a master pistol instructor, I've been to intelligence school, a course called intelligence and combating terrorism . . . Everything, been to LAPD advanced SWAT School, TEES—Tactical Explosives Entry School.

Hunter paused for breath. "All that—but I'm not an operator anymore. Now I'm a handler. So, are you looking for guys?"

"Let's talk about what you have," Geraldo said, encouraging him toward specifics.

Hunter said he had been recruiting some new mercenaries for his security team. To prove to the Colombians that he was professional and thorough, like any first-tier security company, he went to pains to demonstrate his vetting process. He pulled out a stack of resumes. The first belonged to Dennis Gögel.

"Okay, this guy right here is the number one guy I recommend," Hunter said. ". . . He's a sniper qualified in the German military. And he's ready to go for anything, and we want this guy working for us . . .

Afghanistan . . . lots of trigger time . . . He was recommended to me from a friend of mine that is an American sniper instructor. . . . He's gonna do great things for us."

The second resume was Gögel's friend Michael Filter, also a former German army sniper and a veteran of the war in Afghanistan. The rest of the candidates were veterans of U.S. or NATO military services.

"I picked them because they are sniper qualified and that gives us opportunities for other stuff," Hunter said. "And they are motivated. They want to get in with Paul."

"Money is a motivation for everyone," Diego said dryly.

Geraldo said he and Diego would make decisions after they ran background checks on the candidates. He said they had to be sure that the men would keep their mouths shut "because they will see a lot of things."

"Things" was understood to mean violent deaths.

"Exactly," Hunter said. "Yeah, we make good money. But, like myself—you know—I miss what I used to do. It's the same way with these guys."

He said he told his men, "You're not a door buster any more. Now you're a magician. . . . You go and do stuff that nobody knows how it happened." He had picked up LeRoux's trick of planting subliminal hints that he had supernatural powers.

Cindric and Stouch waited in a Bangkok hotel room for the informants to wrap up the meeting and deliver the recording devices.

"Christ, they all want to be Jason Bourne," Cindric said when he listened to the recordings. "They have a troubled life and they're in a tug of war for their souls. They romanticize. Too much TV. Too many video games."

After a long email chain with LeRoux, Hunter scheduled a meeting with Diego and Geraldo in Phuket for March 8. Cindric and Stouch took the two informants to Phuket several days ahead of the meeting.

They were met by Pat Picciano from the DEA Bangkok office and some technical people, there to help the Thai police install a closed-circuit video and audio surveillance system inside Hunter's safe house. On March 8, Picciano had Bee, his Thai assistant, pose as a chauffeur hired by the Colombians to collect Hunter at the Phuket airport.

Later that day and over the next few days, Hunter went to the hotel where Diego and Geraldo were staying, at first alone, then with three of the mercenaries—Gögel, Filter, and Slawomir Soborski, an ex-commando from Poland.

Diego and Geraldo told the mercenaries the same story they had given Hunter earlier—that they represented a Colombian trafficking group and were looking to hire security to protect their business. They said the security team members would be involved in moving drugs, weapons, and money and would be asked to kill untrustworthy members of the organization.

After meeting with the Colombians, Hunter and his men returned to the safe house, sat down in the common room, and had a roundtable discussion about the Colombians' proposal. The surveillance system recorded Hunter explaining who LeRoux was and how he had partnered for years with the Colombians. The DEA summary of the tapes said, "Hunter detailed all of the jobs he did for PCL to include weapons trafficking, surveillance, intimidation, and murder."

Working for LeRoux was good money, Hunter said, but no one should steal, or Hunter would find him, by which he meant, kill him. He told the men what happened to Dave Smith—dead because he stole from LeRoux. He explained that "bonus job" was code for contract hit.

Hunter's performance on the surveillance tape answered the question—who was Rambo Hunter? What kind of man was he when he thought no one was watching?

The tape made clear that Hunter was somber and purposeful. He didn't celebrate the act of killing. He was not a crazy serial killer who got something like an erotic thrill from killing. He treated killing just as a car mechanic would regard cleaning a carburetor or changing brake fluid.

Cindric and Stouch watched the tapes and realized they had solid gold evidence. The agents had instructed Diego and Geraldo to repeat the meaning of the term "bonus jobs" several times. The reason was, if the case came before a jury, it had to be crystal clear that every man in the group knew that he was being asked to commit murder and had made a conscious decision to do it. As they watched the tapes, the agents didn't think any judge or jury could see and hear them and believe that these men didn't know they were agreeing to kill strangers for money.

Over the next couple of days, Diego and Geraldo met with each of the mercenaries individually and, with their recorders running, asked each man if he understood what he was being asked to do. Each mercenary said he was in.

Diego and Geraldo gave the men their first assignment for the LeRoux-Colombian partnership. It was a simple task—to guard one of LeRoux's yachts, supposedly loaded with guns or drugs. The purpose of the job was to produce evidence that Hunter and his team willingly and knowingly participated in a drugs and arms smuggling conspiracy.

Cindric, Stouch, and the informants returned to the States, thinking the plan was going smoothly. Then a snag developed. The agents took LeRoux to the federal courthouse, went through their routine, and opened his email. They spotted a message from Hunter, dated March 18:

There are strange issues here at the house. The guy that picked us up at the airport, came to the house a couple of days before we arrived with three other thais and tried to break into the safe. Do not know if you are aware of that. Also, received a call from a woman asking about the owners car, wanting to know when it will be back. I did not know what she is talking about, because there was never a car there. The maid, said the same guy came and took the car and said he was taking it to the shop and not to tell anyone.

The agents sat down with LeRoux and then talked with Picciano, who was back in Bangkok, and tried to piece together what had happened. They determined that the maid, hired by Hunter to clean the safe house, had relayed a mangled version of the facts. It was true that Bee, Picciano's Thai helper, had led the Thai cops to the house a few days before Hunter arrived. He stood by as the cops installed the bugging system. It was also true that Bee and the cops opened the safe, looking for LeRoux's fake passport.

Cindric and Stouch cooked up a response, which they emailed to Hunter under LeRoux's name. The message informed Hunter that Bee was a local handyman who did odd jobs for LeRoux at the house. In an email dated March 19, 2013, they wrote:

> the guy that picked u up at the airport . . . is the one that handles small things for us locally, there was a 4x4 at the house, it was bought about 5 years ago, i told [him] to take it to get it repaired, they will repair it and return it to the house to save on transportation costs, relax the maid, our guys opened the safe because smith left my passport in that house somewhere (the one the house is registered under) that is what we were looking for (if u find it let me know it is a venezuelan passport)

Hunter wasn't convinced. He swept the house, poked his head up into the attic, and spotted the electronics controller box that led to the closed-circuit video system. He pulled the plug.

He returned to his computer and fired off a frantic email to LeRoux:

> We found the cameras and DVR Recorder and stuff in the house!!! The guys will not return back to the house, they want to rent another house, asking for 30K for that. They are hesitant now about the job and want to know whats going on!!! I will continue to stay in the house, the guys go to another one. They also, want their pay up to 10K each, as the job has already went from protecting funds to all kinds of stuff and now their [sic] freaked about the house. They are

requesting bonus work ASAP. These guys will do anything if you let me handle it, but this situation now causes problems.

"Oh fuck, did this whole thing get blown?" Cindric said. He looked at Stouch, and both men started to panic. How could they fix this? *Could* they fix it?

Yes, they could, LeRoux said. He was calm, as usual, even smirking.

"Ah, it's normal," LeRoux said. "I always have security cameras in my stash houses to keep an eye on things."

The agents relaxed a little. It might work. They had to try it. What choice did they have?

They sat LeRoux down in front of his laptop and stepped out of camera range as LeRoux rang Hunter on Skype. What Hunter had found, LeRoux said blandly, was an ordinary home security system. As a homeowner, LeRoux would be crazy not to have one, since he might have very valuable contraband inside. What was he going to do, call the cops? Besides, Phuket was full of thieves because it was full of blind-drunk tourists, begging to be robbed.

Hunter didn't buy it. He'd seen the cameras and he didn't think they were routine.

"I know who they're from," he growled. "It's the Colombians."

"No, no, no, you're just seeing the security cameras," LeRoux replied. But if Hunter wanted a different house, LeRoux said, he could rent one and LeRoux would pay.

LeRoux ended the call and turned to the agents, laughing.

"Guys, it's just as good," he said. "He thinks it's the Colombians."

"Paul had such street cred as a bad guy that even when things could potentially look like cops, nobody believed it," Cindric said. "We had the fat man. He trumped everything. He was such a bad guy, nobody would believe he was working for law enforcement."

Hunter was not too freaked out to try padding his expenses. He asked LeRoux for $30,000 a month to rent a house. The agents and

LeRoux knew that he could rent a big beach house for $2,000 a month. Hunter said he wanted to raise the gunmen's pay to $10,000 a month. LeRoux agreed. Later, the agents learned that Hunter told the men they were getting a raise to $9,000 a month. Hunter had skimmed $1,000 a month from each of them.

The good news was, the DEA tech in Bangkok had downloaded the security system shortly before Hunter discovered it. Hunter's speech describing the dirty work he had done for LeRoux had been preserved.

The next step was to give the mercenaries riskier assignments. The agents didn't think it would work to ask them to go from zero to sixty—murder—in a short span of time. They had to become accustomed to obeying orders.

Meanwhile, Shackels and Stammers had showed up in Phuket, eager to make drug deals and arms deals. As usual, they had lots of irons in the fire. On March 9, 2013, at a hotel in Phuket, Stammers introduced Diego and Geraldo to a Chinese man named Chen, who was willing to sell a large quantity of small arms. Speaking through an interpreter, Chen offered, among other things, HN-5 missiles, Chinese-made knockoffs of Soviet Stingers, sought after by militant groups everywhere. Chen and his partner, an Englishman, said they could deliver at least 100 shoulder-fired surface-to-air missile systems, including a launcher and two missiles, for a mere $25,000 per unit, or $2.5 million. The informants started negotiations.

Shackels and Stammers, sniffing fat commissions for brokering arms to the Colombians, set up a series of meetings with more arms dealers of various nationalities. In April, they invited Diego and Geraldo to accompany them to Mauritius to meet some of their contacts in the Serb mafia—men whom Shackels and Stammers had nicknamed "the war criminals." Cindric and Stouch approved the meeting, seeing it as an opportunity to open a window into a seldom-seen underworld of arms merchants. The agents decided to have LeRoux order the mercenaries Gögel, Filter, and Soborski to go along, ostensibly to provide security for the Colombians. The mercenaries' willingness to participate might eventually serve as evidence against them.

The agents, working with the police in Mauritius, set up bugs in the meeting rooms and took photos. To their astonishment, the session turned into a gun-runner summit. Four Serbs showed up, representing Serb mafia organizations in South America, Europe, Africa, and Australia. They seemed deeply entrenched on each continent. They expressed interest in forming a partnership with the Colombian cartels on cocaine deals and with the North Koreans and Chinese triads, moving meth and ecstasy.

A second meeting, convened strictly to educate the agents about the international arms business, involved a well-known registered arms dealer, Johan Erasmus, a South African who helped governments and reputable security contractors acquire arms legitimately, and Erik Iskander-Goaied, a Swedish-Tunisian businessman. Cindric and Stouch wanted to pick the men's brains about how the Iranian Defense Industries Organization made arms deals. Interviewed later by the author, Erasmus recalled that he explained to the agents that he didn't deal with Iran himself, but, for business reasons, he did try to monitor that nation's arms deals, particularly in Africa. "Iran has a very good small arms industry," he said. "Their equipment is superior to the Chinese. However their range of weapons is very limited. Their ammunition is also of a good quality. In return for the weapons and ammo they supply to West Africa, they get oil and gold. Lots of it. Plus, due to sanctions, they have got very good delivery channels set up." Erasmus added that during the meeting, Billy Meintjes, LeRoux's South African lawyer, pressed him on LeRoux's behalf to help collect some or all of the $100 million the Iranians had promised for the missile navigation system. Erasmus said he demurred.

One objective of the Mauritius sessions was to test LeRoux's theory that arms dealers would snap up his missile navigation system, under development for Iran, and also a small surveillance drone design. The theory went that the arms dealers would compete to broker these systems to small governments and large militant groups. The agents decided to find out more about the potential market for this technology and perhaps develop other useful leads into the world of gray- and black-market arms dealers. They had LeRoux draw up highly technical descriptions of his navigation systems. To explain them and answer questions, the agents introduced a new undercover operative, a Canadian pilot named John. He was a genuine expert in sophisticated small weapons systems and could geek out endlessly on the latest and greatest innovations in the field. Sure enough, the Serbs were impressed with LeRoux's achievements in navigation technology and wanted to know more.

But backstage, things were tense. Georges, the French bush pilot, accompanied the mercenaries to Mauritius to make sure they got where they were supposed to go. He was delighted to encounter Erasmus, with whom he had bonded when both had worked for Joseph Mobutu, president and military dictator of the Democratic Republic of the Congo. Erasmus, once with South African intelligence, was a military advisor to the strongman; Georges was his pilot. "The old croc!" Georges hailed the arms dealer.

Georges did not have warm feelings for his supposed partner, John the Canadian. Georges enjoyed swashbuckling, drinking, and checking out the ladies of Mauritius. John was quiet, detail-oriented, somewhat guileless, and devoutly religious. Things went bad when John took it into his head to try to save Georges. Georges emphatically did not want to be saved, and if he talked to God, he didn't want to say so. Also, he thought John was wrong about some aspects of the weapons system and was about to blow the undercover scenario.

"If you guys keep putting me with him, I'm going to fucking kill him," he warned the agents. "This idiot nearly got us caught. I had to use all my military skills to get out of this shitty situation."

Fortunately, no blows were exchanged or shots fired before everyone had to head back to Phuket.

Tensions worsened during the next undercover meeting, in Phuket on May 18, 2013. That day, Diego summoned Hunter and the team to his hotel to hear good news. "Finally, you guys were asking for it, we have a bonus job," he announced, using the group's term for contract murder. "There is a leak on the inside."

Geraldo piped up that the leak was connected to the "boat that ran ashore." He referred to the wreck of LeRoux's yacht, the *JeReVe*, on Tonga and the loss of its cargo, 204 kilos of cocaine. The discovery of the wreck had made the Australian papers. Diego claimed that after the *JeReVe* incident two more of his group's loads were seized. His organization was investigating the losses and possible leakers. He would soon reveal the details of the bonus job.

"We will take care of it," Hunter said solemnly.

That should have been cause for celebration at the safe house. The mercenaries were enjoying traveling around on somebody else's dime. Diego spoiled the mood by giving Hunter a tongue-lashing for arriving late. He insulted the mercenaries as "little bastards" and "dogs" who would lie down and get up when he said so.

This was not in the scenario Cindric and Stouch had discussed with Diego. The Colombian was improvising. He had gotten caught up in his character and decided he wanted to portray his cartel guy as an overbearing asshole.

On May 20, 2013, Hunter fired off a blistering email to LeRoux about Diego's high-handed behavior:

Diego said he was disappointed in me, because he gave us one hour to reach his destination. It was impossible to do this. First, not even Delta Force has a one-hour recall. There is a two hour recall, and that's just to get everyone assembled, and does not include movement. We do not have taxi service where the house is. We have to ride double on 125cc motorbikes except for one guy and their hotel was 35 kilometers away. All Diego gave us was an address and we did not know where it was, there was an electricity outage at the house and we could not even look the address up on the Internet because it was not working. We busted our ass to get there, and then we here shit about being late and what if we were needed. If they might need us in an emergency situation it has to be planned in advance, it is impossible to get everyone together and move to an unknown location in a hour!!! . . . The guys will get the mission done. Diego needs to lighten up, we are here to [do] missions, not play around and be told we have a mission at the end of June. Give us the mission and the guys will do it, they do not need to be treated like their [sic] owned. I'm not being disrespectful, but the guys are professionals and will apply their selves to the mission, when they are needed.

Georges agreed with Hunter. Diego was making trouble needlessly. Georges went straight from the meeting with Hunter to the room where Cindric and Stouch were holed up, waiting for the audio and video feed, and told the agents he was appalled at Diego's over-the-top performance. He didn't think American and European military veterans were going to stand for that kind of bullshit.

"The way he talks, it's going to blow up," Georges told the agents. "The situation is very volatile. Diego is really talking to them like shit. I can read it in their eyes. They're ready to do something."

"Do you think you can hold them?" Cindric asked.

"*Bien sûr*," Georges said with a Gallic shrug. "I can play a game with them and get them back on track."

The agents fired up LeRoux's smartphone, which they carried with them, and sent Hunter this message under LeRoux's name:

i will discuss the issues with Diego. relax i know he can be a arrogant colombian but he is good at making money. i will take care of him

They juggled the assignments. From then on, Georges would play LeRoux's right-hand man and alter ego in Africa and Asia and would take over as the point of contact for Hunter.

Diego and Geraldo would deal with the drugs-and-arms trafficking crew—Stammers, Shackels, Lim, and Reyes Peralta. The traffickers didn't know the mercenaries because LeRoux had kept the branches of his organization stovepiped, as a security measure. There was no chance they would gossip about the Colombian informants or anything else.

Diego wasn't happy, but he had no choice. The agents explained that it was for the good of the operation; it wasn't an option.

The day after the disastrous meeting, Georges strolled into Hunter's rented villa, all brisk competence. He said he had spoken to LeRoux, who agreed that Diego's behavior was "unacceptable." They were changing operational management. From that time on, Georges would handle all coordination and planning.

Hunter looked relieved. "We just want the mission," he said.

Georges smiled sympathetically and distributed smartphones with a PGP encryption key that double-coded text messages. He asked the men to use these phones to communicate with him and the Colombians. These were the phones that Cindric and Stouch could tail virtually, with a satellite-based cell phone tracking system.

In June, the mercenary team was dispatched to Nassau to stand guard while 300 kilos of cocaine, actually benign powder, were loaded onto a private plane heading for the United States. The gig went without incident.

Just when Cindric and Stouch thought they had gotten everything back on track, things went off the rails again. On August 15, Hunter pulled up to Georges's hotel in Phuket. With him were Gögel and Tim Vamvakias, Hunter's army buddy, a Californian who had worked for LeRoux since 2009. He was a compact man of forty-two. He must have been good-looking once, but his face said he'd seen hard times.

"I need to talk to you for a minute," Hunter told Georges. He wasn't smiling. "We're gonna use advanced security measures, right? So, what we're gonna do, we're gonna go to your room, we're gonna search everybody. Leave all the phones, everything there, get whatever paperwork you need, we'll go talk out at the beach."

Georges was worried. Would they discover the body bug he was wearing? Georges tried to avert the search of his body by saying that he was there simply as a messenger, to convey information from LeRoux about the "bonus job." But Hunter insisted.

"When you start working with people, you know, you might be good today but two months from now . . . I mean, like him"—he gestured toward either Gögel or Vamvakias, Georges wasn't sure which—"like he might be a rat tomorrow. I don't know. Checks and balances."

Georges took a close look at Hunter's eyes. They were glassy. He looked stoned. And he stunk. His hygiene was terrible. Hunter told people he didn't drink, but he was on something now, Georges was pretty sure of that. Or maybe the stress was getting to him. Georges thought Vamvakias looked drunk, and Gögel looked like a fool, but Hunter looked the worst. They started to make their way to Georges's room.

Georges had heard the recording in which Hunter boasted about all his firearms and tactical training. Georges thought Hunter was not only stoned but also a coward. If he was such a hot operator, why was he hiding in the back? Why didn't he go out with his men and lead from the front? Besides, Georges had figured out that he was embezzling and padding from everyone. What kind of leader would steal from his own men?

"He is a real fucking piece of shit," Georges said to himself. "If I could kill this guy myself I would."

It wouldn't be the first time Georges killed someone.

As Georges walked through the hotel with Hunter, Gögel, and Vamvakias, he considered the fact that he wasn't in a position to kill any of them. There were three of them and one of him. There was no way to break away from them without risking getting shot. He didn't know whether Hunter had a sensor that would find his wire. He had never worked with this new kind of body bug before, and he didn't know how it functioned.

When they reached room 4305 on the third floor, Georges looked at the windows. One was directly over the pool. Good. He thought he could jump out of a window and into the pool. On the other hand, you could get shot in a pool. . . .

Non. He needed a Plan B. If they found the wire, he decided to say that LeRoux and Georges didn't trust Hunter—that LeRoux insisted that Georges tape the meeting and send him the audio for analysis. Georges knew that Hunter was terrified of LeRoux and his Colombian partners and would believe it.

Hunter told everyone to set their belongings in the room to be searched. Gögel ran a small scanner up and down Georges's body. He slid the device over the wire in Georges's pocket and pronounced Georges clean. Georges relaxed momentarily.

Hunter summoned the group to follow him to the beach so that they could talk freely. Though he had swept the room for bugs and found none, he wasn't totally confident there wasn't a recording device still hiding someplace.

"You're fucking paranoid," Georges growled. "They can pick us up on the beach. You're going to kill a DEA agent!"

Hunter insisted, so off they went. When they returned to the room, Georges handed Hunter the fake surveillance photos of Casich and Sammy and a document with details of their daily routines in Monrovia. The document was formatted as if drafted by a cartel surveillance team.

"This is the number one subject," Georges said. He showed the mercenaries a photo of Milione/Casich by himself and a second photo of Milione/Casich and Taj/Sammy.

"Joseph Casich with his friend," he said.

Hunter pointed to the image of Taj. "He looks a little different with his beard."

He ran his finger down a list of cafes and restaurants the pair supposedly frequented. He pointed to one name.

"Before this place, before the restaurant," Hunter said. "All right, this is going to be no problem."

"Oh yeah, this is looking good," Vamvakias said.

"Do they have a car?" Hunter said.

"Yes."

"We will need the license number and the car."

Georges said they usually took cabs.

"So, they're walking around a lot?" Vamvakias said.

"They feel very safe there, huh," Gögel said.

"According to your intel these guys are out eating and drinking every day? And they're together?" Vamvakias said.

"Yes."

"Okay, good."

Georges said that the agent and the Libyan drank a lot and chased women.

"Perfect," Gögel replied.

There was a brief discussion of the latex masks that Hunter had bought to transform the pale German and American into black-skinned Liberians. They were theatrical-quality, moved like flesh, and cost $1,400 apiece. The mercenaries dared not travel to Monrovia with them. Customs agents might raise questions. Georges said he would get them into the country. He promised they would have cars and motorbikes to move around Monrovia.

"And a couple [of] helmets if we need them because we might just do a motorcycle hit," Vamvakias said.

They turned to their favorite topic, "tools," meaning guns.

"I think the two biggest weapons we need, two apiece, would be the MP7 with suppressor and two .22s with suppressors," Vamvakias said. "So two MP7s and two .22s with suppressors."

Georges asked if they wanted a .308 sniper rifle. This was a precision long-distance weapon, standard for U.S. and NATO military snipers.

"That's just a contingency, if we use it," Vamvakias said, "But, the bottom line is I think we're probably gonna have to get up close to them, you know what I mean, to make sure it gets done. And that's why, if we have, you know, automatic MP7s. . . ."

"The thing with the .308 is it's fucking loud," Gögel said. "You can't suppress a .308. You know if we use the weapons with a suppression system it's gonna be easier for us to get in, eliminate the subject, and get out."

"Yeah, the whole point in having the .22 is to finish the job," Vamvakias replied, "or, if I have a weapons malfunction with my primary, that's my secondary. You know, we gotta do this, hit it hard, hit it fast, make sure it's done, and get the fuck out of there. That's all that's to it. If we got the right equipment we're good to go. You'll take the masks; we got a motorbike and a car. We're all set."

"Oh, one last item I was thinking of off the top of my head, was latex gloves," Vamvakias added. "You know those cheap latex gloves . . . if you got some of those, that's for handling the equipment, make sure we don't get gun residue on our hands or anything else."

The tension seemed to have eased somewhat. Vamvakias said, somewhat apologetically, that their original list of guns needed was extensive because they weren't sure how it would go down. Now that they knew more, perhaps they could shrink the list.

Georges said relax, he had good contacts in South Africa to get the weapons they wanted.

"That would be sweet if we can get the MP7s," Vamvakias said. That's when he referred to the waterfront bar where the assassinations would likely occur as the "kill zone."

"The most important thing is to have a suppressor and automatic to get as many rounds into them as possible," Vamvakias added.

Business done, they went to the hotel bar, ordered beers, and talked about Africa, women, and French politics.

Georges excused himself, went into the bathroom, peed, and sang Frank Sinatra's signature song to himself—and to the bug.

> *Regrets, I've had a few*
> *But then again, too few to mention*
> *I did what I had to do and saw it through without exemption*
> *I planned each charted course, each careful step along the byway*
> *And more, much more than this, I DID IT MY WAAAYYY.*

When Cindric and Stouch listened to the recording, they got Georges's point. Diego had been the wrong man to talk to mercenaries. You can send a doper to talk to a doper but when you're dealing with a merc, send a merc. Georges had done it his way and come up a winner.

Back in the room with Hunter, Georges considered how he could establish control over him. Since his character was supposed to be Le-Roux's shadow—his eyes and ears on the ground—he needed to sound like the man in command. Having been a real commander in the fighter wing of the French navy, this wasn't a stretch.

Georges told Hunter sternly he would appreciate not being patted down and searched ever again. There was no sense checking each other. He understood checking "external" people, but not the team. They needed to protect one another and the mission, of course, but that didn't mean they should suspect one another.

"Well, it's going to happen," Vamvakias said sulkily.

"I'm a straightforward guy," Georges said. "I will need to report to Paul that there was a check. Do you have an issue with that?"

Go ahead, Hunter said. "I am always going to do it my way."

"And so am I, my friend." Georges smiled coldly.

After more talk of the women of Phuket—"adult Disneyland," the mercenaries called it—they left the bar. Hunter went off on his own.

Vamvakias and Gögel turned to Georges and apologized for Hunter. They said the search was Hunter's idea. They assured Georges that they trusted him, but they answered to a "higher power," meaning Hunter. They made a date to meet the next day.

Georges saw real fear in their eyes. It reinforced his initial impression, that they would follow Hunter's orders. If he said kill, they'd kill, no questions asked. Georges gave them a wave of his hand and a wolfish grin and took his time making his way to the DEA agents' room—where he slumped down, mentally spent.

"Holy fuck, man," he said.

Cindric handed him a beer. He was sorry they hadn't told Georges how the wire worked. It didn't emit a signal. It captured sound and stored it on a chip. The advantage was that it was completely passive. The disadvantage was the agents couldn't help Georges if shooting started. They all knew that even if he had worn a device that was transmitting, if somebody in the room had pulled a gun, nobody could get to the door and kick it in fast enough to save him.

Georges shrugged and softened. He never expected anyone else to save him. He had gotten out of a lot of tight spots—Argentina, Mali, Ivory Coast, Malta, Sierra Leone, and so many other places—and he had some stories to tell. It was the life he had chosen, more interesting than that of his father, a schoolteacher. He worried that by chewing out Hunter, he might have blown the deal.

The agents told him they didn't think Hunter would walk away from the mission. Judging by the number of times he had begged for "bonus jobs," he had to be desperate for cash. Sooner or later, one of the mercenaries would realize that Hunter was stealing. They could easily kill him on the spot and no one would care.

Cindric and Stouch agreed with Georges that it was a volatile situation. All the guys seemed to be skating on a thin edge of reason, with the exception of Soborski, who had that thousand-yard stare that said he'd seen some things and could handle anything.

The agents told Georges to go relax, if he could. He liked a good stiff Scotch. He wandered off to find one. The agents had more work to do, downloading the listening device.

The recording told them they had another problem. Hunter was setting up the hit in Monrovia as a two-man job, with Gögel doing the sharpshooting and Vamvakias backstopping him. The agents had hoped Hunter would send Filter and Soborski to Monrovia as well. Leaving Hunter and two mercenaries in Phuket would be dangerous for the Thai police making the arrests.

How about luring Filter and Soborski to Estonia? The DEA agents in Copenhagen had excellent contacts in the Estonian counternarcotics police and the SWAT team there. The Estonian government was eager to prove its worth as a recent addition to NATO and the European Union. How about sending the two mercenaries to Tallinn on a mission to guard Diego at a meeting with a Serbian trafficker? It sounded plausible.

Cindric sent Hunter a text from LeRoux's smartphone:

> We will need your two other guys around mid-Sept for a local
> surveillance job and then possibly in the Baltics for personal security
> for a meeting with the Serbs.

They scheduled Takedown Day for September 25, 2013. They couldn't space out the arrests because the men might have a signaling system, such as a sort of panic button on a cell phone that automatically broadcast a key word that meant "get lost." They might have set up a negative signal—if someone didn't call in at such-and-such a time, consider him compromised, and scatter. The same day, they would roll up LeRoux's drugs and arms trafficking.

Diego and Geraldo were deep in negotiations with Shackels and

Stammers to buy North Korean meth and ship it to "the Apple," meaning New York. During those meetings, which were recorded, Lim implied that the Pyongyang regime approved the manufacturing and sale of the meth.

"The NK government already burned all the labs," Lim said. "Only our labs are not closed . . . to show Americans that they [the North Korean government] are not selling it any more, they burned it. Then they transfer to another base . . . It's only us who can get it from NK." This information was notable because Lim and his Triad were dealing directly with meth producers inside North Korea. Lim was saying that the Pyongyang regime's claims to the international community that it had clamped down on meth trafficking were false. The reality was, the regime was still sanctioning the manufacture and sale of meth by permitting certain favored North Korean lab operators to operate.

LeRoux had already bought 100 kilograms of North Korean meth through Lim. It was being stored in Thailand and the Philippines. Lim told Diego and Geraldo that his Triad group was prepared to offer much more, drawing from a ten-ton stockpile of North Korean meth it had already warehoused. This was a mind-boggling amount that would bring in enough hard currency to finance, well, just about anything the North Koreans desired.

Stammers and Shackels pronounced themselves ready to move massive quantities of meth for LeRoux. In a dry run to test the smuggling route, they shipped a container loaded with 4.7 tons of tea leaves from China to a warehouse in Bangkok. If it had been real North Korean meth, it would have been worth at least $300 million wholesale and several times that on the street. The dry run worked beautifully. Stammers and Shackels were eager to start shipping the real thing.

Diego and Geraldo asked the four traffickers to travel to Phuket and meet them at a certain hotel on September 25, supposedly to make final preparations for a big shipment to New York.

In mid-September, Cindric and Stouch moved into a Marriott resort on Phuket and set up their command center. They had long lists of details to coordinate, laid out in notebooks, computer files, and their whiteboard, propped against one wall, next to a map of the world.

Every day at dawn, Stouch put in his thirteen miles, no matter what. He had a route down a path and along the beach, zigzagging around naked bodies, passed out or drowsily grinding on companions. One rosy dawn, a pack of feral dogs chased him and one bit him, drawing blood. Picciano took him to the emergency room, where the doctors started him on a series of anti-rabies shots.

Cindric practiced his Muay Thai moves and ran wind sprints on a soccer field near the hotel. The day before Takedown Day, some water buffalo wandered out from the woods while he was ripping across the grass. A hotel guard came out and shooed them away.

There was something about the water buffalo that got to Cindric. He started giggling and couldn't stop. Stouch ran up in time to find him tomato-red in the face and almost hyperventilating with laughter. He couldn't explain, except that it was probably the tension that hadn't let up for months. The care and feeding of the informants and sources demanded constant attention. LeRoux was worst of all. He was making nice for now, but they could almost hear those gears in his peculiar brain clicking noisily. What was he plotting and when would he spring it?

What if the whole case fizzled like a dud firecracker?

Suddenly Cindric stopped laughing, stood up, and turned to Stouch. "I had a vision," he said. "It's all going to be good."

Stouch rolled his eyes. A vision and a dollar wouldn't buy you a cup of coffee in Phuket.

CHAPTER FOURTEEN

NINJA STUFF

THE VISION WAS RIGHT. THE GOD OF COPS HAD SMILED.

Against the odds, three police forces, three justice systems, and three border control agencies did what they were supposed to do. Presidents, intelligence services, and defense ministers didn't interfere. Airplanes didn't break down. Nobody tipped off the bad guys. They were all where they were supposed to be, except for Hunter, and he wasn't far, or armed.

By dawn in New York on September 26, 2013, LeRoux's enforcement and meth operations had been flattened like wings of an outdated factory after controlled demolition.

The mercenaries and meth guys were in jail. Call center workers, pilots, and other gig workers, paid over the past year to maintain the fiction that LeRoux was in business as usual, were out of jobs and on the street. Houses, condos, and yachts sat vacant.

A old-school businessman would weep to see his life's work in shambles. LeRoux smiled. In the Age of Innovation, entrepreneurs didn't go bust. They pivoted. They moved on to other ventures. He was ready to pivot.

When Cindric told LeRoux that all his men and all his systems were down, he grinned and said, "Ah, it worked good. It's good work."

He paused. "That's good for me?"

"Yep, that's good for you."

At this point, all LeRoux wanted, all he *needed*, was a break. He had built a string of fabulously lucrative businesses from nothing, and he was confident he could do it again. But he had to get free, which meant he had to satisfy every demand of the agents and prosecutors so they would recommend to the federal judge hearing his case that he get another chance at freedom. The judge didn't have to take the prosecutors' recommendation, but if he or she did, LeRoux could get off with a sentence of twelve to fifteen years or so. Counting time served, he could be out in 2024, a vigorous fifty-two-year-old, and still very rich. The agents assumed he had secret stashes all over the place.

LeRoux was desperate to get to sentencing and set a date for the end of his lockup. Hunter's performance wasn't going to make it easy. On the DEA flight from Phuket to New York, Hunter melted down. "I'm not a bad person," he sobbed. "The people that I hurt deserved to be hurt. These people stole from my boss. They're thieves. I felt like they had to pay."

He didn't bad-mouth LeRoux. To the contrary, he spoke of the Boss almost worshipfully. Yet in his passive-aggressive way, he painted LeRoux as bloodthirsty. His utter loyalty to LeRoux was toxic, not only for his victims, but for LeRoux.

Hunter said that shortly after he signed on with LeRoux, he stumbled into the middle of one of the Boss's most durable vendettas—a feud with LeRoux's own family. In 2008 or 2009, LeRoux's cousins Mathew and Garry Smith, who, like LeRoux, were born in Rhodesia, had moved to South Africa with the general white exodus and had returned to Zimbabwe to pursue mining-related business, introduced LeRoux to their friends Steve and Andrew Hahn, who had a gold mine and expertise in the gold trade. LeRoux hired the Hahns to help him buy African gold.

The Hahn brothers got involved in a losing gold-buying venture in Mali. They claimed they put down a big pile of LeRoux's money to pay for gold that was never delivered. LeRoux didn't believe them. He suspected them of faking the loss and swindling him out of at least $800,000, maybe more. He summoned them to Manila to explain.

The Hahns blamed the Smiths. LeRoux doubted them. Instead of pursuing the facts in an orderly and legal way, he jumped straight to punishment. He told Dave Smith (unrelated to LeRoux's Smith cousins) to set up the Hahns by planting cocaine in Andrew's luggage. As the Hahns headed back to South Africa, Philippine border control authorities found five grams of coke in Andrew's bag and arrested him at the airport. He languished in a Philippine prison for two and a half years, until he and his brother convinced the authorities to dismiss the charges.

During Andrew's incarceration, Steve Hahn returned to South Africa to figure out a way out of the dilemma. LeRoux sent Dave Smith and Hunter to South Africa to track him down and punish him for his role in the screwup.

Hunter later recounted the story to Gögel and Soborski in a conversation captured by the DEA bug in the safe house:

> I said, "Steve, they want me to . . . to shoot you." He's like, "No."
> I said, uh, I told him, "Don't worry about it 'cause after I shoot you, everything is gonna be good." . . . We had people go to his house and stay with him to watch, right? I said, "There's no more people in your house. Nobody's gonna bother you anymore. You know, this . . . your, your life will go back to normal." He said, "Yeah. No problem." . . . And then I was thinking, "You know, he's saying that, right? But if I shoot him, he's gonna go to the police and they're gonna get me in the airport." So I . . . made up a story because I was thinking about it for like three days. "How am I gonna get out before he gets to the police?" And I told him, "Steve, this is the deal. I'm flying from here to South Africa. When I get to South Africa, I have to make a phone call. I have two guys in a townhouse in your, in your town . . . .If I don't call them back, they're going for your family."

With that powerful inducement, Hunter claimed that Hahn allowed himself to be shot.

When Hunter told the story to the DEA agents who flew with him to New York, he portrayed Hahn as remorseful and himself as a reluctant enforcer.

"The guy said, 'I know why you're here,'" Hunter said. "'I know you're the enforcer, I know I was bad to your boss. Do what you gotta do.'" Hunter said that Steve Hahn held out his hand to be shot, so Hunter pulled the trigger. Hunter said that Steve Hahn thanked him for not killing him and even drove him to the airport so he could make his plane back to Manila.

"I was sweating bullets until wheels up," Hunter told the agents. He claimed he felt bad about the whole thing, but how else could the Boss maintain discipline? Call the cops? File a lawsuit? No, in his view, enforcers were a necessary and accepted workforce in the dark economy. Hunter rationalized that the Hahns knew the rules of the road. He claimed he saw Steve Hahn a year later, doing business with LeRoux in the Philippines, and Hahn said, "No hard feelings."

But around other mercenaries, Hunter showed no regret for the assault on Hahn. "He just told me he shot him in the hand [and] he dumped him off at a hospital," Vamvakias said.

Meanwhile, LeRoux shifted his attention to his cousins the Smith brothers. He sent three of his mercenaries—Dave Smith, Hunter, and Chris DeMeyere—to Zimbabwe to find and terrorize them for their part in losing LeRoux's money. According to Hunter, he threw a Molotov cocktail into Mathew Smith's house. No one was hurt, but the house burned. LeRoux hired South African hitman Marius to firebomb Garry Smith's house in Johannesburg. He considered having Marius kill the Smith brothers but changed his mind.

"I decided since they were family members, I couldn't go through with it," he said, somewhat sanctimoniously, since he mentioned that the other factor was, the hit man wanted too much money for the murders.

LeRoux left other strong-arm jobs to Dave Smith and his mercenaries. In 2008 or 2009, he suspected Moran Oz, who was managing the RX Limited business, of stealing. Hunter said he, Smith, and DeMeyere took Oz out on a boat, threw him into shark-infested waters, and shot into the water near him. After Oz begged for his life and promised not to offend again, the mercenaries pulled him out and let him straggle back to shore.

Hunter told the investigators that LeRoux was open to all sorts of revolting moneymaking ventures. One was a money-laundering operation on behalf of Charles Taylor, the former Liberian president-turned-warlord who terrorized his own country and neighboring Sierra Leone. (In May 2012, Taylor was convicted in The Hague of war crimes and sentenced to fifty years in prison.)

Hunter said that LeRoux sent him to Pemba, Mozambique, on his private plane, with orders to go to a warehouse in Brussels, pick up $300 million amassed by Taylor, either stolen from the Liberian treasury or raised through the blood diamond trade, and deliver it someplace in South Africa. Hunter's job was to guard the money. For some reason, LeRoux's pilots, an Israeli and a Russian, left Hunter in Mozambique and flew on to Brussels alone. Hunter didn't know what became of Taylor's $300 million, if indeed it existed. LeRoux, who presumably would have received a sizable commission for securing the money, dropped the subject.

On another occasion, Hunter said he traveled to Sri Lanka to buy a cache of grenades stolen from a military base. The deal fell through when the seller panicked.

Hunter said LeRoux was starting up new operations in Yemen and North Korea. He didn't know what they were, exactly. All he knew was, LeRoux was hiring people with the nerve to travel to Sana'a and

Pyongyang, navigate the opaque cutthroat political factions in each hellhole, and emerge with a moneymaking deal for LeRoux.

During his rambling and self-serving confessions, Hunter portrayed himself and his mercenary mates as loyal soldiers just carrying out orders. That they came from a capricious underworld tyrant didn't matter to Hunter. The agents doubted that they could believe this man, who obviously had a fractured conscience and not much judgment.

Still, now that Hunter was confessing, he might drop some facts that could be checked against LeRoux's confession and vice versa. Hunter had a better memory for certain details about the murders than LeRoux. LeRoux insisted he didn't know the names of the men who killed the realtor Catherine Lee.

Hunter knew. On February 26, 2015, after months of queen-for-a-day debriefings and negotiations, Hunter made a plea deal, and he told the whole story of Catherine Lee's death. He identified Adam Samia, cover name "Sal," as the triggerman and Samia's friend Carl David Stillwell, cover name "JT," as the wheelman. That, he said, was the meaning of his email to LeRoux, dated January 24, 2012, assuring him that "Sal" and "JT" would each be paid $35,000 "upon Mission Success," meaning the assassination of Catherine Lee. Hunter said that LeRoux pushed hard for Samia and Stillwell to eliminate not only Lee but several others on LeRoux's kill list. LeRoux, he said, was involved in every intimate detail. Confronted, LeRoux admitted he had lied when he claimed not to know much about the Catherine Lee hit. He said he feared that if he told the truth, he might be extradited to the Philippines, where he would be convicted and locked up for the rest of his life, or just shot for knowing too much about official corruption, in which he had played a starring role.

Unlike LeRoux's ideal mercenaries, Adam Samia had no military or police experience. As he would eventually testify in his own defense, he grew up on a farm outside Leicester, Massachusetts. After graduating from high school, Samia worked as a mechanic on a used car lot and as a plasterer for his brothers' construction business. In search of adrenaline fixes, he took up Okinawan martial arts and got so good at sparring and kickboxing that when one of his brothers joined the local police force and made the central Massachusetts SWAT team, Samia, twenty-three or twenty-four at the time, was invited to play the bad guy at SWAT training sessions. While punching and ducking his way through scenarios, he got to know a visiting trainer—Dave Smith.

Over drinks and dinner, Smith regaled the cops and Samia with tales of his days as a British commando, CIA operative, bodyguard, and security contractor. He claimed to have protected Elton John, Gianni Versace, Steve Jobs, and various superstar athletes and entertainers. How much of this, if any, was true is unknown. But it was clear that Smith knew his way around the netherworld of guns for hire.

When Smith offered Samia a private security job coming up near Washington, D.C., the younger man jumped at the chance. The job wasn't glamorous— as Smith put it, "halls and walls," meaning checking identifications of people attending a conference and making sure nobody went where he wasn't supposed to go. But, said Samia, "It was easy. It was exciting, a little different, something I was never used to." Best of all, it was lucrative. Samia was paid $1,000 a day, a fortune for a young guy just starting out in the building trades.

Smith encouraged him to become a security contractor, a growth field because of the rising threat level. "Mr. Smith . . . gave me some tactical training, taught me how to dress, how to act around executives, stuff like that, some motorcade stuff," Samia later recalled. At Smith's urging, he took a hundred-dollar "crash course" in bodyguard skills at the Executive Protection Institute in Berryville, Virginia, about fifty miles west of Washington, D.C. He followed up with other weekend training sessions and shooting courses. From time to time, he got jobs on temporary security gigs at special events.

In 2004, when Samia was thirty, his father, who was retired, decided to go into farming full-time. To stretch his savings, he looked to the rural South. In Roxboro, North Carolina, population 8,362, he found a five-bedroom house and fifty-six-acre horse farm on sale for just over half a million dollars. He bought and renamed the place Samia Son Stables.

Adam Samia joined his father, the father's second wife, and the father's mother, Adam's grandmother, on the farm, but life in a one-saloon, one-Confederate-statue town was not very rewarding. He kept up an email correspondence with Smith. In 2008, Smith offered him a job with Echelon Security, the front company he had set up to handle LeRoux's strong-arm work. Smith explained, as Samia later recalled, that "he has a very rich client. They had a lot of money in the pharmaceutical [business]. . . . He wants to diversify his money and get into gold and diamonds and timber and stuff like that." Smith offered $7,000 a month to start and $10,000 once the job got going, many times Samia's earnings as a plasterer. Samia didn't hesitate. He flew to Hong Kong, where he was met by one of Smith's men, a Canadian security contractor named Lachlan McConnell, and was introduced to Hunter and other mercenaries. Smith called the operation Midas. He named it for the Greek king who allowed his desire for gold to destroy his life. The job involved traveling to the Republic of the Congo, the neighboring Democratic Republic of the Congo, and Papua New Guinea, transporting gold and bribing local officials for timber concessions. LeRoux used these business activities, which were, for all practical purposes, impossible for outside investigators to trace, to disguise proceeds from his illegal pharmaceutical sales.

At first, the other mercenaries were wary of Samia because he was inexperienced. "I didn't want to partner up with him," Vamvakias said while testifying for the prosecution at Samia's murder trial. "I had a big issue, too, with the fact that he didn't have a military background. I felt he didn't have the firearms training, the hand-to-hand combat. I knew we were involved in stressful situations and I felt like he could potentially put our lives at risk and in danger or the mission in danger. And because he didn't have the military background, I also felt like there might be some sort of issue with him having the ability to follow orders."

"Don't worry, he's a good guy and he's a gamer," Smith replied, according to Vamvakias. A "gamer," Vamvakias explained, was "somebody who was willing to commit the same crimes that we were committing. . . . Any type of violence and anything else."

By way of vouching for Samia's eagerness to do dirty deeds, Smith added, according to Vamvakias, "Can you believe he actually mentioned wet work to me?" By "wet work," Vamvakias said, Smith meant "assassinations but up close and personal."

After the gig, Samia returned to North Carolina and worked at a gun store called the Arsenal with David Stillwell, who made and sold handcrafted holsters and gun concealment devices such as a bra holster called the Bosom Buddy. Samia and Stillwell launched a venture they called Grandfather Oak Training Group. Samia described himself in the marketing materials as "Assistant Instructor & Security Officer" and instructor in the "Advanced Combat Shooting Class," a "tactical shooting, engaging multiple targets at once, use of cover, tactical loads and combat loads." These were pretty bold claims for two guys who got all their information about warfighting from videogames and surplus stores. Samia applied for a job with the first-tier security firm Triple Canopy but without true military experience, he couldn't qualify. He continued to look for employment as a gunman, advertising himself on LinkedIn as a "security contractor" and networking at shooting events.

Samia got crossways with Smith in late 2008 or early 2009. While on R&R in the Philippines, Samia got into a fistfight with a bar girl and got arrested. Smith had to bail him out. He was furious. He fired Samia and sent him packing back to North Carolina.

Hunter kept up his correspondence with Samia. They had bonded over their mutual contempt for their bosses. On March 9, 2009, Hunter emailed Samia to grouse, "Still working for Dave and Paul and everything is still the same with those two. No planning and the planning they do is shit." Two months later, Hunter wrote Samia, "Adam, still with the same idiots. I'm in PI [the Philippines] right now and I'm supposed to head out to Africa again next week. Nothing has really changed. Still doing the same thing. Trying to hold out as long as I can."

Which, as it turned out, was indefinitely. LeRoux paid well, and Hunter didn't have any better prospects for employment.

As Cindric and Stouch pieced the next chapters together, from the confessions of LeRoux and Hunter, subpoenaed emails, and emails and texts from various seized electronic devices, around December 2009, both Smith and Hunter began to talk to Samia about handling some of the contract murders LeRoux wanted carried out. Their communications were always couched in an informal code that was open to interpretation, but the agents didn't have any doubt about what they were saying. They just had to prove it to a judge and jury.

The emails depicted Samia as eager for dirty work. On December 17, 2009, Hunter wrote Samia, "I just got here in the U.S. for the holidays and I will give you a call. This is something other than what I told you about. It is for doing the serious thing in Africa." To which Samia responded: "Roger that, bro. Give me a call."

A couple of weeks later, Smith wrote Samia: "The job is simply 9k a month plus 25k bonus on each job done as u know what joe does for us clean up with our problem people. You will work with joe. Need answer." Samia expressed interest and asked for more details and the price.

Samia's contacts with the LeRoux team became more intense after LeRoux had Smith killed in December 2010. In early 2011, LeRoux promoted Hunter to Smith's old job, chief of security. Sucking up to LeRoux, Hunter congratulated him on killing Smith because, as LeRoux later testified, "Dave Smith spent more time drinking and womanizing and wasn't really actively planning anything." By "planning," Hunter appeared to mean setting up contract hits.

Hunter reorganized the mercenary band into what he thought would be a more efficient killing machine. "Things are going to be different this time," he told Vamvakias and DeMeyere in the spring of 2011, as Vamvakias later recalled. "The business is going to be split in two. There's going to be the ninja side of things this time and the business side of things."

Vamvakias would take the "business side," which meant organizing a group of men to smuggle Tramadol, an opioid pain medicine, from northern Mexico to El Paso.

DeMeyere was working on the "ninja side." He strong-armed, threatened, and, on occasion, did worse, Vamavakias told authorities.

"Paul LeRoux had a list of people to be murdered," Vamvakias said. "And Chris was going to be the first one on board to be taking part in that list and murdering people and he was also going to help [Hunter] find other people to fit that position so he'd have more ninjas."

When LeRoux ordered Hunter to set up assassination teams, Hunter nominated DeMeyere and the New Zealander known as Mack Daddy. "I met Chris DeMeyere, Daddy Mack with Joseph Hunter at a meeting in the Philippines," LeRoux testified at the trial of Hunter, Samia and Stillwell. "And they were introduced to me as the new kill team put together by Joseph Hunter." LeRoux approved. According to the transcript of Hunter's bugged conversations in the Phuket safe house, the plea agreements of both LeRoux and Hunter and LeRoux's sworn testimony in court, they murdered Noemi Edillor in June 2011 but then refused to return and kill more people on LeRoux's hit list. Their departure left Hunter in a panic. He knew plenty of guys who would work on the business side of LeRoux's empire, carrying out routine bodyguard duty and smuggling, but fewer who would commit cold-blooded murder.

On July 29, 2011, Hunter emailed Vamvakias, "Hey, bro, looks like

Chris and the other guy that was working here for me took off. They got some money in their pocket. I know one has quit. Chris is bullshitting me. I know he's trying to set it up where it looks like he has to quit. I don't know what will happen here without a crew. I might be out of a job. I'll be keep you updated when I know more."

By the fall of 2011, frantic to get LeRoux off his back, Hunter contacted Samia via Skype and offered him "ninja work." Samia was definitely available, even eager. He was in Roxboro, still living with his father, bored out of his skull, occupying his time by having affairs with two or three local women, all of whom were seeing other guys, according to local lawmen, and playing war games with his buddy Stillwell. He was getting fat and spiraling downward into bleak middle age. He responded to Hunter immediately, accepting the job and proposing Stillwell as his driver and wingman. Stillwell had lied to Samia, falsely claiming that he had been a U.S. Army ranger and a sniper, and that he had gone to South America on U.S. special operations counterdrug missions. Actually, he had never been outside the United States. He didn't even have a passport.

Ever the micromanager, LeRoux said he wanted to discuss the Lee hit with Samia in person. LeRoux summoned Samia to a meeting in Rio. Samia didn't show. He failed to apply for a Brazilian visa in time to make his flight. Hunter began to regret his decision to reactivate Samia. He suspected that Samia was really trying to pocket the money LeRoux had sent him for the airfare to Rio, and they both knew what LeRoux did to people who skimmed. On October 14, 2011, Hunter wrote Samia a pointed email:

> . . . you fucked this up. You didn't got your visa. Now you read every word I say carefully. You get a refund on ticket. If there is no refund available, then you are expected to pay for the cost of the ticket. We are not paying for a ticket because you did not get a visa. The second thing is you and your guys work for me here in PI or the

states. You do not work for the boss directly unless he puts you on
an independent job that does not involve me. Your job and one of
your other guys is here in PI following my order. No negotiations.
No complaining. No bullshit. You'll be paid to do a job with a result.
The key word is "result." We do not pay for thinking about it. We do
not pay for trying. We do not pay for your time. We pay for the end
result. Do you understand? [Y]ou and one other guy prepared to
ninja stuff. Get your shit ready and stand by. I will tell you when to
get on the plane. No fucking delaying. No availability issues. If you
want to work do what I say.

Hunter followed up with an email to LeRoux, arguing that Samia's
misdeeds weren't his, Hunter's, fault:

The guy is crazy with attitude, so I had to set him straight!!! He
said he wanted a sit down with you before the other guys came on
board, and I explained to him that he is hired to do a job with an
end result!!! I told him he does what he is told and he gets paid. I
told him we are not paying for him to think about doing the stuff,
we are not paying him to try, we are not paying him for his time,
I told him we are paying for the result, period. I then told him to
quit fucking around and if he wanted a job, to pack his shit and
standby with his partner. I also told him he has to pay for that
ticket, because he failed to get the VISA. He says he can exchange
the ticket for a ticket to PI [the Philippines], but that's bullshit.
What he is going to do is buy a cheap ticket to PI instead of paying
the 1,600 back. That is what I think his plan is. Anyway, he said
he understands and he is ready to come here but the other guy
cannot come for a month.

But Hunter needed Samia for the moment, so all was forgiven. On
October 19, 2011, Hunter sent an email to Samia giving him a green
light to proceed with the murder:

Boss says you are on standby until the other guy is ready and you guys will come here together for Ninja stuff. . . . We want you guys, but are just waiting until you and your partner can get on the same time table.

Samia landed in Manila on January 9, 2012. At thirty-seven years old and six feet, one inch tall and paunchy, with coal-black hair and a stubbly beard, he was unmistakably an American, a head higher than the crowd of Filipinos on the Manila streets. Stillwell, forty-four, who landed a day later, was even more of a standout—blond, pale, and built like a fireplug.

Hunter told the pair to meet him at the Howzat Sports Bar in downtown Manila, near the boxing gym where Hunter worked out. It was a deafening, twenty-four-hour expat hangout with fifty-inch TV screens, live satellite feeds of American football, soccer, cricket, hockey, basketball, and golf, plus burgers, wings, and steak and only a few prostitutes. Hunter had often stopped by there with Dave Smith, and fellow mercenaries John O'Donoghue and Tim Vamvakias, when they were around. There were bedrooms to rent upstairs. Nobody would notice three more American guys having a beer at a table in the corner.

"Okay guys, this is how you do it." Hunter said, as he later recounted, according to court records. "Have her meet you at McDonald's. They call it Jolly, like a Jo, Jolly B. It's like McDonald's, right? Have her meet you in the parking lot at Jolly B. Get her into your car and take off so nobody saw you guys together. Maybe a couple of people in the restaurant that they won't remember. Right?"

Samia and Stillwell must have struggled to stay focused. They were still jet-lagged and trying to get acclimated to driving around greater Manila, a bewildering warren of neighborhoods, gated communities for the wealthy and *barangay*s, slums.

"As soon as she gets in the car, drive down the road," Hunter instructed. "Drive down the road maybe a quarter mile, a half kilometer.

Turn around and shoot her. It's done. Nobody saw anything. Just kill her in the car. Take a blanket with you and wrap her up. And then, just keep driving and find a place to dump her."

Hunter gave them a thumb drive that contained a "target package" for Dazl Silverio, an RX Limited employee whose name topped LeRoux's kill list. It consisted of digital photographs, addresses, and other intelligence compiled by a surveillance team of Filipinos hired by LeRoux. As well, he handed them a "weapons kit" that contained a .556-caliber rifle and a Smith & Wesson pistol and silencer from the Red, White and Blue Arms warehouse. Hunter loaned them a Toyota Innova van and a car that belonged to the RX Limited/RWB fleet. He told them to buy some stolen license plates for the van.

Samia and Stillwell couldn't find Silverio, because she had multiple addresses, including a place some distance from the city. They asked for more target packages. A few days later, Hunter supplied them with data for Catherine Lee and two other people, Fitch Penalosa, a low-level employee at RX Limited, and Manuel Jalos, whom LeRoux blamed for tipping the Philippines Coast Guard that the *Captain Ufuk* was running guns. "He cost me a lot of money," LeRoux griped.

According to court documents, Samia and Stillwell stalked Catherine Lee for a week, driving by her house and office in a community called Las Piñas. They spoke to a neighbor about her. They emailed her, posing as Bill and Tony, a pair of Canadian tourists who were interested in looking at rental properties. She agreed to take them around.

Around February 4 or 5, 2012, they picked up Lee at the Jolly B, also known as the Jollibee, a fast-food joint. She jumped into the back of their van as they drove around Manila, looking at houses. It was all very friendly and routine for a real estate agent. This went on for days.

When they weren't on the street with Lee, Samia and Stillwell studied the craft of killing. Stillwell read how-to guides they had downloaded on how to be a mercenary and how to be a hit man. ("When using a small-caliber weapon like the .22, it is best to shoot from a distance of three to six feet. You will not want to be at pointblank range to avoid having the victim's blood splatter on you or your clothing.")

Samia googled cyanide, grenades, and explosives and watched YouTube videos called "homemade silencer tutorial," "homemade wireless detonator," "how to build a grenade," and "how to make and explode a bomb." He searched for an answer to the question "How does ricin work?" Ricin is a deadly poison made from castor beans. Samia would later deny that these searches were his; someone else must have used his laptop, he claimed, without explaining who else would have had access to it in a hotel room in Manila.

As time passed, Hunter grew impatient. "Hunter was really ticked off," Vamvakias testified, "because during the day Adam Samia and his partner are riding around town with Catherine Lee and they're looking at properties and the murder is not getting done. And so at some point Adam Samia ends up calling to check in with Hunter and Hunter is ticked off that it's not done yet. He says, 'What have you guys been doing?' [Samia] says, 'Well, look, we haven't had the chance. People have seen us. She's run into friends. It started raining and there were people inside the buildings that they were looking at and they just hadn't had the opportunity to Hunter was pissed off about that and he basically told them don't call me back until it's done."

On February 12, 2012, Samia and Stillwell asked Lee to show them some more expensive places in Cavite, an upscale community outside Manila. She hopped in the backseat of the van as usual. It was a pleasant afternoon—sunny, balmy, and barely 80 degrees, and clear. Toward dusk, as Stillwell drove, Samia whirled around and leveled the muzzle of LeRoux's Smith & Wesson .22 at Lee. It couldn't have been more than a foot from her face. That's when Samia shot her in the face twice, one bullet under each eye. The two men wrapped Lee's head in a cloth to try to catch the blood. Samia took photos of her head and body with his phone.

They drove for several hours in the dark, looking for a place to dump the body. They settled on a pile of garbage in Taytay, Rizal, a sweat shop district twenty minutes from their apartment in the Mayfield Park Residences.

A trash collector reported finding the body at 7:15 a.m. the next day. Besides her jewelry, the police found Lee's Nokia C3 cell phone, which contained identifying information and an email trail between her and a man who called himself Bill. They located eyewitnesses who had seen her with two men in the Innova van, driving toward Manila at 5:30 p.m. on the previous evening. The witnesses described the men to a sketch artist.

The next day, Samia met Hunter and handed him Lee's driver's license and a memory card with the gruesome photos of Lee's head, mutilated and beginning to swell, and body. About a week later, Hunter gave Samia an envelope full of hundred-dollar bills containing the bonus payments for himself and his partner. The two hit men went to a Western Union just a mile from the spot where Lee was killed and wired $54,500 back home. The money, sent in small increments, was addressed to one of Samia's girlfriends and Stillwell's wife.

Hunter was not happy. "When they contacted Hunter afterwards, he was ticked off," Vamvakias later testified, "because they didn't do the way he told them to do it and also they ended up leaving her purse, her cell phone, her jewelry. He wanted them to make it look like a robbery and they didn't do any of that."

Hunter emailed LeRoux that the hit had "gone wrong . . . there were witnesses," LeRoux later testified. "The individuals had been sketched." Hunter also complained to the other mercenaries, in the bugged conversation in the Phuket safe house in March 2013, "They went to all these different houses with her, where there was people living in the houses. So every house they went to, people saw them together. They saw their faces. They saw the real estate agent. They did this for like three different days. . . . And then I was watching the news and they had the sketches, but the sketches didn't look like them so everything was okay. One guy kinda looked like an Asian and the other guy looked like a cartoon character."

LeRoux put $70,000 in a bag, hand-carried it from Rio to Manila, and gave it to Hunter to pay Samia and Stillwell for the Lee hit. But he didn't send them home. Despite their greenhorn performance, LeRoux wanted the pair to move ahead with the other hits on his list.

Samia and Stillwell seemed blissfully unaware of the consternation over their bumbled performance.

Two days after killing Lee, according to court documents, Samia sent a friend a message on Facebook that said, "My [dog] is going on 11 [years old] so it is coming for me to[o] . . . dreading that day . . . much easier to put down a person than a dog!!"

Samia and Stillwell proceeded to stalk their next victim. On February 27, Hunter messaged LeRoux that the pair had gone to the house of Fitch Penalosa "for a couple of days and are going to his office today." But for some reason, they didn't pull the trigger. On February 29, Hunter messaged LeRoux that Samia and Stillwell were "going home for tax filing" but were "definitely coming back." Stillwell departed on February 29; Samia, on March 5.

LeRoux set about destroying evidence. Samia had returned the murder weapon to Hunter. "Please get the .22 barrel changed," LeRoux emailed Hunter. He told Hunter to take the pistol to a gun club in Angeles City, which had a relationship with Red, White and Blue Arms, and have one of the staff members replace the barrel so that if the gun were subjected to ballistics tests, it wouldn't be linked to the murder. The staffers said no, they didn't have the tools or know-how to replace a pistol barrel. LeRoux told his aides to return the gun to the Red, White and Blue Arms warehouse.

The bloody van was a bigger problem. Samia and Stillwell drove to public parking lot near the Howzat, intending to return it to Hunter. Hunter peered inside and saw quarts of Lee's blood soaked into the backseat and on the floor, plus blood spatters all over the steering wheel and driver's door handle. The gunmen clearly had no idea how much blood would pump out of a human being's head. The little towel they had brought with them to soak it up was useless.

Hunter left the van in the lot for three or four days. LeRoux sent a young Filipino assistant to retrieve it. He panicked and disappeared. Two Israelis on LeRoux's staff took over. They drove the van to one of LeRoux's houses south of Manila. LeRoux started hosing down the van himself, then turned the job over to his aides, supervising them as a cascade of water and suds poured out of the vehicle. The stains were still deep. LeRoux had the middle seat pulled out and the rest of the rear seat reupholstered. After he was satisfied that the evidence was gone, LeRoux told the aides to return the van to his warehouse in Cavite. This was not a smart move. The warehouse was also the location of his pet project, his clandestine research lab for the Iranian missile venture.

Back in Roxboro, Samia tried to wipe his computer. He messaged Hunter that he was "on standby" for more jobs. Despite all the trouble Samia caused, LeRoux didn't give up on him, perhaps because people with U.S. passports were valuable. LeRoux told Hunter to give Samia another task—go to Miami and buy an oceangoing vessel that Stammers and Shackels could use to transport cocaine across the Pacific from Peru to East Asia. Samia refused, on grounds that the pay, $166 per day plus $40 a day for expenses, was ridiculously low. He couldn't find a cheap place to stay in South Florida for that kind of money, much less feed himself. "It's just not worth it for me," Samia wrote Hunter.

LeRoux blamed Hunter for Samia's lack of discipline and subservience. He cut Hunter's pay. Hunter fired off a furious email to Samia, dated May 18, 2012:

Maybe there is some miscommunication or something, because I sure do not understand. First, when I say I need you there ASAP, I meant two days ago or yesterday. I have been more the lenient with you as far as your wishes. Either, you want a job or you do not. But, you seem to have it in your mind that you're going to squeeze our balls on any issue you can find. But, thats [*sic*] your personality, and I will put up with it to an extent. You are not answering my emails in a timely manner and you are not answering my phone calls at all. I need team members that can get a job done!!! Not someone who thinks there [*sic*] in a position or have the experience to fuck this thing up!!!

Let me explain, you signed up for a job . . . in which I am responsible for both of you. I am expected to get these things done. You said you wanted the job. First, I waited a year for you to be available because of your other plans. Then you finally come onboard, do one sloppy job which could have endangered everyone and left. . . . Dave [Smith] would not have you back because of this exact reason. He told me about you and I still had faith that you would do a good job because I worked with you for a month and thought you were OK. So I will put it to you like this: Either you are with us or you are not. Interested. If you want a job, you will answer your telephone whenever I call and you will answer my email in a timely manner, because I have no time to waste with you. Your salary will be as stated above. If you accept this job, get your ass on the plane and quit fucking around.

Hunter and Samia negotiated over email for a while, but in the end, they couldn't come to terms.

Hunter, meanwhile, set out to assemble a proper kill team, this time made of experienced former military men with skills and discipline. He prided himself on possessing these soldierly virtues and wanted to hire people who would take orders unquestioningly. Midway through the recruitment process, LeRoux was arrested. As part of his cooperation agreement with the government, LeRoux started manipulating Hunter from the federal courthouse. Hunter's next hires were being approved by LeRoux with Cindric and Stouch at his shoulder.

The murder of Catherine Lee haunted the agents. During the plea-bargaining process, the prosecutors had agreed not to charge LeRoux with that murder or others he had set in motion. They decided they did not have jurisdiction, since the homicide of a foreign citizen overseas was normally a matter for the justice system of the nation where the crime was committed. There was a federal law permitting the prosecution of someone who conspired within the United States to commit a murder abroad, but LeRoux was never inside the United States when the seven murders he admitted to were being conceived.

But Hunter, Samia, and Stillwell were Americans. The evidence showed that they had planned aspects of the Catherine Lee murder on U.S. soil, in violation of federal law. They couldn't claim that they didn't know better. They weren't, for example, child soldiers whose minds had been twisted by deprivation and ignorance. They were relatively well educated and privileged, with all the opportunities afforded by American citizenship. The agents were determined that their crimes would not go unpunished.

"If we don't get them, nobody else will," Cindric said. "The Philippines is incapable of prosecuting that case."

Besides, he said, "I think Samia has done this before and for other people. We've tapped into a global murder-for-hire ring." If Samia went unpunished, Cindric was convinced that he would kill again and again.

Using Hunter's debriefings, the agents obtained search warrants for the two men's AOL, Facebook, and Gmail accounts. Incredibly, they had not deleted their email trails *even after* they read worldwide headlines heralding Hunter's arrest. Their "private" messages on Facebook were highly incriminating.

On November 20, 2013, one of Samia's friends sent him a link to a DEA press release announcing that Hunter and the mercenaries had been arrested:

MALE-1: you hear bout Tim [Vamvakias] and Joe [Hunter]?
SAMIA: . . . no what happen
MALE-1: read this

MALE-1: http://www.justice.gov/dea/divisions/hq/2013/hq092713.shtml

SAMIA: Wow . . . holly Shit . . .

MALE-1: That is crazy stuff . . .

SAMIA: very stupid people

SAMIA: they are done . . . they will never get out

MALE-1: yeah I would imagine not . . . I can't believe that they are that sloppy.

SAMIA: they got blinded by greed

On December 11, 2013, Samia hinted to another friend online that he had killed somebody:

SAMIA: . . . any new ideas to get rich quick!! Lol

MALE-2: Murder, sex, and drugs lol

SAMIA: did those already;) . . . well no drugs lol

MALE-2: Lol im guilty

SAMIA: Yep . . . like you said that why we get along so welllllllll . . . lol

Nine days after that, Samia forwarded to Stillwell a link to the U.S. attorney's office press release, dated September 27, 2013, announcing the arrest of Hunter and the other mercenaries for "conspiracy to murder a DEA agent" and other crimes.

On January 22, 2014, Samia wrote another friend about Hunter's arrest:

SAMIA: How are thing going in [the Philippines] Bro?!

MALE-3: Feels a little chilly even though its 76F . . . Other than that, same old stuff. . . . I suppose you've already heard about Joe Hunter?

SAMIA: ya that is crazy shit

SAMIA: Got greedy an sloppy

MALE-3: Yep . . . They're gonna put him in a cell UNDER the prison

SAMIA: Ya him an Tim [Vamvakias] . . . dont know the others . . .

On September 22, 2014, one of Samia's friends alerted him to a news report that LeRoux was cooperating with the DEA. Up to that time, LeRoux's cooperation had been kept secret. Samia scoffed, implying that he wouldn't get in trouble so long as he wasn't dealing in drugs. Illusions could be very sturdy things.

SAMIA: well that's good news Bro . . . .how are you doing . . . anything new . . . I am going crazy need to get back out!!

MALE-1: Nothing going on. Lachlan [McConnell] indicted in the Minneapolis case against RX Limited employees by the Feds and will be arrested soon

SAMIA: what for what

MALE-1: Stuff he did for [the leader of the Organization]

SAMIA: wtf . . . how many years ago was that from

MALE-1: Does not matter

SAMIA: did [the leader of the Organization] get pop too

MALE-1: [He] got lifted by the Feds in Brazil in 2012 and sang like a canary and set all his guys up

SAMIA: Wow

SAMIA: scary shit dude

MALE-1: So far there have been ten guys who worked for him lifted in diff countries and extradited to US

SAMIA: wow holy shit

SAMIA: that is fucking BS

SAMIA: that's to[o] bad for Lachlan he is a good guy

MALE-1: He's in a bad way at the moment

SAMIA: have they picked him up yet

MALE-1: Not yet

SAMIA: wonder if we r going to get brought in to this shit

MALE-1: No

MALE-1: They were all involved in drugs and taken down by the DEA

SAMIA: dumb I would never fuck around with that shit

MALE-1: They got greedy and stupid

SAMIA: I told joe that too

Samia and Stillwell didn't seem to think they were going to be found out. Two months after they got word that LeRoux was in jail and was talking, Stillwell posted a snapshot of himself on his Facebook page, reclining on a motorcycle, with this caption:

Welcome Blood Money to the family! She is wearing her winter color for now. SOON to show up in her new warpaint!!

The photo showed a police edition Harley-Davidson Road King, the model the company manufactured for police forces. Police Harleys were always white. Stillwell must have bought a police chopper that had been sold as surplus. Did he mean he intended to paint it with some of the cash Hunter paid him for the Lee murder?

The prosecutors in Manhattan presented the case to the federal grand jury and filed a sealed indictment of Samia and Stillwell on July 14, 2015. The pair was charged with conspiracy to murder and kidnap a person in a foreign country, using a firearm in a crime of violence and conspiracy to commit international money laundering.

Cindric and Stouch went to Roxboro and explained the situation to Sheriff Dewey Jones of Person County and Sergeant Mark Massey, who ran the sheriff's Special Operations Division and Special Response Team, a SWAT-like unit that handled dangerous arrests. Massey and his deputies would take the lead in arresting Samia and Stillwell. It would be an amazing bit of luck if the men were even around Roxboro.

But if they were there, the situation was risky. Cops all over America were getting shot at traffic stops, by people who didn't have criminal records. These men had already killed, and the emails indicated that Samia, at least, was actively looking to do it again. Together, the two men probably owned more guns than some small countries.

Massey said, no problem, Samia was a regular at Dalton's, the saloon across from the sheriff's office. That was the way it was in a small town. The deputies all knew him and knew all about his huge gun collection. They came up with a plan for avoiding a shootout with him.

On July 22, 2015, Massey had the sheriff's assistant telephone Samia and tell him to come by the department to renew the paperwork for his license to carry a concealed weapon. She was a gentle, soft-spoken woman whom Samia would not suspect of lying. When Samia showed up, shortly after 9:30 a.m., Massey, Cindric, and Stouch were there to meet him. They told him he was under arrest for conspiracy to commit a kidnap and murder in a foreign country, carrying a firearm in a crime of violence, and conspiracy to commit money laundering. They relieved him of the handgun on his hip.

Stouch read him his rights. Samia denied he knew anything about Catherine Lee. He told several conflicting stories about why he was in the Philippines. He said he wasn't "Sal," the cover name Hunter had used for him, and he didn't know a "JT," Stillwell's cover name.

After close to an hour of ducking and weaving, he said he wanted a lawyer. But he didn't stop talking. He started regaling them with his many connections in law enforcement. He said his uncle and brother were police officers in Massachusetts, and he was a reserve deputy sheriff there. That shiny, official-looking badge in his pocket proved it.

He added that just the previous week, he had been having beers with "a buddy of mine, another DEA agent" from Albuquerque.

What was his buddy's name? Stouch asked.

"Joe," Samia replied.

So that was Samia's get-out-of-jail card? Joe from DEA, no last name?

"Joe," Stouch repeated. He was struggling to keep a straight face. "Okay. All right, well, look, um, obviously it's your right to, to stop this and, and request an attorney."

Samia tried another angle. "You want a job with the former chief of police of Roxboro? He moved to Iraq, doing a job in security."

No, Stouch did not want to go to Iraq.

Samia asked to call another "good friend," the county district attorney.

"You can call whoever you like when you have your phone call," Cindric said. He added that Samia was going to be prosecuted for murder in federal court in New York City, so he would need a defense lawyer who could practice there.

"I've never even been to New York," Samia said plaintively.

While Cindric, Stouch, and Massey were parrying with Samia, they got a call from one of the deputies staking out Stillwell's home, a double-wide trailer. Stillwell had walked out of his front door and was heading toward his vehicle, and the deputies were following him. Because they knew the trailer was packed with guns, the deputies planned to pull him over at a traffic stop. When they did, they found him armed, but he didn't pull his gun. They delivered him to an interview room in the sheriff's department. As before, Cindric and Stouch introduced themselves and read him a Miranda warning. Stillwell waived his rights and said he wanted to cooperate. He denied involvement in the murder. He admitted he had been in Manila but claimed he had traveled there "to get the hell away, my father had died the previous year, and I just needed stress relief—went drinking and whoring, basically." He claimed that a month in the fleshpots of the mysterious East had wiped his memory nearly clean.

Over the hours, as the agents revealed their detailed knowledge of his movements in Manila, he broke down in tears and finally confessed.

"Did Adam Samia pull the trigger on that woman?" Cindric asked.

"Yes," Stillwell said.

"Were you present?"

"Yes."

"Did it happen in a van?" Stouch asked.

"It was in a vehicle."

"Who was driving the vehicle?"

"I was driving."

"Were you shocked he pulled the trigger?"

"Yeah."

Stillwell hung his head and sniffled that he was "a stupid idiot in the wrong place at the wrong time." He gave permission for the deputies and some agents from the federal Bureau of Alcohol, Tobacco, Firearms and Explosives to search his home, where, he said, they would find "rifles, pistols, knives, suppressors, machine gun."

"Anything else there that we should know about?" Stouch said. "Is there any type of explosives there? Do you have any grenades?"

"No, no. I have ammo, but . . ."

"How many guns are we talking?" Stouch asked.

"Over a hundred," Stillwell said.

"Oh boy," Stouch muttered. He turned back to Stillwell and asked again if he was absolutely sure there were no explosives. He didn't want the deputies to stumble into a booby trap.

"I have powder for reloading," Stillwell said. "I guess you can call that an explosive."

Stillwell's trailer yielded 159 firearms. As the agents walked through it, their boots crunched on guns scattered all over the floor. They found a digital camera memory card, with Stillwell's trophy shots of Catherine Lee's bloody face and body still on it. Stillwell's laptop at the Arsenal contained the same images. Stillwell had tried to erase the photo of Lee's bloody head and target package for Catherine Lee from that laptop, but deleting all traces of a digital image is not easy. Thomas Song, an investigator with the Justice Department's cybercrime laboratory, would pull up the digital documents and photo without much difficulty.

At Samia's house, the DEA agents, sheriff's deputies, and ATF agents found about thirty guns, some legal to own, but also a .50-caliber sniper rifle that had been illegally modified to fire fully automatic, like a machine gun. It was set up on a tripod on the pool table. They found a laptop similar to Stillwell's, with the target package for Catherine Lee. They found a massive pile of pocket litter connecting Samia to LeRoux—business cards, phone numbers, and travel receipts linking him to Hunter, McConnell, and O'Donoghue and a business card for Kelly Reyes Peralta, LeRoux's North Korean meth broker. LeRoux's name was written on one document. They found a password Samia used for communicating with Hunter—"joegoesbad-ass." They found a lease for a condo in the Mayfield Park Residences, near the Catherine Lee murder scene in Manila.

They found a Toyota Innova van key.

Back in Manhattan, with Cindric and Stouch watching, LeRoux got on the computer and sent messages to his former employees in Manila until he located someone who knew the location of the Toyota van in which Catherine Lee had been murdered. Steve Casey flew to Manila and tried the key in the van's ignition. It fit. Samia had saved the van key as a trophy.

In April 2018, Hunter, Samia, and Stillwell were tried for the murder of Catherine Lee. Samia denied all knowledge of the crime and suggested that Stillwell had done it. Stillwell didn't testify but stood by his confession, in which he fingered Samia as the triggerman.

LeRoux testified against all three mercenaries. He admitted, while perhaps not every crime he had ever committed, nonetheless many crimes, including ordering the death of Catherine Lee.

"The agreement requires me to tell the truth, not commit any more crimes, and testify if asked," LeRoux said. He did not say he regretted anything he had done. The prosecutors saw no point in asking him to feign contrition. Assistant U.S. Attorney Rebekah Donaleski told the jury, when vouching for his credibility, "He is a sociopath. He is evil. He has done horrendous things in his life. . . . We're not asking you to approve of what he's done, nor could you. We are asking you to listen to him. We're asking you to listen to what he says, to think about how he said it, to consider whether his words are backed up by emails, by things found at Samia and Stillwell's homes, by the other testimony at trial. Is what he told you corroborated? Because when you do that, you'll see that what he told you is corroborated and is backed up."

On April 18, 2018, a jury found all three men—Hunter, Samia, and Stillwell—guilty of conspiracy to commit murder in a foreign country, murder through use of a firearm, murder-for-hire, and murder-for-hire conspiracy. Samia and Stillwell were also convicted of money laundering. LeRoux was taken back to the lockup in Brooklyn to await his own sentencing, which could range anywhere from ten years to life in prison.

And when he got out, what then? On the stand he said he would not commit any more crimes. His eyes said something else. They were as deep and still and stony as a quarry lake.

Privately, the agents wondered. Would anything stop LeRoux from more crimes except a bullet?

CHAPTER FIFTEEN

BURNING IT DOWN

"HE'S RUNNING THAT FUCKING JAIL," CINDRIC SAID.

He was guessing, but his cop gut, which he trusted because it had been right most of the time, told him that a white Rhodesian/South African/Australian with a build like a rugby player and an epic superiority complex had become a leader in a federal lockup in Brooklyn. It made no sense but that's how it looked.

Even in lockup gray threads, LeRoux still had that old black magic. His spirit had revived, and he had dropped some dozens of excess pounds. With his shoulders squared, his chin high, and his gaze even, he looked even more Brando/Kurtz than when the agents first met him.

"He gets in there the first day," Cindric said. "Somebody called him a snitch and shoved and punched him and he didn't report that."

Why not? Because he planned on asserting command himself. He didn't intend to share control with the U.S. Marshals Service. On paper, the Marshals Service was in charge of the Brooklyn facility. It was not technically a prison. It housed people who had been arrested for federal crimes and who had agreed to become witnesses. The practical effect of this situation was to place them in legal limbo. They weren't inmates yet. Nearly all were awaiting sentencing, which would be contingent on their truthful testimony.

Other prisoners in the lockup surely concluded that LeRoux was an important government witness. He came and went hundreds of times, always with an escort of deputy marshals. He didn't get beaten up again. There was only one way to read his survival: as respect paid him by his fellow inmates. All the more remarkably, he got it without a gang or posse.

"He doesn't have to have a whole team around him," Cindric said. "They just know he has power. Paul exudes power. It's power to help people, power to hurt people. He's playing chess when they're playing checkers, and if they're playing chess, he's playing three-dimensional chess."

LeRoux had negotiated a bed in a favorable spot, out of the way of the air-conditioning system so it didn't blow on him. He bragged that he had arranged to have ten egg sandwiches a week delivered to him in the lockup. Two sandwiches every weekday.

He played spider-and-fly with the brighter prisoners. He made a point to size up men arrested for white-collar crimes, because they could play chess with him for real.

In Mir Islam, a young black-hat hacker, LeRoux found a chess partner and soul mate. Islam was a Bangladeshi American from the Bronx. (Despite his name, he told the court he was Jewish.) The first time he was arrested was in 2012, when he had just turned eighteen, for stealing and trading stolen identities. He was released and rearrested in 2013, for "swatting"—making false reports that dispatched SWAT teams to victims' houses; "doxing"—posting personal information about celebrities and officials on the Web; and cyber-stalking a young woman who had caught his eye.

According to LeRoux's testimony in the Hunter/Samia/Stillwell trial, LeRoux met Islam in 2015, when the younger man was incarcerated in the Brooklyn facility, awaiting sentencing. They struck up a friendship. LeRoux gave Islam money for food, a cell phone, and a laptop. When Islam was sentenced to two years and transferred to a federal facility in Virginia, he and LeRoux kept up their relationship via a covert communications channel, using a telephone that was supposed to be reserved for calls to defense lawyers' offices. In mid-2016, LeRoux was on the phone with his young buddy, discussing going into business together. "I discussed with Islam, using Islam to assist me in legal research and we also discussed opening a legal call center business with legal E-commerce operation," LeRoux testified in the Hunter/Samia/Stillwell trial.

Since Islam would be out of jail first, he would be the active partner in the call center enterprise. LeRoux would be the silent partner, putting up the funding.

LeRoux inveigled a paralegal worker at a law firm that represented him to visit him and make three-way calls so that he could talk directly to Cayanan, still his girlfriend and business partner.

The scheme fell apart in the summer of 2016, when FBI agents in Northern Virginia got wind that Islam was having strange conversations with some guy named Paul. The phone conversations were recorded. The FBI agents called the U.S. Marshals Service. Somebody there realized that LeRoux was a criminal defendant and a star witness for the DEA and the Southern District and alerted Cindric and Stouch. The agents investigated and determined that LeRoux had used the arrangement to communicate with a Filipino programmer who had worked for RX Limited. Through the IT man, LeRoux had set up a new server. He intended to use it to regenerate his pharmaceutical business and to serve as a platform for a new online gambling venture and possibly other businesses. He planned new call centers and new financial channels.

When called to testify in the Hunter/Samia/Stillwell trial, LeRoux insisted that he wasn't planning to resume his life of crime. "We discussed a variety of legal e-commerce businesses," he said.

Maybe. But his plans had all the hallmarks of an incipient criminal enterprise, communicating at the speed of light with nodes throughout the world. LeRoux had the new server programmed to erase itself every twenty-four to forty-eight hours, so that it wouldn't leave an electronic trail. It wasn't illegal, yet, but it looked devious.

LeRoux got a stern lecture and for a while, isolation from the agents. He shed a few real tears over that one. He had gloried in being the center of attention and "leader" of the winning Team America. Power, control, and attention were smack, crack, and crank to a narcissist. LeRoux was always chasing the rush, so the agents had been giving it to him as long as they needed his help tracking down his associates in his criminal network.

After they wrapped up the man-hunter phase of the investigation, the spotlight shifted to the prosecutions. The agents didn't need to pull LeRoux out of his cell every day or so. He went sullen and moody. When they saw him, they sensed the beast inside him, clawing and hissing. During one interview session, LeRoux spent most of the time ranting about some minor misstep by one of his women.

"I'm under attack," he raged.

"Fuck, dude, she's five foot nothing and a hundred-and-nothing pounds." Cindric laughed.

LeRoux was in no mood to kid. His "friendship" with the agents was situational. The agents knew he would switch it off the minute he didn't need them.

"Did you see his eyes?" Stouch asked Cindric afterward.

"Oh yeah. We better check our cars."

They shared an inside joke that LeRoux was going to figure out a way to build a remote-control detonator so he could blow up the agents' cars from his cell. They were sure that when they weren't around, LeRoux was sitting in his cell, pushing his chess pieces around, ruminating on ways to beat them, beat the system, take revenge on a world that gave him nothing.

Nothing but money, women, children, yachts, cars, airplanes, houses, beaches, an island for a while, and whatever else struck his fancy.

Many times, LeRoux was calm and smiling when other people would have panicked. The agents wondered, was he one of those people whose feet didn't touch the same earth everybody else's feet trod? Sometimes they had a sense that they were looking at a remake of *Apocalypse Now*, that LeRoux was a twenty-first-century Colonel Kurtz. LeRoux couldn't match the charisma of Brando as the renegade warrior-king of Francis Ford Coppola's iconic 1979 film about the madness of the Vietnam War, but he was far worse than Kurtz in some ways, because he possessed real scientific know-how and lit up when he talked working day and night to make it possible for Iran to destroy a lot of Israel and any other place the radical regime's leaders didn't like.

Was he born this way, or did something twist him around? The agents didn't probe deeply his childhood and possible motives for his misdeeds. There was too much else to do. Those questions were best left to the psychologists and, frankly, every crook they'd ever met had a sad story about mama or a daddy issue.

Even then, LeRoux managed to surprise them. During a routine debriefing, one of the agents from Minneapolis questioned LeRoux about the identities of other black-market pill merchants. Asked to examine a photo lineup with mug shots of suspected pill peddlers, LeRoux pointed to a photo of a middle-aged man and said, "Yeah, I know that guy. He's my biological father."

"What?" Stouch said.

"Yeah, he's one of my biggest competitors in the pharmaceutical business. He stole from me. He definitely stole $60,000 from me."

LeRoux said that soon after he got into the Internet pill game, he connected with the white Rhodesian he had been told fathered him. He didn't say how he knew. He said they became business partners, and Hornbuckle went to the southern United States to sign up pharmacies to fulfill the bogus prescriptions ginned up by LeRoux's paid doctors.

LeRoux suggested he trusted the older man, because he made Hornbuckle a cosigner on one of his business bank accounts. Things went well, he said, until sometime in 2007, when LeRoux realized that $60,000 was missing from the account. LeRoux told the agents that from that moment on, the man was his archenemy.

In a twisted way, LeRoux's father, or at least, father figure, might have inspired him to ascend to greater heights in business. That the business was on the dark side was no accident. That's where he thought his dad had tried to make his mark and where he wanted to crush the older man.

"His father being that much of an asshole lent itself to risk-taking," Stouch said. "Obviously, he was trying to prove he was better than his dad."

He didn't have a good word to say about his adoptive parents. He didn't know where his adoptive father was. Maybe gone, maybe dead. It didn't matter. He didn't care about his adoptive mother, either. Some months after his arrest, a message landed in LeRoux's email box from his younger sister, the biological child of the LeRoux couple. She wrote that Judith LeRoux had died. Since Cindric and Stouch were reading all LeRoux's email, they brought him the bad news and offered condolences.

LeRoux shrugged. "Guys, she's been dying for years," he said, and changed the subject.

Being simultaneously indifferent and insatiable is what narcissists do. It's the reason narcissists make excellent innovators. They don't stop, and they don't yield to logic or compassion.

The agents concluded that Paul LeRoux was intercepted before he realized his full potential as a villain. Still, he left an enduring legacy. He had laid the foundation for something new—a new form of transnational organized crime that transcended categorizations such as "drug trafficker" and "gun runner." It didn't have a name yet. It was fluid and seeped into cracks. LeRoux and his disciples, acolytes, and imitators functioned like a swarm of jellyfish. They looked like discarded bits of tissue paper, if you could see them at all. But try swimming in a bay they occupied.

Investigative agencies and legal systems weren't built to grapple with this protean menace. LeRoux's world only seemed unorganized because it didn't fit the traditional template of a solid, squared-off structure with an identifiable hierarchy and command-and-control apparatus.

LeRoux didn't get caught up in a massive structure of camaraderie, like the Mafia. He created a virtual reality that allowed him to dispense with the need to meet people face-to-face most of the time. He insulated himself in original ways.

"When you marry that brilliance with someone who has no qualms, that's what's so scary," Milione said. "He will not stop, and people will not see it coming with him."

Milione and his agents built the plane while they were flying it. They found a way to peer into LeRoux's world, then retooled their tradecraft and improvised to get inside, first with Jack, then with other informants, all the while playing LeRoux, the master manipulator. Their street-cop guts served them well. They didn't always guess right, but they managed it often enough to gain a narrow edge over their adversaries.

"We knew that Paul is a very complex business guy with a truly multifaceted criminal empire," Cindric said. "He's a much more sophisticated model than the cases we had worked before. It's like making the jump from Triple-A ball to the major leagues: you're taking everything you learned, and you gotta be able to hit the curveball this time."

The chilling thing was, the 960 Group had gotten Viktor Bout as he was on the downslope of his career. LeRoux was on the rise. "If we hadn't gotten Paul when we did, God knows what he would have been able to do," Cindric said. "There'd be a lot more people dead."

Milione saw LeRoux as a logical extension of the concept of the entrepreneurship movement, the way of thinking personified by Elon Musk. "You see how Musk has grown and how Tesla has grown and how it's completely changed how everybody else is doing business," Milione said. "LeRoux is applying almost that kind of disruption on the dark side. He's so brilliantly psychotic that he can apply that dis-

ruptive frame of mind to business. Guys like him are the engine behind all the bad things that are going on in the world, whether it's
drug trafficking, money laundering, arms trafficking, fake documents,
terrorism. He crosses over all kinds of things, into terrorism, weapons,
drug trafficking. If he hadn't gotten into the power he felt from killing
people and burning it all down, he might still be out there. Those who
know how to operate in the virtual world and have a ruthless brilliance
about them will be very hard to catch."

Milione and his agents knew that a smart international kingpin employing Paul LeRoux's methodology could win at this game. With rare
exceptions, government bureaucracies are too hidebound and rife with
internal rivalries to encourage risky, expensive, boundary-breaking investigations like the one that caught LeRoux.

"Does LeRoux have a plan for the future?" said Jack, who probably
knew LeRoux as well as anyone living. "Damn right he has, and he's
planning it while he is in prison. Does he have the money and contacts
to succeed? Of course he has, because he would never give up all his
assets and information. He knew he will walk out again one day. Only
this time he has learned a lot more about the system, and he will be
even more careful than ever. We have not heard the last word about
him for sure. When he walks out he could collect and retire on a nice
beach and enjoy the rest of his days in great luxury, but that's not Le-
Roux. Nope, he will need something that feeds his brain constantly,
and it wouldn't surprise me that he will go to Asia or South Africa."

Jack believed that when LeRoux got out, he was going to be pre-
occupied with his own safety. He had made enemies of his own, by
naming names of important Asian and African figures he had bribed.
Some of them ran death squads. And then there were the gunslingers
he had hired for gigs. He'd gotten five of his mercenary snipers locked
up, but there were others still out there.

Cindric and Stouch agreed with Jack that LeRoux was treating
his prison time as an interlude, something like a forced postgraduate

course in the system and how to beat it. They suspected that he had every intention of emerging from prison, then immediately disappearing into a black cloud of money. He hinted malevolently to them that he had no interest in going straight.

"Paul, when you get out, what do you think you'll do?" Stouch asked one day.

"Girls."

"What?" Cindric said.

"Girls. Yeah, you know the Arabs. They want the girls."

"So he thinks his next business," Stouch said with disgust, "is going to be trafficking women."

"When he gets out of jail, he's going to be the worst enemy for the next group of guys who've gotta chase him," Cindric said, "because he knows some of the game."

Yet Cindric and Stouch stubbornly persisted in the belief that LeRoux, and people like him, were not beyond the reach of the law.

"The same thing that took Paul down before will bring him down in the future," Cindric said. Hubris. Excess. That thing inside him was still scratching and clawing to get out and hurt somebody. Whenever it did, Cindric and Stouch believed LeRoux wouldn't be able to resist showing himself, one way or another.

"He'll think, there can't be two more Erics and Tommys," Stouch said. "But there are."

NOTE TO READERS

MOST INDIVIDUALS WHO WORKED ON THE INVESTIGATION OF PAUL CALDER LeRoux and his associates are identified by name and title. Interviews for this book were conducted on the record, with very few exceptions. I have enjoyed rare access to firsthand witnesses. This book is drawn from thousands of hours of interviews over six years with people who had direct participation in and knowledge of the events described in the book and from thousands of documents, including government documents, personal notes, diaries, emails, texts, timelines, photos, transcripts, undercover audio and videotapes, and documents seized from people investigated and prosecuted for crimes.

When I have used exact quotations, dialogue, thoughts, or conclusions, I have derived that information from firsthand witnesses to the events or from documents, including transcripts, emails, and texts among the participants.

To protect innocent lives, I have used cover names to conceal the identities of a few people who were and are working undercover or are living and working in dangerous situations. These include:

Taj, a DEA agent who frequently works undercover;

Jack, a former LeRoux employee who penetrated LeRoux's organization as an undercover DEA informant in order to stop LeRoux's murders and bring him to justice;

Anya, Jack's fiancée;

Leo, a European mercenary associated with Jack;

Diego, a DEA informant who posed as a Colombian cartel representative in order to bring LeRoux to justice;

Geraldo, a DEA informant who posed as Diego's Colombian partner;

Georges, a professional pilot who served as a DEA source in Africa and Asia and who helped bring LeRoux to justice;

Bee is a code name for a Thai employee of the DEA office in Bangkok. His whole name has been withheld for security reasons.

Paul Calder LeRoux has not been interviewed for this book. He is incarcerated in a secure federal facility, has pleaded guilty to certain crimes, and has served as a government witness against those he hired to commit murders, to traffic in drugs and arms, and for other crimes. I have submitted requests to interview him but have not been permitted to do so.

To date, all the individuals charged in the U.S. for agreeing to carry out contract murders for LeRoux or for trafficking in North Korean methamphetamine for LeRoux have pleaded guilty or have been convicted in the U.S. District Court for the Southern District of New York.

Elaine Shannon, Washington, D.C.,
October 18, 2018

NOTES

INTRODUCTION: MALIGN ACTOR

5   **His first venture generated**: The estimate of LeRoux's RX Limited sales comes from a plea agreement signed by John Wall, a former RX Limited employee. It disclosed that DEA agents calculated that from June 2007 through August 2011, RX Limited shipped over 2,973,374 orders valued at $297,337,400. Source: U.S. District Court, District of Minnesota, Criminal No. 13-273 (4), *USA v. Jonathan Wall* (4), Dec. 7, 2015.

CHAPTER 1: SEPTEMBER 25, 2013

16   **His mother died**: Dennis Gögel's personal history comes from his letter to federal Judge Laura Taylor Swain, filed in U.S. District Court, Southern District of New York, on Aug. 27, 2015.

18   **He hired mercenaries**: The quotes from LeRoux come from an email from Paul LeRoux to Joseph Hunter, dated January 4, 2013, and obtained by the author.

CHAPTER 2: MURPHY'S LAW

33   **Hunter took to the job**: The quotes from Hunter come from a transcript of a conversation that took place March 8, 2013, in Phuket, Thailand, and was filed in U.S. District Court for the Southern District of New York on March 16, 2018, in Case 1:13-cr-00521-RA.

38   **They and other conservatives and libertarians**: The history of the Intercollegiate Society of Individualists, later, Intercollegiate Studies Institute, is described in Lee Edwards, *Educating for Liberty: The First Half-Century of the Intercollegiate Studies Institute* (Washington, DC: Regnery, 2003).

38   **By the time the Reagan Revolution**: The quote from President Reagan comes from the ISI website at https://home.isi.org/about/about-isi.

42   **As Milione hoped and expected, Kassar's arrogance**: Monzer al-Kassar's crimes are described in *USA vs Kassar,* filed on June 21, 2007 in the U.S. District Court for the Southern District of New York.

43   **Kassar was sentenced**: Benjamin Weiser, "An Arms Dealer Is Sentenced to 30 Years in a Scheme to Sell Weapons to Terrorists," *New York Times*, February 25, 2009, http://www.nytimes.com/2009/02/25/us/25arms.html.

51 **It was a surprising development**: According to interviews of DEA agents by the author, Estonian law required an extradition proceeding. The two accused men were extradited to the United States in April 2014. Once the Estonian court ruled, Casey, Cindric, Stouch, and Taj flew to Tallinn in a rented executive jet to pick up Soborski and deliver him to court in Manhattan. "How did you take the cuffs off?" Casey asked him. "Training," he said. He turned his back to them and stared out the window. When Casey, Cindric, Stouch, and Taj photographed Soborski shirtless, they noted a big scar on his abdomen, clearly, from a major operation. They said he complained at length about the miserable food and frigid cell in the Estonian prison, but he didn't mention being beaten. However, once in the United States, Soborski accused the Estonian SWAT team of beating him during the arrest. In the end, the U.S. court did not determine how the Pole became ill or injured. Soborski and Filter pleaded guilty to one count of cocaine trafficking.

CHAPTER 3: THE RHODESIAN

65 **Today, only 17,000 people**: Information about Zimbabwe's population can be found in the "Zimbabwe Inter-Censal Demographic Survey, 2017," www.zimstat.co.zw/sites/default/files/img/publications/Census/ICDS_2017 _Report.pdf, and Ian Phimister, "The Collapse of Rhodesia, Population Demographics and the Politics of Race," *Journal of Imperial and Commonwealth History* 39, August 15, 2011.

66 **Liberation brought no peace**: Authoritative information on post-independence atrocities can be found in the "Report on the 1980s Disturbances in Matabeleland and Then Midlands," compiled by the Catholic Commission for Justice and Peace in Zimbabwe, March 1997, http://www.rhodesia.nl /Matabeleland%20Report.pdf.

67 **The LeRoux family would have avoided**: Paul LeRoux's father's employment as an asbestos mine supervisor was reported by Evan Ratliff in an online article, "He Always Had a Dark Side," https://magazine.atavist.com /he-always-had-a-dark-side/.

67 **Available accounts of the period**: The Shabanie and Mashaba asbestos mining complex was owned by Turner and Newall of Manchester, England, Britain's largest asbestos company. In the 1970s, Shabanie was considered the world's largest underground asbestos mine, employing 12,000 people. According to a seminal academic research study published in 2003 and titled, "Asbestos Mining and Occupational Disease in Southern Rhodesia/Zimbabwe, 1915–98," these workers were exposed to far more potentially lethal asbestos dust than allowed in comparable operations in the industrialized world. "To be profitable Zimbabwe's mines had to run at full capacity, but the limitations of the plant meant that the more ore that was put through the mills, the higher the levels of dust and the higher the incidence of disease," Professor Jock McCulloch, the study's author, wrote. "The mines were so profitable because they were so dangerous." McCulloch, a historian at the Royal Melbourne Institute of

Technology University in Australia, himself died of mesothelioma in January 2018, probably from exposure to asbestos in the same Zimbabwe mines where Paul LeRoux the elder may have worked as a manager.

67 **Rhodesians labored under a stigma:** Life for whites in Rhodesia is described by Piers Brendon, *The Decline and Fall of the British Empire, 1781–1997* (New York: Knopf, 2008); Robert Blake, *A History of Rhodesia* (New York: Knopf, 1978); and Frank Clements, *Rhodesia: The Course to Collision* (London: Pall Mall Press, 1969).

68 **LeRoux's father reportedly parlayed:** Paul LeRoux's employment in South Africa is reported by Evan Ratliff in an online article "He Always Had a Dark Side," https://magazine.atavist.com/he-always-had-a-dark-side.

69 **The teenage years:** The demography of South Africa during LeRoux's teenage years is detailed in Padraig O'Malley paper "Demographic Characteristics of South Africa in the late 1980s," https://www.nelsonmandela.org/omalley/index .php/site/q/03lv02424/04lv03370/05lv03389.htm.

73 **Hafner wanted to launch:** The significance of the project undertaken by LeRoux is explained by Kim des Zetter, in "Hacker Lexicon: What Is Full Disk Encryption?" *Wired,* July 2, 2016, https://www.wired.com/2016/07 /hacker-lexicon-full-disk-encryption/.

73 **And then do them:** In December 1998, LeRoux had published a freeware disk encryption program he called E4M—Encryption for the Masses. He released not only the E4M application itself but the underlying source code that made it and invited other programmers to improve on it. When Hafner and his programmers looked at LeRoux's source code closely, they spotted a string of code they had written for an early stage of Hafner's project and shared with LeRoux in 1997. LeRoux dismissed his appropriation of Hafner's code as an oversight. Hafner accepted his explanation because LeRoux had valuable skills.

78 **Except for a brief unresolved dispute:** In February 2004, a collective of anonymous programmers calling themselves the TrueCrypt Team published a full disk encryption system as freeware. The TrueCrypt website announced that the program was based on LeRoux's E4M program. Since TrueCrypt competed head-to-head with SecurStar's DriveCrypt, Hafner immediately suspected that LeRoux was behind TrueCrypt and was seeking revenge for his firing and humiliation. Hafner discovered that E4M contained a string of code that had been created by other Hafner programmers and accused LeRoux of "intellectual property theft." The TrueCrypt Team refused to withdraw its product. The dispute, which blew up in geek chat rooms, enhanced the TrueCrypt image as the rebel's choice. Among its famous users was Edward Snowden, the whistle-blower who used TrueCrypt in 2013 to transmit sensitive information he took while consulting for the U.S. National Security Agency. DriveCrypt became the choice of mainstream corporate and government customers, including Citicorp, Exxon, Shell, Volkswagen Financial, Prudential, Scotland Yard, the U.S. Federal Aviation Administration, Motorola, PriceWaterhouse Coopers, and Texas Instruments. "If James Bond had

encryption software he would have the DriveCrypt Plus Pack," Justin Peltier of *SC* magazine raved.

81 **As a child in a whites-only school**: White Rhodesian culture is explained by Richard West in *The White Tribes of Africa* (Cape, 1965) and Brendon in *The Decline and Fall of the British Empire, 1781–1997*.

CHAPTER 4: BLACK CLOUD

82 **Exactly how this stroke of genius**: LeRoux appears to have given different people different stories about what inspired him go into the e-commerce pharmaceutical black market. In 2012 and 2013, when negotiating for a plea bargain, he claimed to DEA agents and prosecutors that Hafner, his old boss and mentor, was already in the illegal online pill business and led him into a life of crime in 2004. Hafner denies this accusation, saying he was a respected and trusted figure in the legal digital electronics, telecommunications, and cybersecurity businesses and, by 2004, wasn't talking to LeRoux. Details of LeRoux's story seem unlikely: he claimed he did web design for Hafner's pill websites. Hafner says LeRoux, while an excellent cryptographer, did not have web design skills and relied on others to build the SecurStar website. Hafner's version of events is supported by LeRoux's own message to TrueCrypt Team chat room in February 2004, in which LeRoux said he "hadn't been involved with SecurStar since 2002." That assertion squares with Hafner's version of events. The author concludes that LeRoux leveled a false charge against Hafner as revenge for firing LeRoux for stealing proprietary code in 2002.

83 **Pills that looked like Willy Wonka**: U.S. pharmaceutical sales in 2003 were $216.4 billion, up 12 percent over the previous year and 44 percent of global pharmaceutical sales of $492 billion, according to a paper by Health Strategies Consultancy LLC. "Follow the Pill: Understanding the U.S. Commercial Pharmaceutical Supply Chain," Kaiser Family Foundation, March 2005.

83 **In 2004, according to an annual U.S. government survey**: Trends in drug abuse were reported in the 2004 National Survey on Drug Use and Health, commissioned by the U.S. Department of Health and Human Services, Substance Abuse and Mental Health Services Administration. Later trends were reported by the 2016 National Survey on Drug Use and Health, also published by the Substance Abuse and Mental Health Services Administration, https://www.samhsa.gov/data/.

83 **The black market**: Global pharmaceutical sales figures come from an article by John Laporte, "Topic: Global Pharmaceutical Industry," Statista, https://www.statista.com/topics/1764/global-pharmaceutical-industry/.

84 **One estimate put Big Pharma**: Pharmaceutical industry advertising is discussed in "Big Pharma Spends More on Advertising than Research and Development, Study Finds," *Science Daily,* January 7, 2008, https://www.sciencedaily.com/releases/2008/01/080105140107.htm.

86 **RX Limited usually had about five:** LeRoux's admissions for his plea
bargain are contained in the Proposed Cooperation Agreement for Paul Calder
LeRoux, drafted by attorneys in the office of U.S. Attorney for the Southern District
of New York, including Andrew Dember, deputy chief, Criminal Division; Michael
Farbiarz and Jocelyn Strauber, Co-chiefs, Terrorism and International Narcotics;
Michael D. Lockard; and Rachel P. Kovner. It was signed February 4, 2013. It was
not made part of the public court record but was obtained by the author.

86 **They were generally unwilling:** The epidemic of opioid abuse is
documented in these government reports: "Vital Signs: Overdoses of Prescription
Opioid Pain Relievers—United States, 1999—2008," Centers for Disease
Control and Prevention, November 4, 2011, https://www.cdc.gov/mmwr
/preview/mmwrhtml/mm6043a4.htm; "Opioid Overdose," CDC, August 1,
2017, https://www.cdc.gov/drugoverdose/data/overdose.html.

CHAPTER 5: MAGIC!

98 **LeRoux had hired Smith:** The source for LeRoux's description of
his relationship with Dave Smith, and his murder of Smith, is the Proposed
Cooperation Agreement.

98 **Dave Smith said:** Paul LeRoux testified about his relationship with
Dave Smith during the trial of Joseph Manuel Hunter in the U.S District Court
for the Southern District of New York, April 4, 2018, 13 Cr 521 (RA).

CHAPTER 6: INVISIBLE CITY

117 **It was the best-selling opioid:** Figures for the expansion of prescription
opioid sales can be found at a DEA website, U.S. Drug Enforcement
Administration, Aggregate Production Quota History For Selected Substances,
https://www.deadiversion.usdoj.gov/quotas/quota_history.pdf; U.S. Government
Accountability Office, "Prescription Drugs, OxyContin Abuse and Diversion
and Efforts to Address the Problem," December 2001.

CHAPTER 7: PAC-MAN AND IRONMAN

154 **Cindric went online:** In 1990 Ari Ben-Menashe was tried in federal
court in New York for attempting to sell three U.S.-made Lockheed C-130
Hercules cargo planes to Iran, in violation of the U.S. Arms Export Control
Act. Ben-Menashe claimed that the sale had been sanctioned by the Israeli
intelligence service Mossad. A jury acquitted him. He moved to Canada.

CHAPTER 9: DAZZLE HIM

193 **By contrast, $1 million in $100 bills:** Weight and volume of U.S.
currency was described in testimony by Assistant Secretary of the Treasury
(Financial Markets) Gary Gensler, House Subcommittee on Domestic and
International Monetary Policy, October 8, 1998.

196 **Meth was much in demand**: Methamphetamine use in Asia is tracked in "The Challenge of Synthetic Drugs in East and South-East Asia and Oceania Global SMART Programme 2015 Trends and Patterns of Amphetamine-type Stimulants and New Psychoactive Substance," United Nations Office on Drugs and Crime, May 2015, https://www.unodc.org/documents/scientific/The_Challenge_of_Synthetic_Drugs_in_East_and_South-East_Asia_and_Oceania-2015.pdf.

CHAPTER 10: "I JUST DON'T WANT TO GET ON THE PLANE"

205 **In 2014, the U.S. government**: U.S. sanctions against the Chinese firm Poly Technologies are listed on a web page, "Iran, North Korea, and Syria Nonproliferation Act: Imposed Sanctions," U.S. Department of State, May 2015, https://www.state.gov/t/isn/inksna/c2883.htm and in a Federal Register notice at: https://www.federalregister.gov/documents/2014/06/26/2014-14935/addition-of-certain-persons-to-the-entity-list-and-removal-of-person-from-the-entity-list-based-on.

205 **Afghan opium accounted for**: Estimates of heroin production and use come from the report "The Global Heroin Market, U.N. Office on Drugs and Crime," https://www.unodc.org/documents/wdr/WDR_2010/1.2_The_global_heroin_market.pdf.

CHAPTER 11: QUEEN FOR A DAY

219 **Iran's progress was hobbled**: Iran's Defense Industries Organization had been cited by numerous sanctions regimes. In 2004, the International Atomic Energy Agency declared that the DIO was involved in producing components for centrifuges meant to enrich uranium to for Iran's nuclear program. In 2007, the UN Security Council sanctioned several Iranian entities, including the DIO, for advancing Iran's nuclear and missile programs. The United States followed suit, sanctioning the DIO for activities relating to the development of weapons of mass destruction and missiles, in violation of the U.S. Iran and Syria Nonproliferation Act, the U.S. Arms Export Control Act, and the U.S. Export Administration Act.

220 **LeRoux understood why**: Iran's efforts to obtain high-tech precision weapons were highlighted in the *Annual Threat Assessment of the Intelligence Community,* February 12, 2009, testimony of Dennis C. Blair, director of national intelligence, before the Senate Select Committee on Intelligence.

221 **The DIO was working on a land-attack cruise missile**: Iran's missile development plans are discussed in a series of reports, *Ballistic and Cruise Missile Threat,* by the U.S. Air Force's National Air and Space Intelligence Center in collaboration with the Defense Intelligence Ballistic Missile Analysis Committee published in 2009, 2013, and 2017.

222 **The ITAR rules at the time required**: The rules applied to unclassified commercial GPS systems. They would be amended in 2014 to drop the 60,000 feet/1,000 knot language and instead bar sales of GPS equipment "specially

designed for military application" and also airborne systems that could deliver a 500-kilogram payload 300 kilometers.

238 **Kobi Alexander, CEO of Comverse Technology**: The charges against Alexander are outlined in a Securities and Exchange Commission press release, "SEC Charges Former Comverse Technology, Inc. CEO, CFO, and General Counsel in Stock Option Backdating Scheme"; and a Justice Department press release, "Jacob 'Kobi' Alexander Sentenced to 30 Months in Prison for Securities Fraud," dated February 23, 2017, https://www.justice.gov/usao-edny/pr/jacob -kobi-alexander-sentenced-30-months-prison-securities-fraud.

CHAPTER 12: ALL THE PIECES ON THE CHESSBOARD

247 **Hunter's first kill team**:
On Oct. 15, 2018, during post-trial proceedings in the murder case of Joseph Hunter, Adam Samia, and Carl David Stillwell, U.S. District Court judge Ronnie Abrams issued a ruling that summarized the evidence against Hunter and others, including DeMeyere, who had been named as an unindicted coconspirator. Abrams wrote:
Indeed, it [*13] was well-established that beginning in early 2011, Hunter became the sole person responsible for managing the murderers-for-hire, which included hiring, overseeing, and otherwise acting as an intermediary between them and LeRoux. Tr. 409:17-410:19; 431:5-8; 432:14-433:7. There was thus a basis for the jury to conclude that Hunter was a member of the conspiracy during these three later trips, particularly the last two, at which point Hunter, as head of the operation, was actively recruiting members to the conspiracy, as well as managing the day-to-day operations of LeRoux's "kill team."
The testimony at trial was that in early 2011, after LeRoux helped kill Smith, Hunter was promoted to Smith's position as head of the mercenaries and was instructed to form a two-person team, the sole responsibility of which would be murders-for-hire. Tr. 407:25-408:4, 409:17-410:19.14 The jury could have reasonably concluded, therefore, that during the February 2011 visit Hunter was actively recruiting the members of this newly founded kill team. Tr. 409:17-410:19; 1182:14-1183:1. Indeed, Hunter immediately went about recruiting Chris DeMeer and "Daddy Mack." Tr. 413:5-13.15 When Samia wrote Hunter in April [*14] 2011 expressing interest in work, Hunter indicated that he "[a]lready ha[d] eight guys working for me on various things," seemingly confirming he had already recruited the new kill team, in compliance with LeRoux's instructions. Tr. 412:8-13; GX 436. DeMeer and Daddy Mack would commit one murder for LeRoux in May or June of 2011 before promptly exiting the organization, leaving Hunter to recruit the new kill team that would eventually consist of Sarnia and Stillwell. Tr. 428:16-22, 1196:21-1197:15; 1199:5-11; GX 406-3

252 **It was signed by Morteza Farasatpour**: Morteza Farasatpour identified himself on the letter faxed to LeRoux on January 29, 2013, as "deputy managing director (commerce)" for the Defense Industries Organization of the Islamic Republic of Iran. U.S. and Western intelligence considered him a significant figure in supplying chemical weapons to the regime of Bashar Hafez

al-Assad, the authoritarian leader of Syria. In March 2017, acting on information from the intelligence community and open sources, the U.S. Treasury Department would sanction Faratsapour for "coordinating the sale and delivery of explosives and other material for Syria's Scientific Studies and Research Center (SSRC), an entity that controls Syria's missile production and unconventional weapons facilities; oversaw DIO's credit line valued at tens of millions of dollars with SSRC." The term "unconventional weapons" referred to chemical weapons the Assad regime deployed against civilian populations during the country's long-running civil war.

257 **The yacht's first mate:** During the investigation of LeRoux, the DEA agents contacted law enforcement agencies in the Pacific region and saw to it that a tracking device was placed on his smuggling boat, the *JeReVe*. It stopped emitting in October 2012. Cindric and Stouch had LeRoux call the captain of the vessel. He made a muffled comment and hung up. LeRoux then called the captain's wife, who said she had spoken briefly with him and he said he was with "the fish people." She took that to mean he was being held by pirates. Since the captain was not on the wrecked boat, there has been speculation he was murdered by pirates but the truth of the matter has never been established.

264 **"He's at minimum a sociopath and probably a psychopath":** LeRoux has never been formally diagnosed with a psychological disorder by a mental health professional. But a strong consensus developed among agents and prosecutors who met LeRoux that he displayed many of the characteristics of a psychopath, as defined by Robert D. Hare, Ph.D., a researcher in criminal psychology who developed a widely used diagnostic tool called the Hare Psychopathy Checklist—Revised. Hare regularly consults with the FBI. In his book *Without Conscience: The Disturbing World of the Psychopaths Among Us*, Hare wrote, "Unlike psychotic individuals, psychopaths are rational and aware of what they are doing and why. . . . Psychopaths feel that their abilities will enable them to become anything they want to be. Given the right circumstances—opportunity, luck, willing victims—their grandiosity can pay off spectacularly. . . . [They] have a narcissistic and grossly inflated view of their self-worth and importance, a truly astounding egocentricity and sense of entitlement, and see themselves as the center of the universe, as superior beings who are justified in living according to their own rules." The seminal 1941 book *The Mask of Sanity,* by pioneering American psychiatrist Hervey Cleckley, described the typical psychopath as profoundly narcissistic, selfish, and ruthless individual, often brilliantly successful because he had no feelings of shame or empathy or desire to help others. LeRoux's grandiose behavior fit that description.

CHAPTER 14: NINJA STUFF

299 **he grew up on a farm:** Details of Adam Samia's history are taken from his testimony, given April 16, 2018, in U.S. District Court for the Southern District of New York, during his trial for murder, in the case, *USA v. Hunter et al.,* 13 CR 521 (RA). More details of Samia's activities can be found in document 524, filed March 16, 2018, in *USA v. Hunter et al.*

INDEX

ACKNOWLEDGMENTS

WHEN YOU TAKE A TRIP TO A STRANGE COUNTRY, YOU NEED A GOOD GUIDE. For this journey into a place off the map, I've been privileged to find the best.

Bill Mockler, who created the DEA's Special Operations Division in 1992, foreseeing a global underground where technology, innovation and organized crime would converge; his successors Joe Keefe, Mary Cooper, and Derek Maltz; Lou Milione, who founded SOD's 960 Group; his deputy Wim Brown; and LeRoux case agents Tom Cindric and Eric Stouch. Others who helped me include Pat Picciano, Steve Casey, Jim Scott, Joe Kellums, Matt Keller, Jim Sparks, Sam Gaye, Carol Dillon and the undercover agent I call Taj, all of DEA; Liberian National Security Agency leader Fombah Sirleaf; Sergeant Mark Massey of Person County, North Carolina; Lieutenant Colonel Rudolph Atallah, USAF (Ret.); and the courageous undercover operatives known as Jack and Georges.

Lissa August and Mary Wormley copyedited and checked facts; Katie Ellsworth tracked down images. Susan McElhinney photographed me.

The unrivaled Shane Salerno of the Story Factory literary agency in Los Angeles placed the manuscript in the able hands of Liate Stehlik, senior vice president and publisher of HarperCollins and her team: associate publisher Ben Steinberg; David Highfill, executive editor at William Morrow/HarperCollins; Chloe Moffett, Molly Waxman, Andy LeCount, Danielle Bartlett, Sharyn Rosenblum, Kelly Rudolph, Andrea Molitor, Nyamekye Waliyaya, Leah Carlson-Stanisic, Bonni Leon-Berman, Jeanne Reina, Yeon Kim, and Chris Sergio.

Special thanks to Michael Mann for many years of honest, encouraging advice, unerring perception, integrity, and fidelity to the truth.

I am grateful to my husband, Dan Morgan, and my son, Andrew Shannon Morgan, for putting up with my long days, longer nights, and working weekends and holidays. We share a passion for getting to the heart of the matter.

—*Elaine Shannon*